JOAN GILLCHREST

(1918 - 2008)

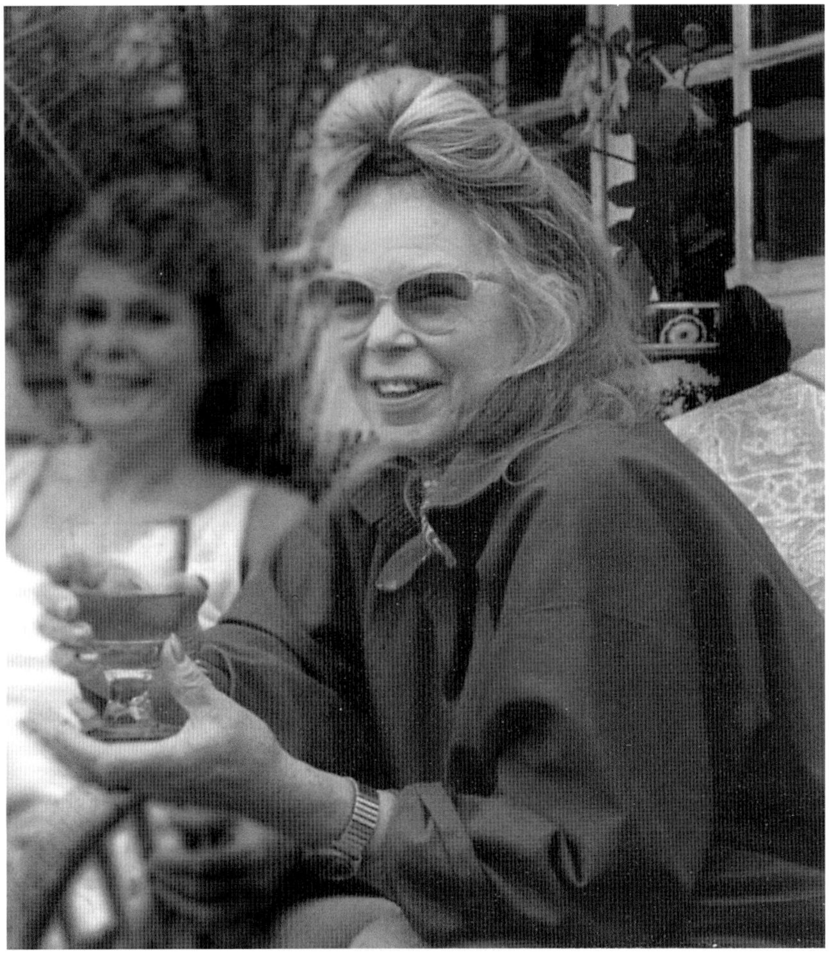

Joan Gillchrest (1918-2008)

JOAN GILLCHREST

(1918 - 2008)

A LIFE IN PICTURES

Gill Mitchell

First published in Great Britain in 2008

ISBN 978-0-9559574-0-6

Published by Wren Gallery, 34 Lower High Street, Burford, Oxfordshire, OX18 4RR, to whom any enquiries should be made.

Printed by Manor Creative Limited, Eastbourne, East Sussex, BN23 6PT

CONTENTS

Introduction

My first meeting with Joan was memorable. Another dealer was to introduce us and we had arranged to meet at "The Wink" at Lamorna Cove. We were standing in the sunshine outside the Pub when the peace of the valley was interrupted by bangs and splutters as an elderly Morris Minor made its way into the car park. Joan got out to greet us.

Those of you who know "The Wink" will remember that the car park slopes slightly downhill to the stream that runs behind the pub - and yes, you have guessed it!! As we said our hellos I caught sight, over Joan's shoulder, of the Morris gathering speed as it rolled backwards towards the water.

Two Art dealers, not known for their athletic prowess, raced to stop the impending catastrophe and found themselves pushing the car with all their might away from the stream. Meanwhile its owner was laughing helplessly and merely remarked that she must have forgotten to put on the handbrake.

This first meeting with Joan set the scene for all my many subsequent meetings. They always started in a pub and were always full of the unexpected, helpless laughter and a lot of good natured gossip.

Many years ago, at one such meeting, we discussed writing her book. She was crystal clear with her instructions. I was to write it but a) not whilst she was alive and b) it was not to be a "boring biography." I was to let her pictures tell her story. It is with great regret that her death has made the book possible. Whether I have satisfied point b) is for others to judge. I hope so.

I have tried, through the wonderful pictures Joan painted, to show how the raw talent first recognised by her father, then by her teachers at Art School and by such institutions as the Royal Academy, developed over the years.

Many words and phrases have been used to describe her work......
"One of the foremost naïve artists of her time"
"Vibrant, colourful, poetic painting belonging to the ongoing Cornish tradition of naïve, primitive art"
"Immaculate paint handling ..."
They are all true but her own description is much simpler... "I observe people, places, buildings...everything that surrounds me and I capture this immediately by sketching. I can't wait to get home and paint from my drawings. My style is born out of a desire to give people some happiness. Life can be so sad."

Joan was often asked "what have been the major influences on your work?" Her reply was that no artist or movement had consciously influenced what she wanted to achieve. There were, however, artists she loved and thought that they must have had an impact on her development. She adored the work of Henri Matisse (1869-1954) and Christopher Wood (1901-1930) became a great favourite after seeing an exhibition of his work at the Redfern Gallery in 1938. Alfred Wallis (1855-1942) and Mary Jewels (1886-1977) were the two Cornish artists Joan held in great esteem.

It is undoubtedly true that most of her work was humorous and mischievous, but she did not shy away from those sad events that touched the people around her. Tragedies such as the Torrey Cannon and the loss of the Penlee Lifeboat were painted with sympathy and dignity. These were never for public consumption, they were Joan's way of expressing how she felt.

Joan was a compulsive sketcher and she left behind reams of sketches, (some doubling up as shopping lists). Her attention to detail was amazing, particularly when drawing the architecture of a church or chapel. Sometimes she would go on to paint exactly the scene featured and it would be instantly recognisable. Other times she would combine several different sketches within a single picture to produce a gloriously detailed work.

I am frequently asked the question "what was Joan like?" The answer is simple, Joan was wonderful. Time spent with her was time well spent. She was full of warmth, compassion, opinions and most of all humour. Just look at any of her paintings and you will see these qualities. She was a great friend and it was a privilege to have represented her over the years.

Gill Mitchell 2008

Chapter 1 The Early Years

Joan Linda Gilbert Scott was born on 2nd November 1918 at Bentinck Street, London W1, one of the family homes. She was the third child of Dr Sebastian Gilbert Scott and Alice O'Hara. The Gilbert Scotts were perhaps the most illustrious family of architects this country has ever known. Joan was brought up in a large house with imposing gardens which swept down to the Thames in Bourne End, Buckinghamshire. She enjoyed all the privileges of a wealthy, successful, upper class family living between the two great wars. Hers was a childhood where parents were rarely seen, nannies ruled the nursery and servants fetched and carried. Brothers were sent to Eton or Harrow at the age of thirteen and sisters were "Presented at Court".

As we shall see somebody as talented, artistic and strong willed as Joan would always find such a life stifling.

The Gilbert Scott Family - A Family of Architects

The family can trace its roots back to a Sir Humphrey Gilbert who was a half brother to Sir Walter Raleigh. Joan's great, great grandfather, the Reverend Thomas Scott (1781-1835) was the first vicar of Gawcott in Buckinghamshire.

Her great grandfather, Sir George Gilbert Scott (1811-1878) was born in Gawcott and started in architecture by designing gaols and workhouses. He travelled around Europe and later studied French Gothic Cathedrals and Churches. He was greatly influenced by Pugin and represented the quintessence of high Victorian Gothic architecture. He was responsible for the design, restoration and conversion of some 700 buildings including Ely Cathedral and Westminster Abbey. Perhaps he is remembered mostly for his work on St. Giles' Church, Camberwell, The Albert Memorial in Kensington Gardens and the Midland Railway Terminus Hotel at St. Pancras.

Joan's grandfather George Gilbert Scott Jnr. (1839-1897) was an innovator and occupied a key role in the development of English architecture between 1870 and 1914. In 1874 he joined fellow architects to set up Watts and Co., a decorating business to rival the influential firm of Morris and Co. Unfortunately he was a chronic alcoholic dying comparatively young and must be one of England's most forgotten architects. He fathered 6 children, 4 of whom survived into adulthood. The second surviving son and Joan's uncle, was Sir Giles Gilbert Scott (1880-1960) who is best remembered for his work on such buildings as Liverpool Cathedral and Battersea Power Station. Another son, Adrian Gilbert Scott (1882-1963) also followed the family tradition.

The dynasty continues to this day with Sir Giles's son Richard who designed the Guildhall Art Gallery.

Joan's father Dr. Sebastian Gilbert Scott (1879-1941)

Sebastian was the eldest surviving son of George Gilbert Scott Jnr. and broke with the family tradition of studying architecture to take up medicine. He qualified in 1904 and was a pioneer in radiology, associated with the work carried out by Marie Curie, research crucial to the development of X-Rays in surgery. He rose to be the head of the radiology department at the London Hospital. Like Madame Curie, Sebastian contracted leukaemia through his exposure to high energy radiation and died at a comparatively young age. Colleagues remembered Joan's father not only for his important scientific work but also as a most accomplished caricaturist. Many of his drawings and sketches survive to this day.

Joan's mother Alice O'Hara (1890-1964)

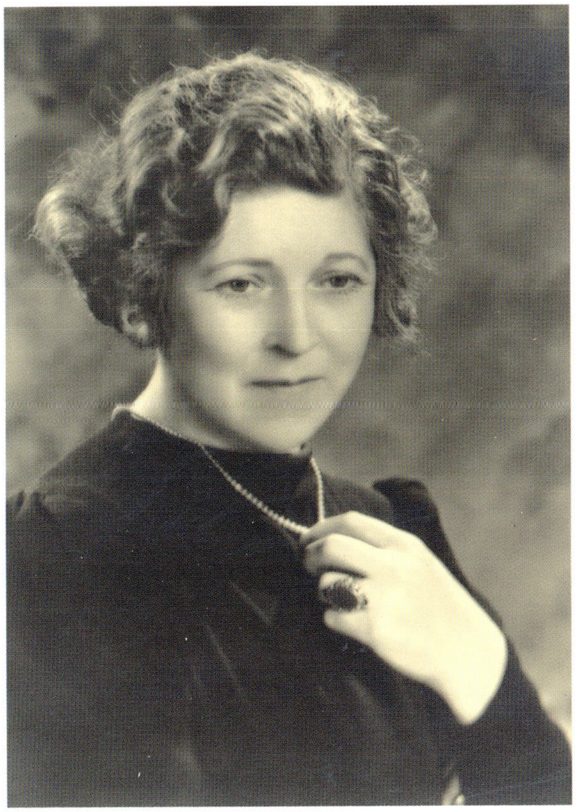

Alice O'Hara (1890-1964), Joan's mother

Joan's mother was brought up on the family cattle station near Sydney, Australia. She and her sister, Linda, were both musical. Joan's mother played the piano and Linda sang contralto. They were both sent to Heidelberg, Germany to continue their musical studies.

It is thought probable that Sebastian and Alice, Joan's parents, met when they were both on holiday in Switzerland.

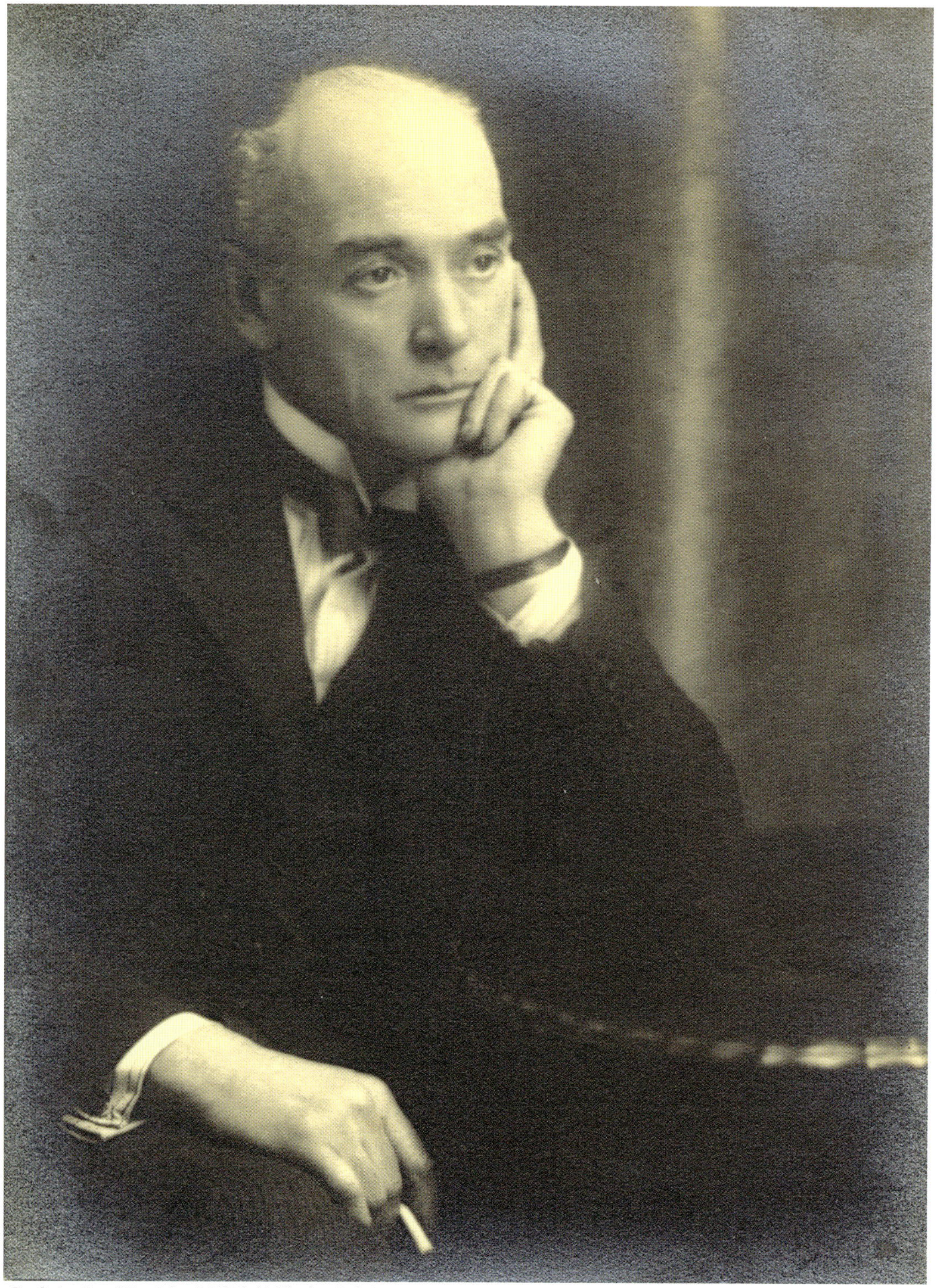

Dr. Sebastian Gilbert Scott (1879-1941), Joan's father

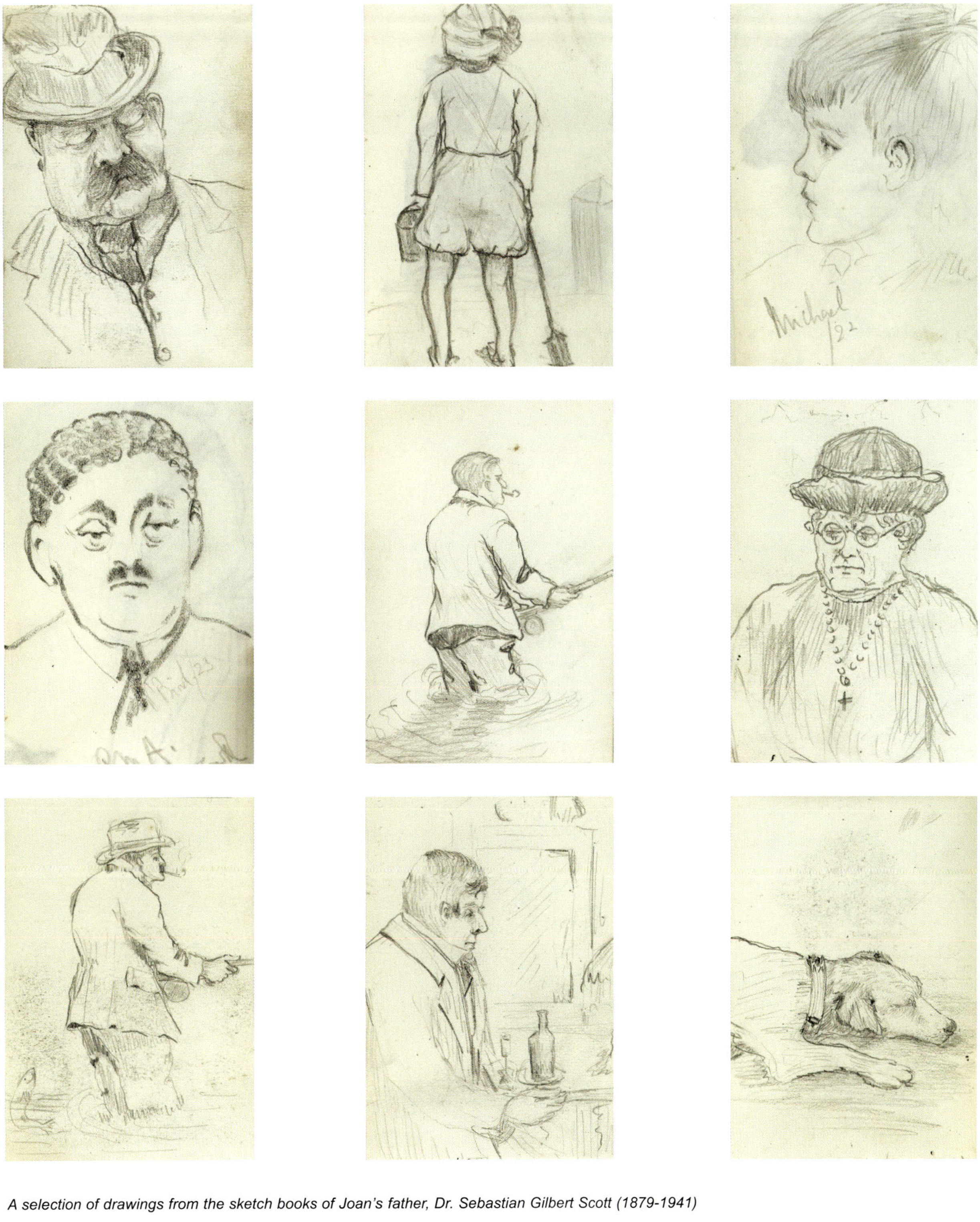

A selection of drawings from the sketch books of Joan's father, Dr. Sebastian Gilbert Scott (1879-1941)

Joan and her Siblings

Elizabeth Louise Gilbert Scott (1915-2001) "Betty" was presented at Court before the war and attended the Rank Organisation 'charm school' in her youth before marrying into the Hoare Banking family. For many years she collected Victorian church embroidery from convents and churches. This superb collection is now housed in the Elizabeth Hoare Gallery in Liverpool's Anglican Cathedral.

Michael Gilbert Scott (1917-1994) was educated at Radley College and studied medicine at Cambridge and 'Barts'. He qualified and practised through the war years. Following in his father's footsteps he became a consultant radiologist.

George Gilbert Scott, (1920-) "Gil" was educated at Harrow where he started pre-medical studies. In 1939 he volunteered as air crew and became a flying instructor in Canada. He retrained on Halifax bombers and flew thirty missions, mostly over Germany, and was awarded the D.F.C. Demobilised, he returned to medical studies at the Royal London Hospital, qualifying in 1952. He worked in general practise in Windsor before moving to France practising in the small town of Argentat-sur-Dordogne. He married Agnes Helgeson in 1942 and they had two sons. His second marriage to Susan Mallows followed in 1977.

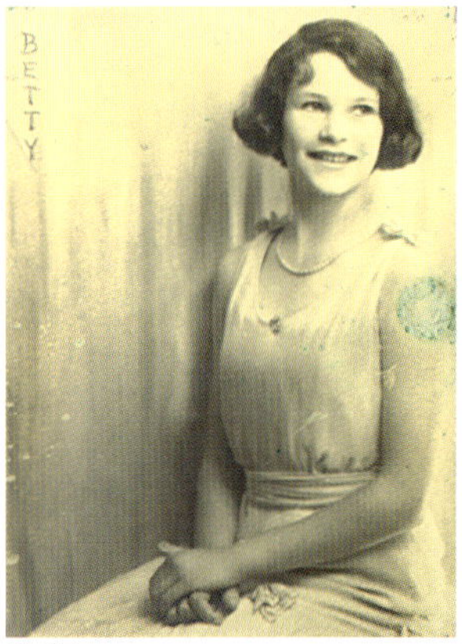

Betty

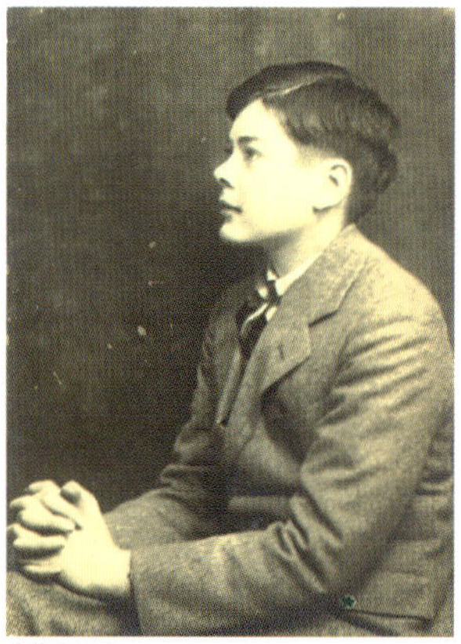
Michael

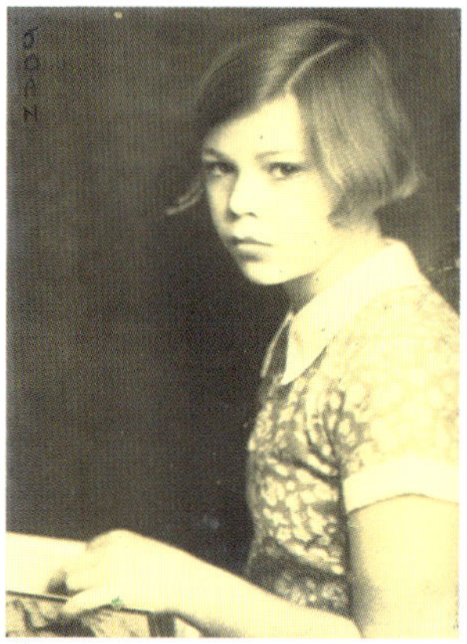

Joan

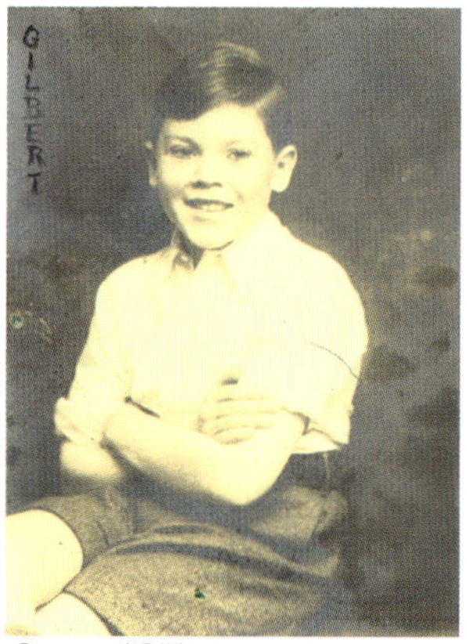

George ('Gil')

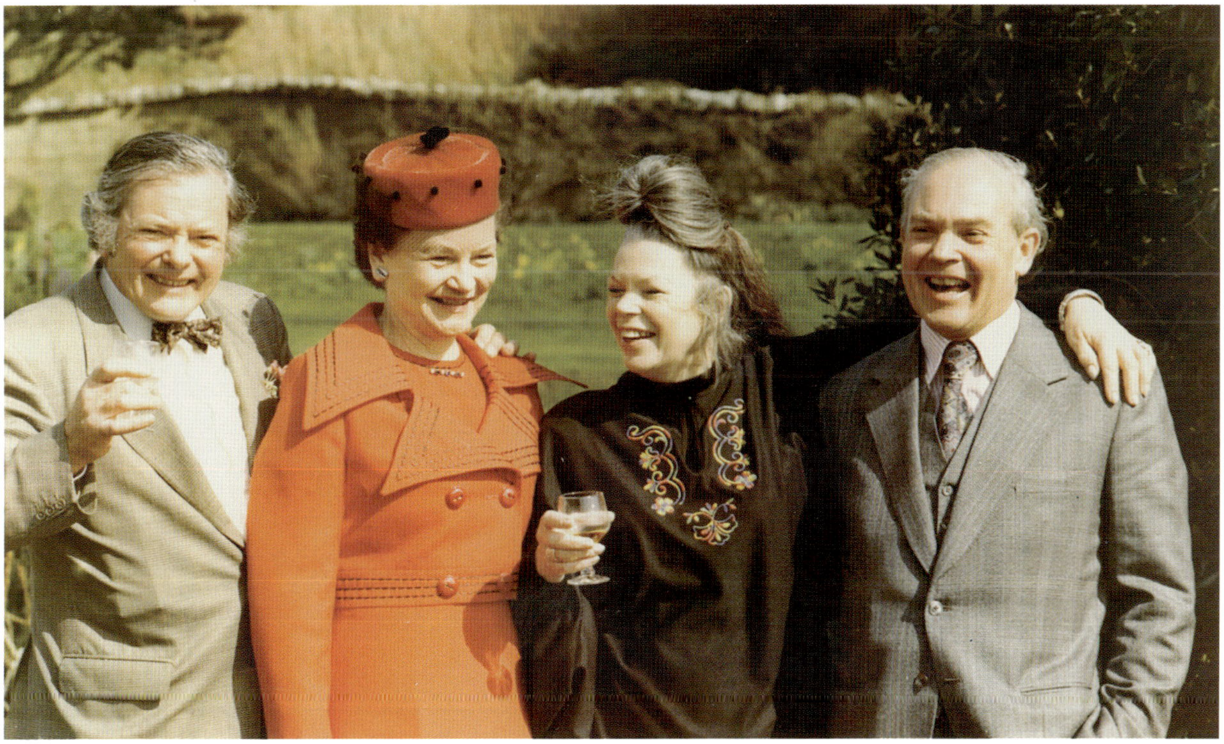

Michael, Betty, Joan and Gil, at Gil's wedding to Susan, April 1977

Childhood and Beyond

By her own admission, Joan was a "difficult" child. It is family folklore that the children had two nannies, one for Joan and one for the rest. She claims to have been sent to various schools to "keep her out of the way" and it is certainly true that she went to boarding school at an early age.

In families like the Gilbert Scotts, the education of sons followed a set pattern of Prep. School and Public School from the age of seven. The education of daughters was not considered important and they seldom received anything more than home study with a governess and perhaps a little "finishing" off in Paris, to learn the language before marriage to the ideal husband. It is therefore quite surprising that Joan attended Rosemead School at the age of six, followed by Upper Chine School on the Isle of Wight and finally Wadhurst Boarding School.

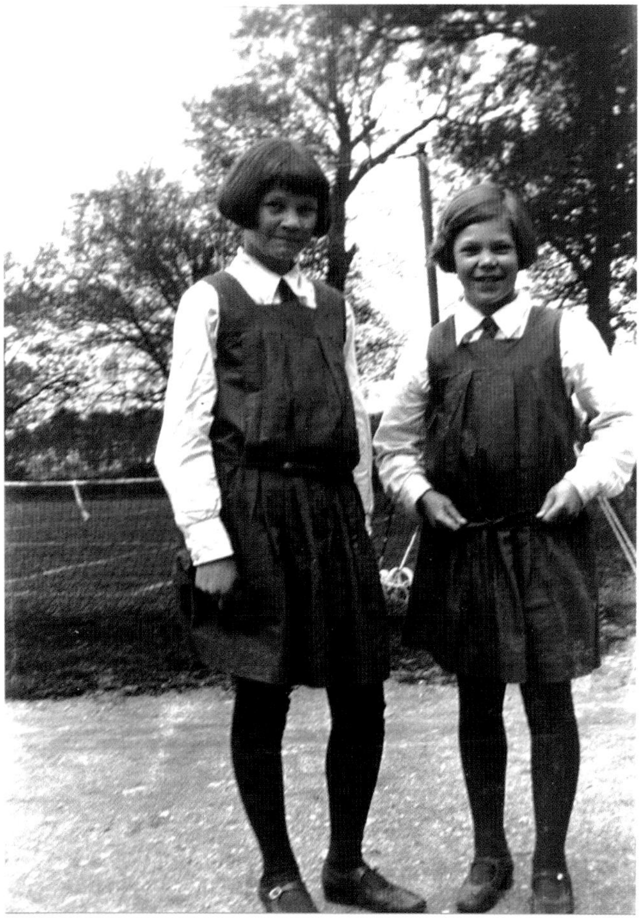

Sister Betty and Joan c. 1930

Although a bit of a rebel and certainly a free spirit she was the apple of her father's eye. With the artistic talents of her parents it is not surprising that Joan developed such a love of drawing and painting and Sebastian gave her every encouragement. All through her life she remained grateful for his support for her art in these early years.

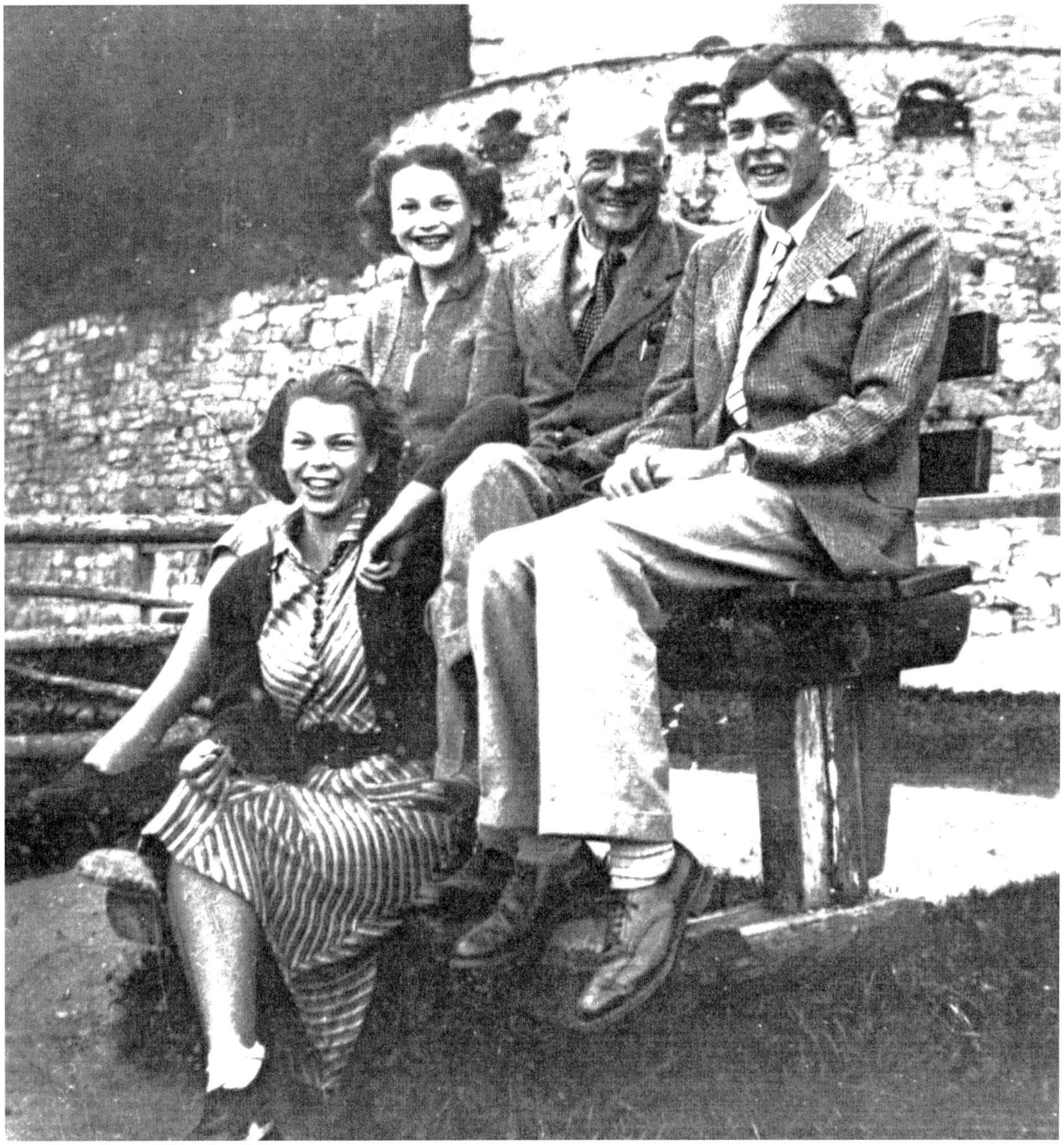

Joan, Betty, Pa and Michael c. 1934

Paris and Art School

Again considering that we are in the early 1930's, the family's position in society and with an older sister about to be presented at court, it is amazing that at the age of fifteen Joan was allowed to go to Paris to learn the language and develop her appreciation of art. She saw and marvelled at the works of the leading French artists of the day, meeting many of them. She visited Gwen John (1876-1939) in her studio. This was only a few years before Gwen died. The John family were to feature in many aspects of Joan's life.

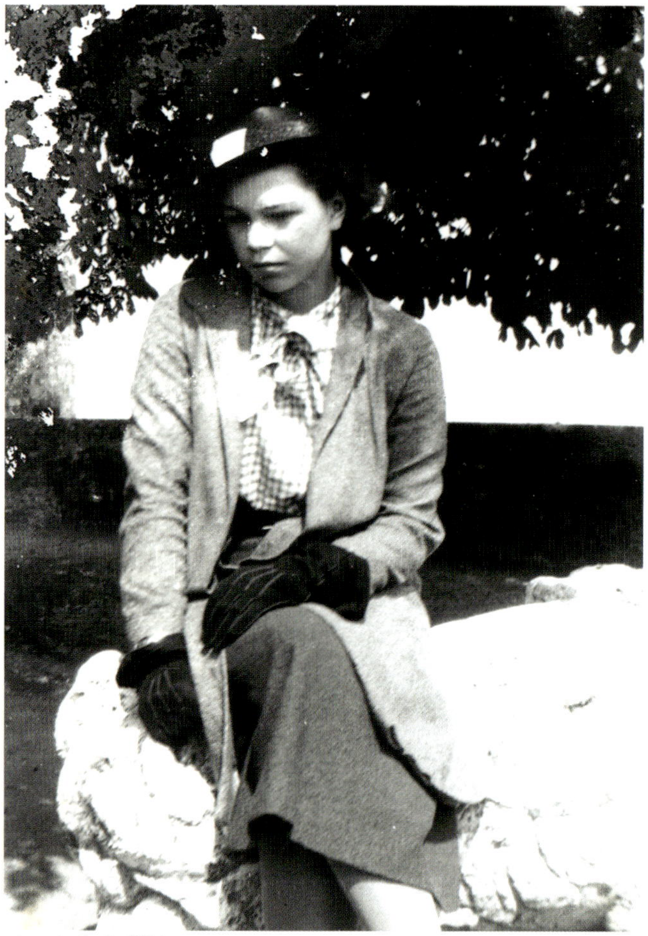

Joan in Paris 1934

To quote one of Joan's many cousins "Her elder sister Betty was presented at court before the war. Joan trod her own path and chose to go to Paris to study art and came home with her hair dyed blonde".

Brother Gil said "She left home as a schoolgirl and came back like a filmstar. When she came to see me at Harrow it was kudos for me."

On her return to London in 1935 she was enrolled at the Grosvenor School of Art which was set up in 1925 by Iain Macnab (1890-1967). He taught Joan, who thought him inspirational, and felt that she owed much of her success to him. She certainly did achieve good things here as she began to exhibit and even sell her work. A painting entitled "Two Girls in Lyons Corner House" was exhibited in New English Art Club in 1937 and "German Scene with Cows" was hung at the London Group in 1938. Joan was only 18 when her first work was exhibited at the Royal Academy. During this time her subject matter was varied, but influenced by what she had seen in France, was experimenting with drawing and painting Still Life using broad brush and palette knife techniques.

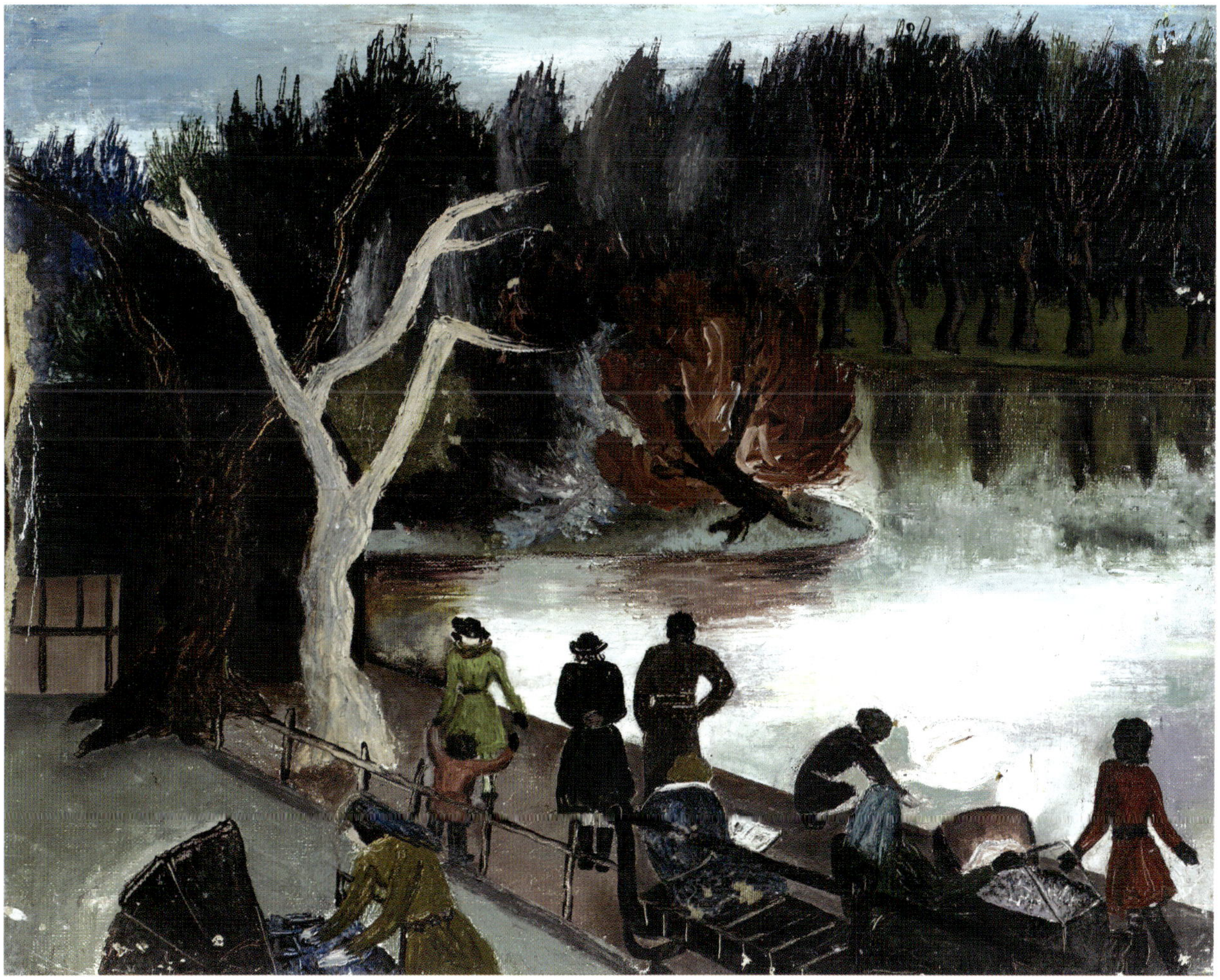

Painted in Paris 1934

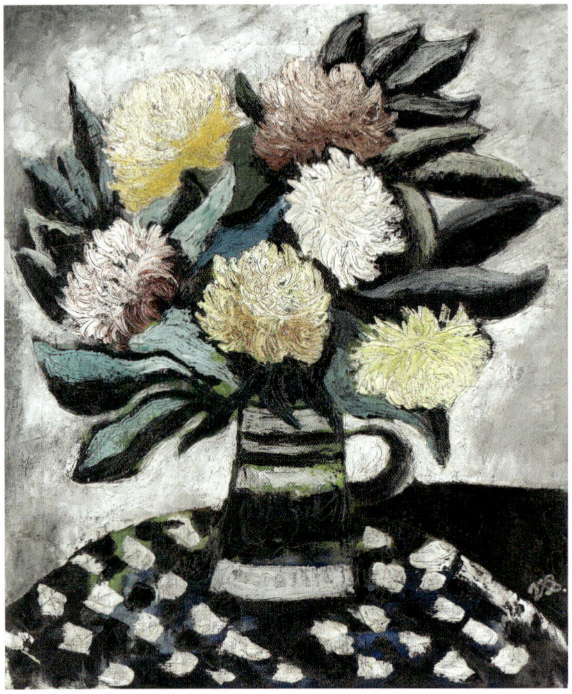

Chrysanthemums, painted at Art School

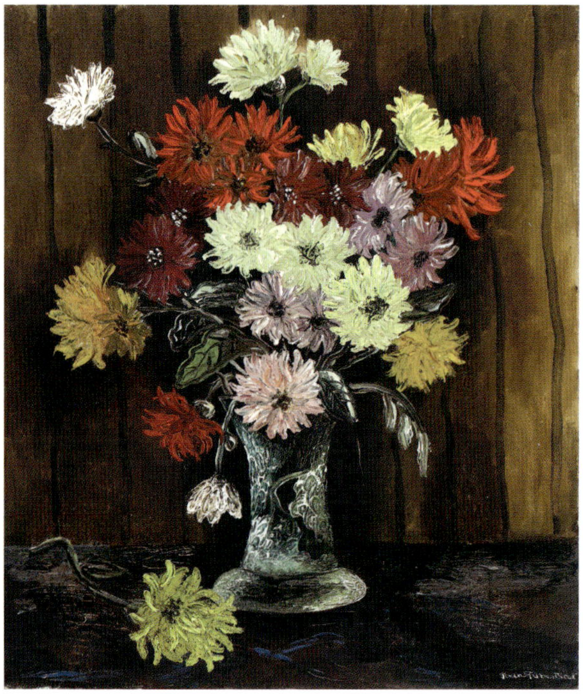

Inscribed on exhibition label 'Flowers Miss Joan Gilbert Scott, Brook House, Bourne End'

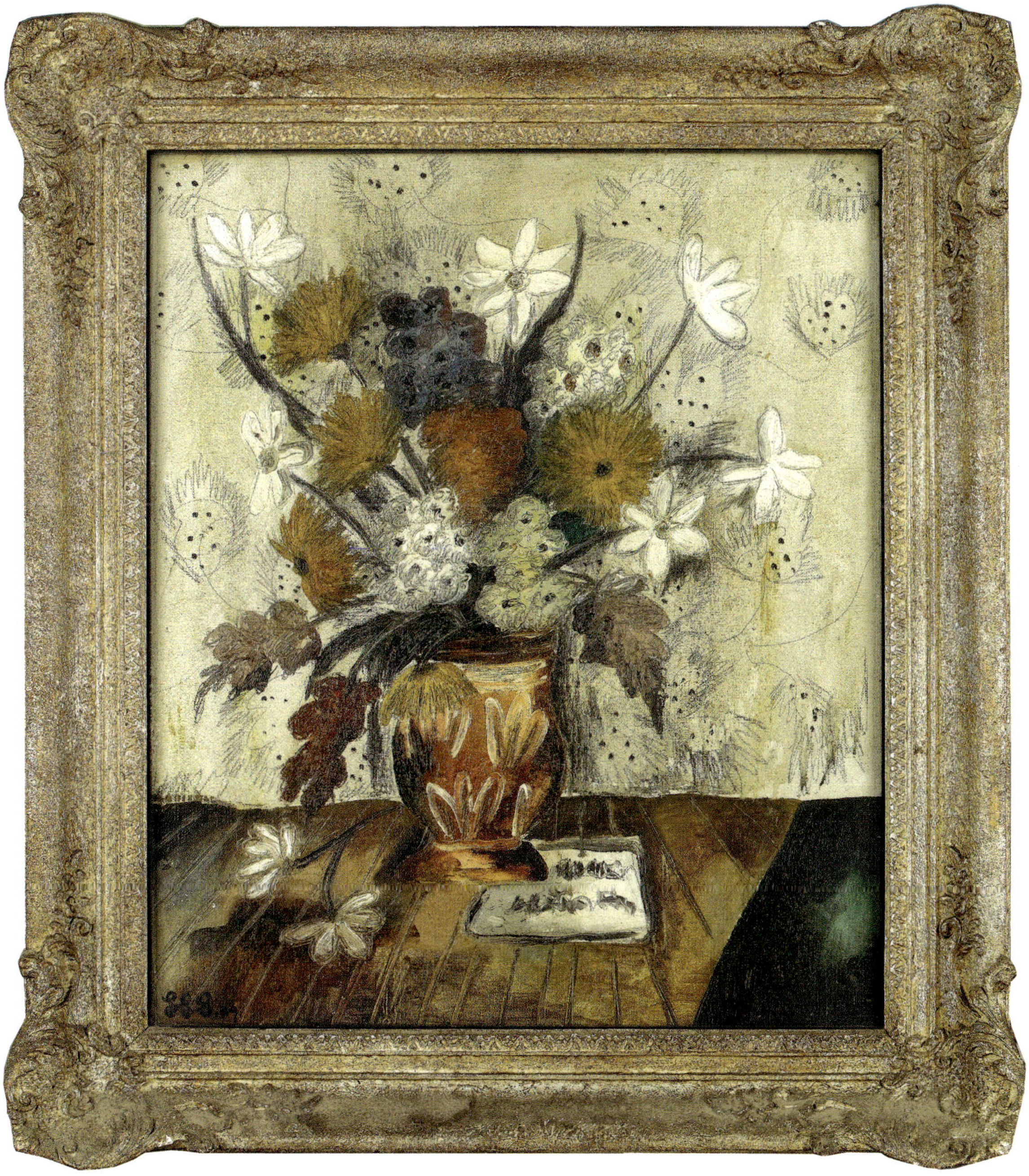

Exhibited at the Royal Academy 1939

Chapter 2 The Forties and Fifties

The Outbreak of War

The outbreak of war in 1939 changed everyone's life. Joan had finished at Art School and had every expectation of painting full time and taking part in public and private exhibitions. Suddenly, brothers and male cousins were being called up and unmarried girls of Joan's age were expected to contribute in some way to the war effort. There were to be no soft options for Joan. She took a crash course in nursing and first aid and volunteered as an ambulance driver for the Westminster Hospital.

Between September 1940 and May 1941 over 20,000 Londoners were killed and many more seriously injured as the Germans blitzed the city. Joan was in the thick of it as a member of a mobile rescue unit and told hair-raising stories of her experiences dashing around the bombed London streets.

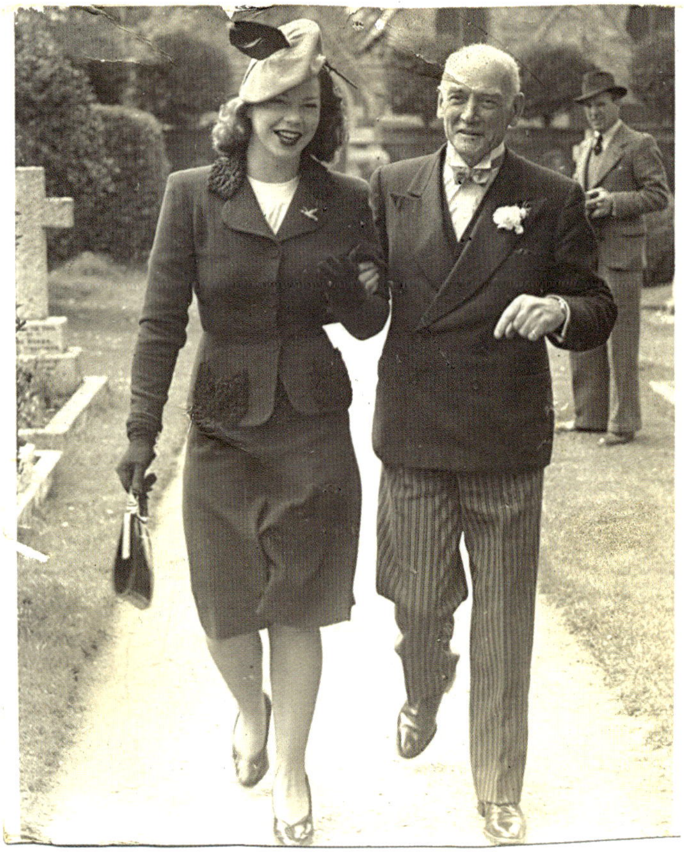

Joan with her father shortly before he died

She painted little during these early war years but kept in touch with Iain Macnab. When the area around St. Paul's was razed to the ground, leaving the mighty church relatively unscathed, Macnab asked Joan and a few other students to paint the scene in situ. Joan's work, painted with a thick palette knife, hung at the Art School for many years.

Tragedy struck in 1941 when Joan's beloved father developed leukaemia, as a result of his exposure to radiation through his research work. Joan with her nursing training helped to look after him in the weeks leading to his death.

Marriage and Children

For a girl from a wealthy upper class family, war or no war, it was important that the right marriage be made. Family background, money, position in society and prospects were vital in determining the suitability of the groom. Joan's sister, Betty had made a good marriage to a member of the Hoare banking family and now it was Joan's turn.

Samuel Gillchrest was a young barrister serving with the Coldstream Guards. His father Samuel Jordan Gillchrest, an American, founded British American Tobacco with Sir Hugo Cunliffe-Owen. Joan and Samuel were married in 1942. The bride was given away by her uncle, Sir Giles Gilbert Scott.

In 1943 a daughter, Marguerite was born and a son Paul in 1947. With a young family and demanding in-laws Joan had little time to paint.

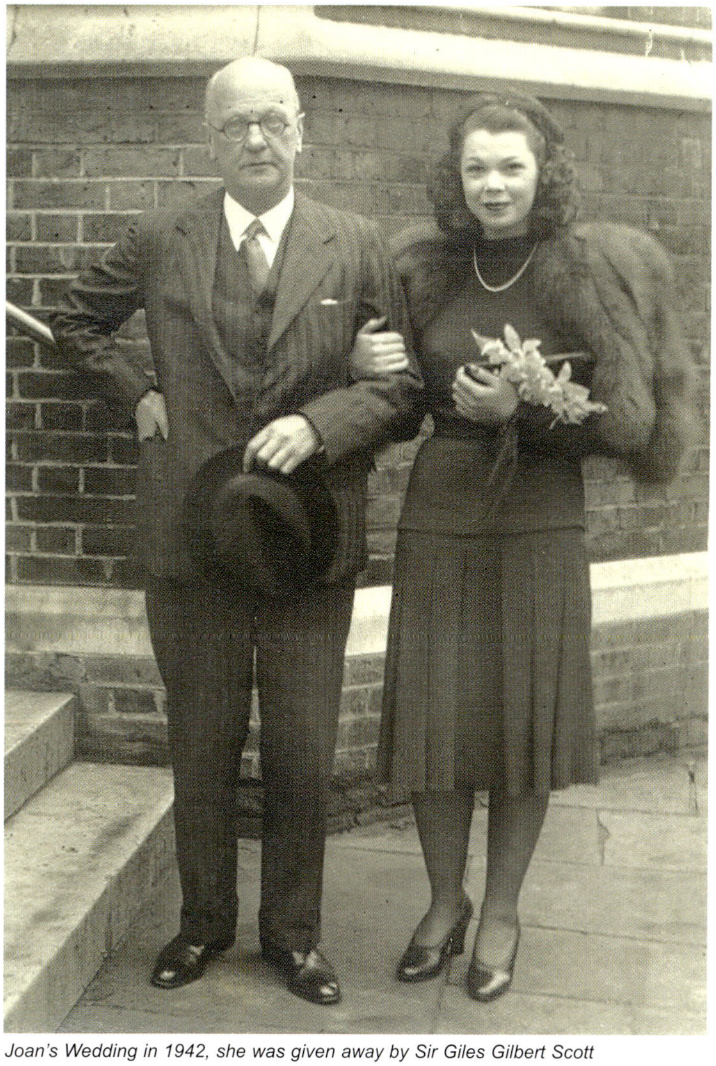

Joan's Wedding in 1942, she was given away by Sir Giles Gilbert Scott

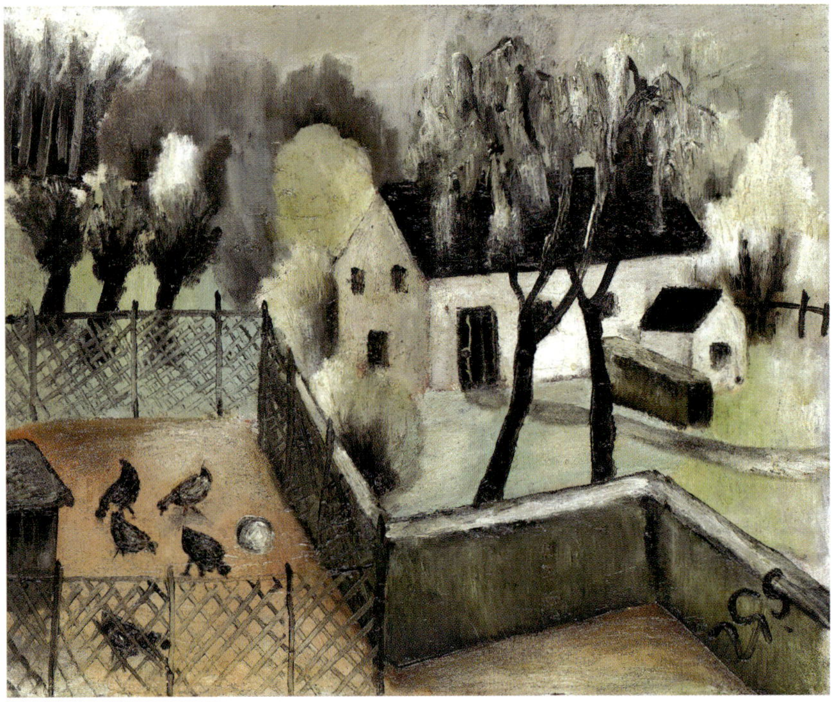

Cottage in Pirbright 1944

The Painting above is inscribed verso with a message to her daughter Mara - “Mara, you sat in your pram as a baby and watched me paint this painting. You were very good, lots of love, Mum.”

In 1944 Samuel was stationed at Pirbright and Joan moved there to be with him. Sam was not keen on her painting as he felt it was ‘beneath him’. However there are paintings which survive from this period, a self-portrait, a garden scene titled "Pirbright 1944" and a third which she gave to brother Gil. This is of sailing boats at the Upper Thames Sailing Club, Bourne End, where Gil was a member. It still hangs in his dressing room in France.

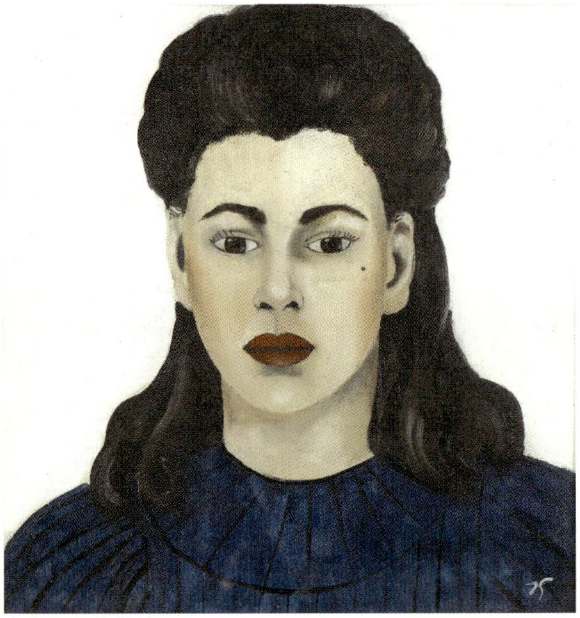

Self Portrait 1944

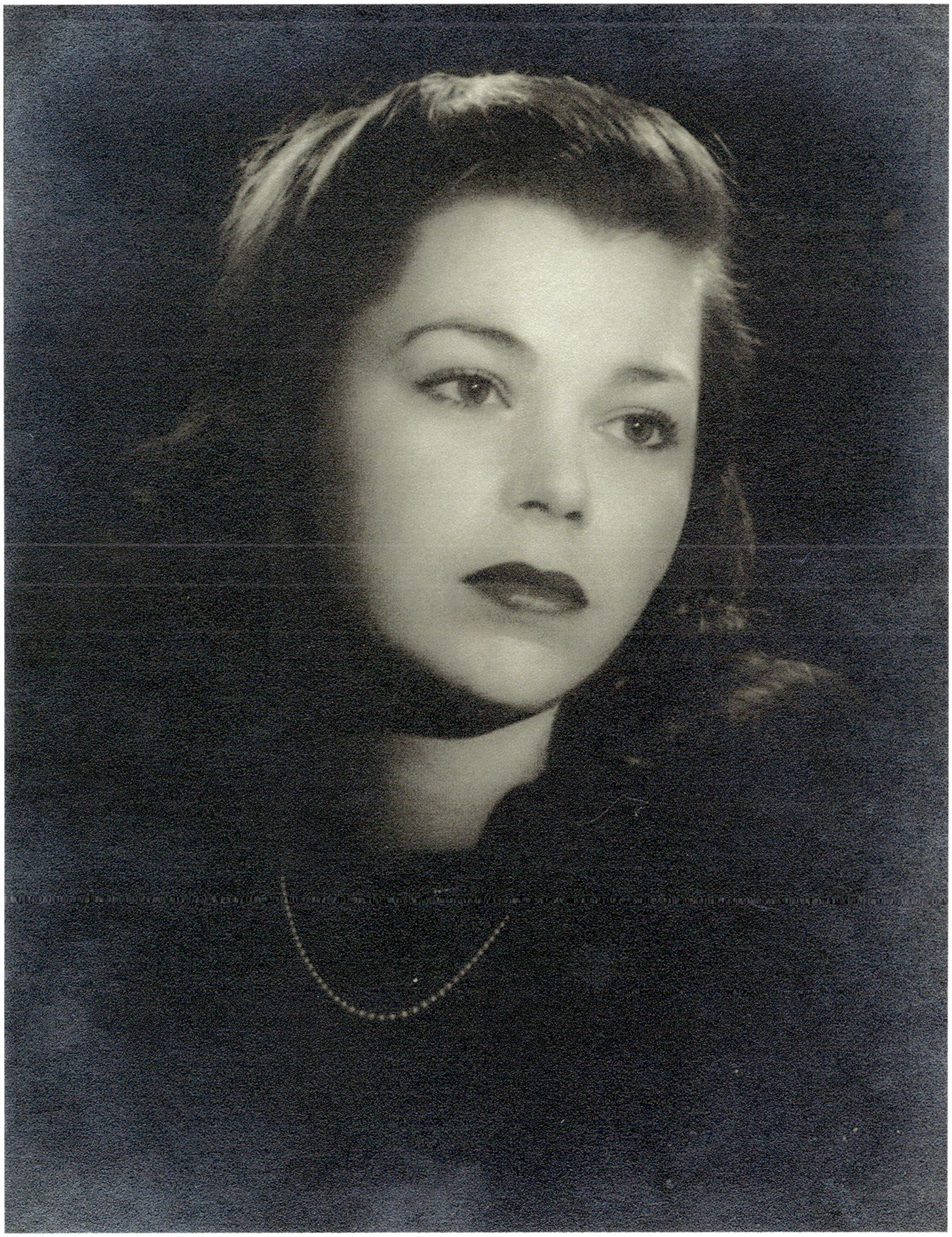

Joan Gillchrest 1944

Separation and Divorce

In the early 1950's Joan and Sam separated and were divorced in 1953. At that time divorced or separated women had few rights and this was particularly so in Joan's case. She had needed to leave a difficult and unhappy marriage but in doing so forfeited money, security and her "rightful" place in society.

Joan had to work to support herself and although her children were at boarding schools she also needed to provide a home for them in the holidays. Her father was no longer around to help but she was close to her younger brother, Gil, who encouraged and helped her at this time. Photographs show Joan to have been a most elegant and attractive woman and she quickly found that she was in demand by the leading Fashion Houses of the day, to model their latest collections. Her daughter, Mara can remember her mother visiting her at her boarding school wearing the most beautiful clothes, hats and shoes. Clearly Joan was allowed to keep or purchase some of these exquisite clothes for she subsequently painted self-portrait studies of these garments.

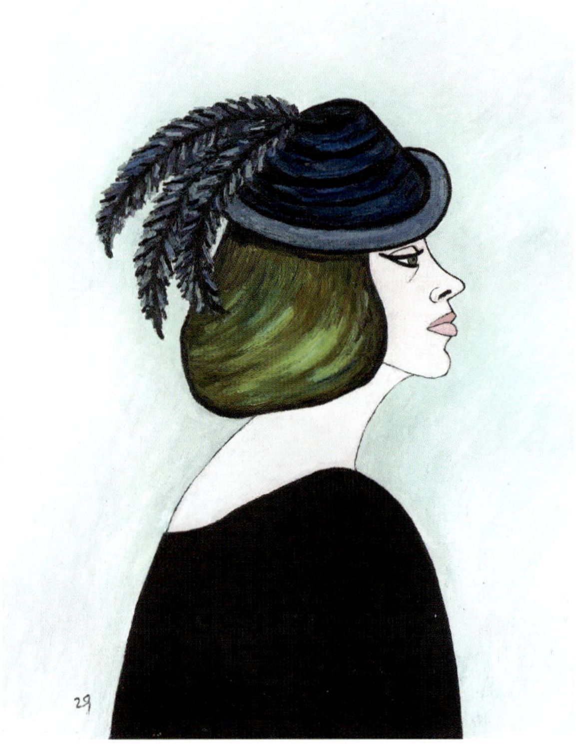

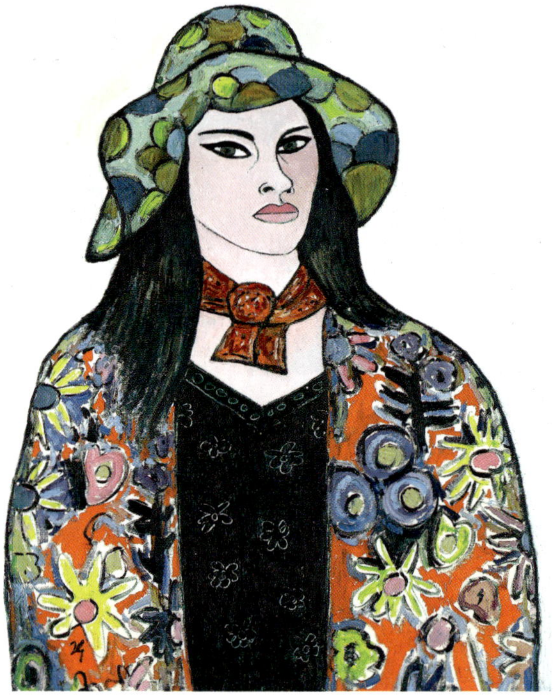

Two of the hats modelled by Joan which remained in her possession.

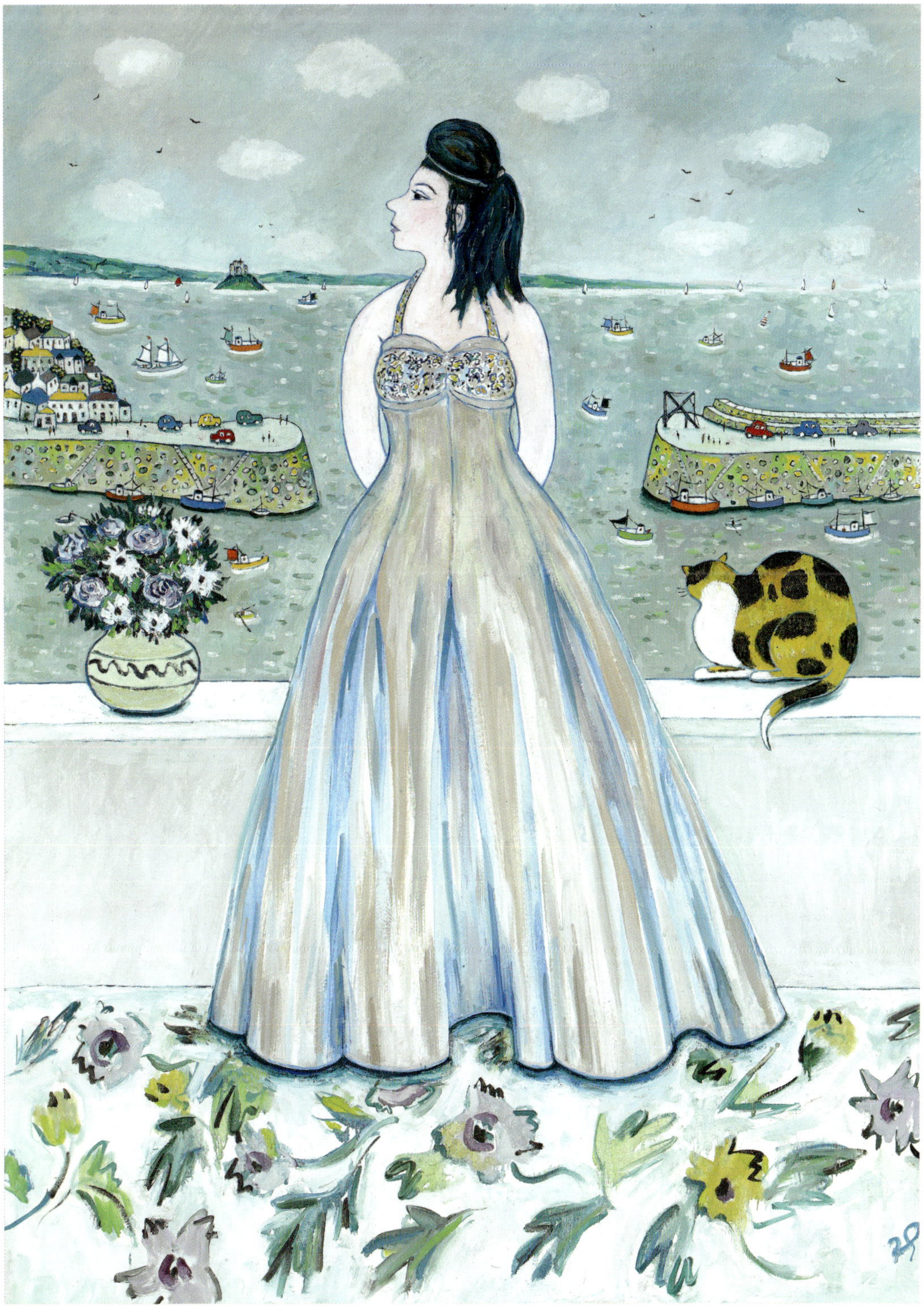

Modelling My Molyneaux Dress at Mousehole

Serious Painting Once More

With all these dramatic changes in her life one thing was constant and that was her overwhelming desire to paint. At last, she had the time and freedom to experiment with colour, style, texture and to explore new ways of expressing herself on canvas. She wanted an artistic life and the free spirit that she was, allowed her to ignore all her disapproving family and friends.

Joan moved to a studio at 48 Tite Street, Chelsea, an area much favoured by the artist community of the day. To help support herself, her children and her painting Joan was finding regular work as an artists' model. She was tall, strikingly good looking in a bohemian way and carried an air of mystery from her rich and privileged past.

It was here that she met the artist Adrian Ryan (1920-1998)

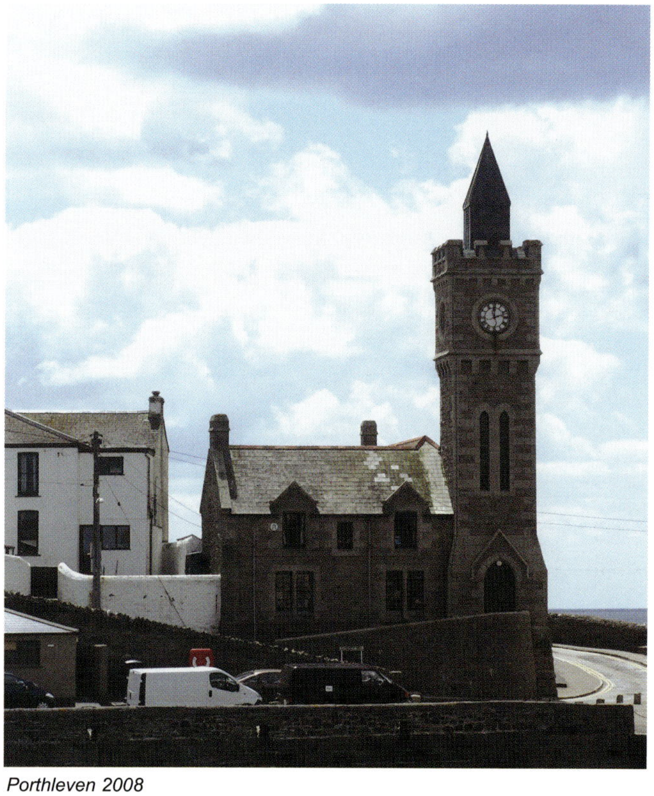

Porthleven 2008

The picture opposite shows Porthleven, Cornwall, which was painted whilst Joan lived at 48 Tite Street. Adrian Ryan had lived in Mousehole with his first wife directly after the war and returned frequently to Cornwall during this period. It seems likely that on one such visit Joan and Adrian went together, staying at or visiting Porthleven. This work is probably one of the earliest indications of Joan's move to her naïve style. Her attention to the architectural detail and construction of the buildings is very noticeable.

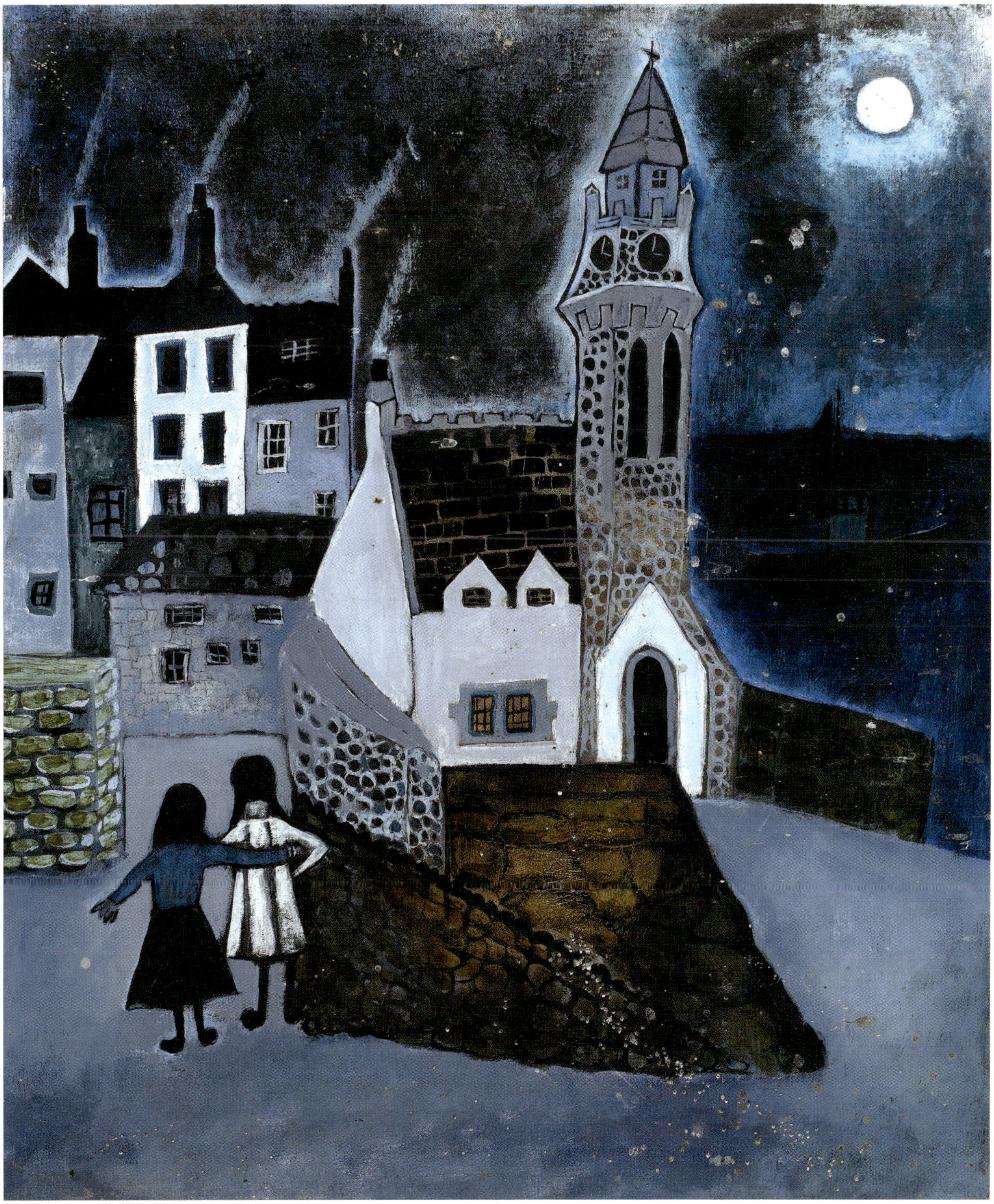

Porthleven, Cornwall

Chapter 3 Tite Street to Mousehole

Joan's first floor studio at 48 Tite Street was directly above the one occupied by the charismatic and fun loving artist Adrian Ryan.

Adrian Ryan (1920-1998)

Adrian Ryan was born in London, the son of portrait painter Vivian Ryan. His mother Kitty was an accomplished watercolourist. He was educated at Eton, the Architectural Association and the Slade. Whilst at the Slade he married a fellow student, Peggy Rose. He was a young man of private means which allowed him to set himself up with a flat and studio in Tite Street mixing with the artistic giants of the day. Ryan first exhibited with the London Group in 1941.

He joined the Army as a private in 1941 but was invalided out in 1943. His first one man show at the Redfern Gallery was an immediate success. He first visited Cornwall in 1943 and in 1945 established a studio in Mousehole, exhibiting with the St. Ives Society of Artists. He was briefly president of the Newlyn painters whilst retaining his studio in London. A failure in the family fortunes proved very costly for Ryan and in 1948 he began teaching at Goldsmiths' College and remained there until retiring in 1983.

Adrian Ryan was a self confessed Francophile who made frequent visits to Paris and between 1948 and 1950 spent much of his time painting in France, when free from his teaching commitments. His first marriage to Peggy was not to last and he married a second time to Barbara Pitt.

Joan and Adrian

When Joan and Adrian met he was teaching at Goldsmith's College and introduced Joan to many of the "trend setters" of the day. Adrian's acquaintances included Francis Bacon (1909-1992), William Scott (1913-1989) and Sir Matthew Smith (1879-1959). Augustus John (1878-1961) also had a studio in Tite Street. He was very fond of Adrian and one of his sons, Edwin was a close friend. Edwin had been left his aunt's (Gwen John) studio in Paris. Joan and Adrian stayed with Edwin and his wife Betty on a number of occasions mixing with many of the celebrated French artists of the time.

Although Ryan was still married to Barbara, his relationship with Joan developed until in 1957 he moved upstairs to her flat. Adrian painted Joan many times in this honeymoon period and some of his best remembered works date from this time.

The Move to Mousehole

Betty John took herself off to Cornwall buying a small cottage in the idyllic fishing village of Mousehole. This was a place well known to Ryan as he had lived there on and off between 1944 and 1948. Joan and Adrian were to make several painting trips to this lovely area between 1955 and 1958 when they decided to move down and set up home in Mousehole. They stayed with Betty for a time, being frequently joined by Augustus John, who was fond of his daughter-in-law.

Selling her two valuable possessions, a sapphire ring from her mother and a sable coat from her mother-in-law and to use her own words, chatting up the Bank Manager, Joan raised the money to purchase a small cottage with spectacular views of Mousehole harbour and Mount's Bay. Adrian moved in with her, dividing his time between here and London.

Life in Mousehole

During holiday times the small cottage must have been bursting at the seams. Joan's two children would be home from their boarding schools and they were often joined by Adrian's daughters. A studio was built in the garden and Ryan produced a series of rooftop pictures which are thought to be some of his best work. Joan was desperate to paint but was vehemently discouraged by Ryan. He was totally unsympathetic towards her need to satisfy the inspiration she was getting from the people and places around her.

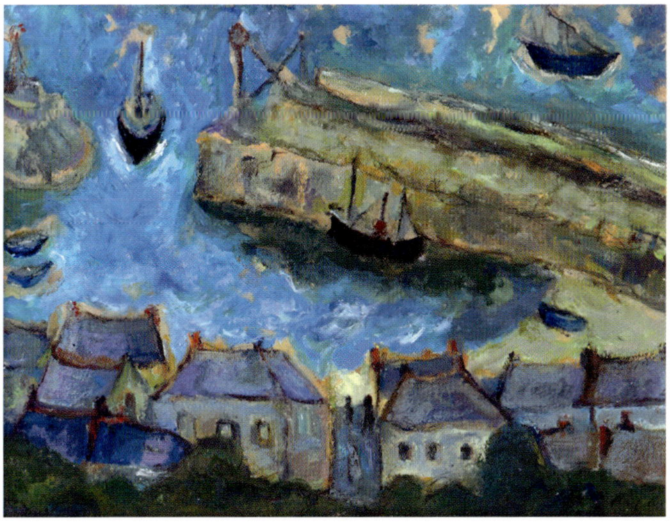

ADRIAN RYAN (1920-1998) Mousehole Harbour

What were his motives for this total opposition? Was he jealous, did he feel threatened; did he require all the attention and praise...? We shall never know.

Freedom to Paint

The relationship lasted nearly eight years but increasingly the years at Mousehole became more difficult. The thing Joan wanted to do above all else was the very thing that Ryan was trying to prevent. Joan wanted to paint.

Although she found him funny, charming, attractive, good company and enjoyed the socialising with his artistic friends, by 1965 she had decided enough was enough.

The end came suddenly. Adrian had taken a new London studio in Camden Town and delivered to this new address came a letter from Joan. In no uncertain terms she told him not to return to Mousehole and that she had forwarded all his belongings and paintings to a depository.

Once rid of Adrian, Joan described feeling as if some explosion had happened within. She suddenly had a new found confidence to paint what she wanted and how she wanted. She was inspired by everything around her, the sea, the buildings, the countryside and the flowers and plants growing in her garden. Work became addictive, detailed sketching first and then creating rich textured paintings, developing the naïve style she was quickly to make her own. Her paintings told stories, they were frequently full of humour and they captured the moment.

At last she was fulfilling her dream. From this time on, painting was to be a major part of her life. Soon she started exhibiting again, firstly at local galleries in Mousehole, the Morrab Gallery (later the Orion) in Penzance and the New Craftsman in St. Ives. Her first solo show was arranged at the Plymouth Art Gallery in 1969, this was made possible by her mentor and friend the art critic, Jack Wood Palmer.

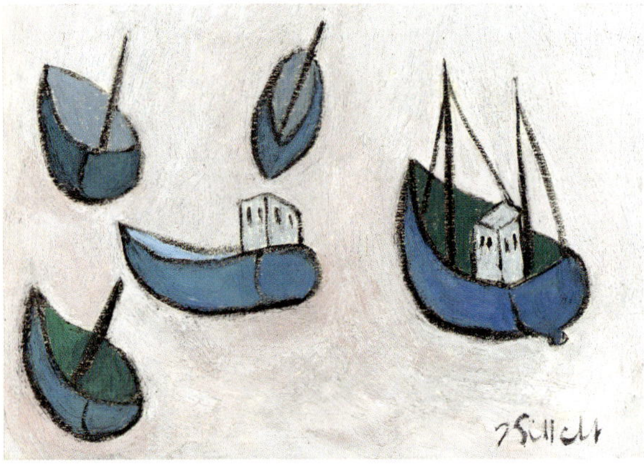

Five Boats

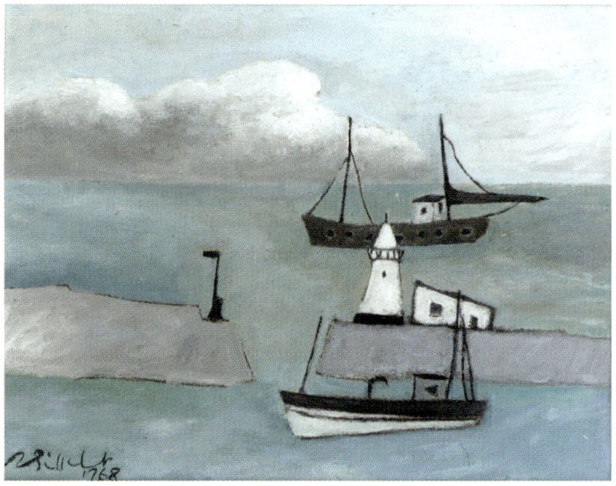

Leaving Harbour

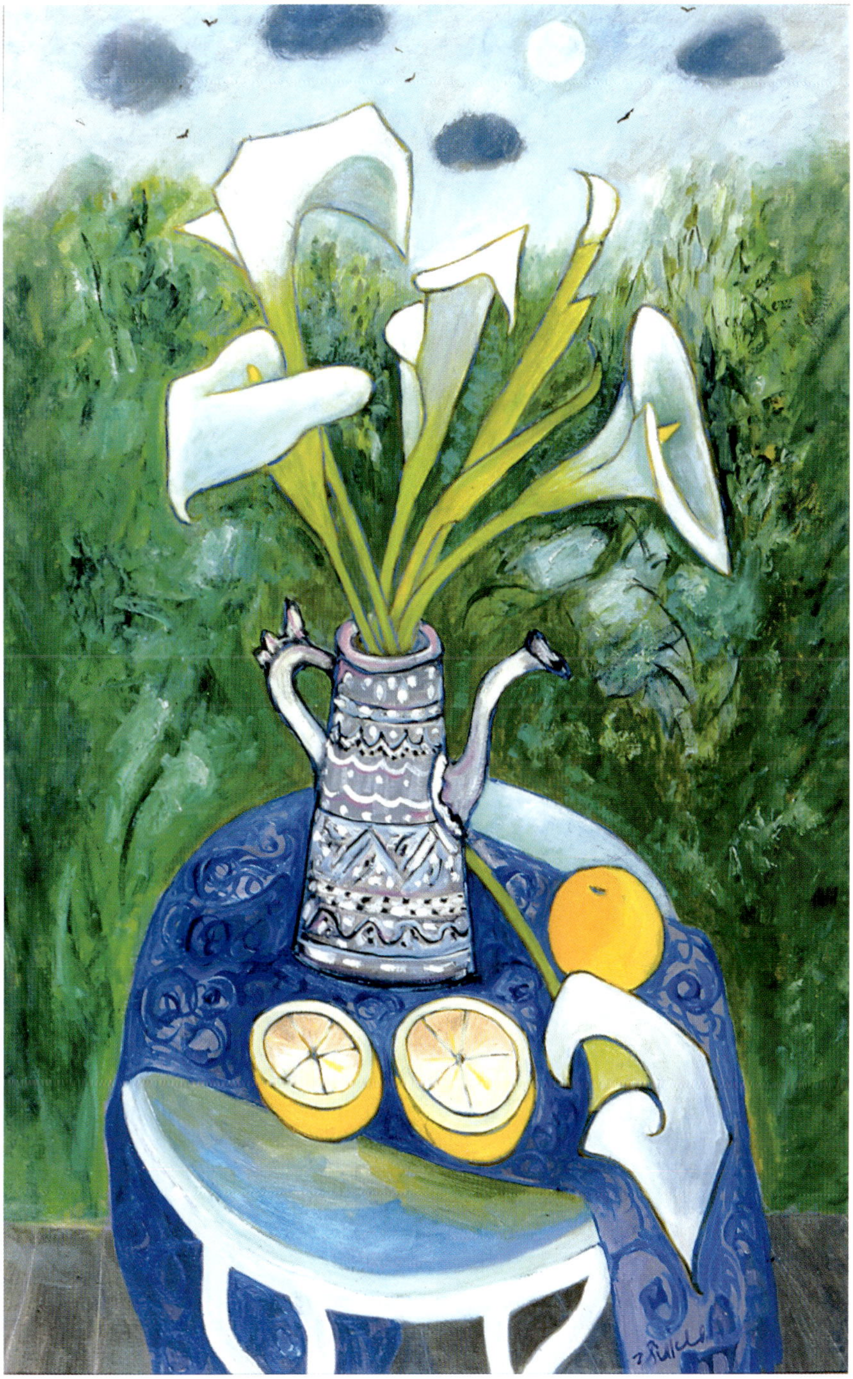

Arum Lily

This still life was painted in 1966 and it is interesting to contrast her style here with the more conventional still lifes of earlier years.

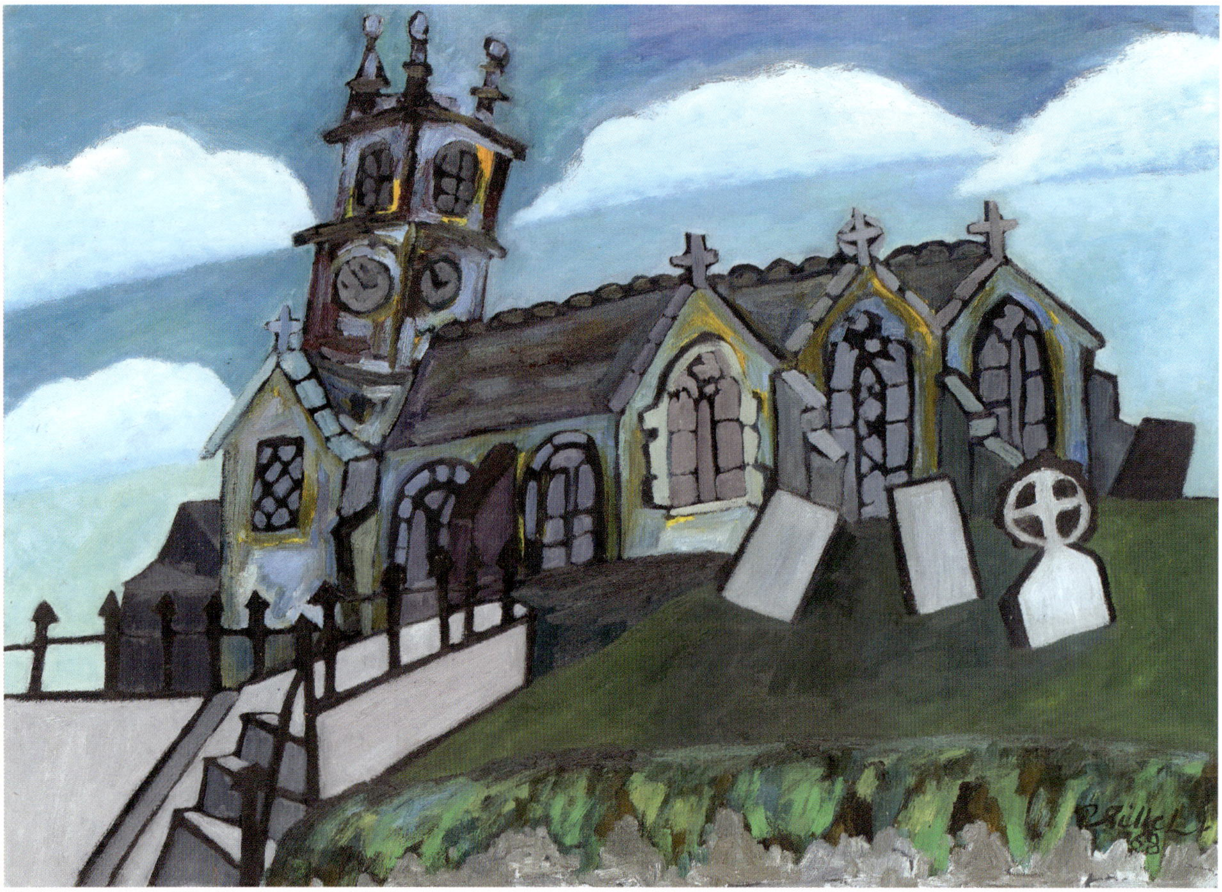

The Church on the Hill, signed and dated 1968

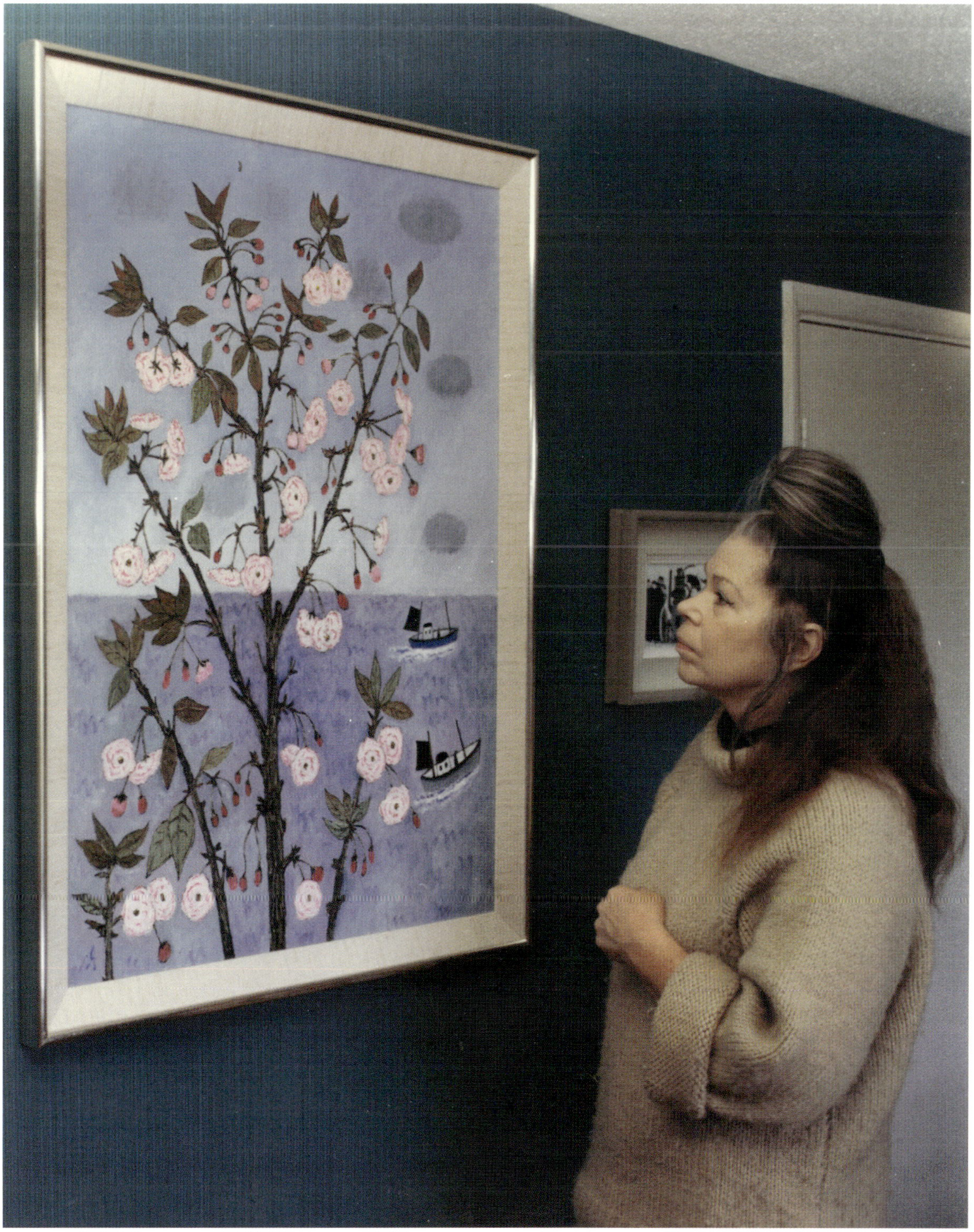

Joan at her first Solo Show, Plymouth Art Gallery 1969

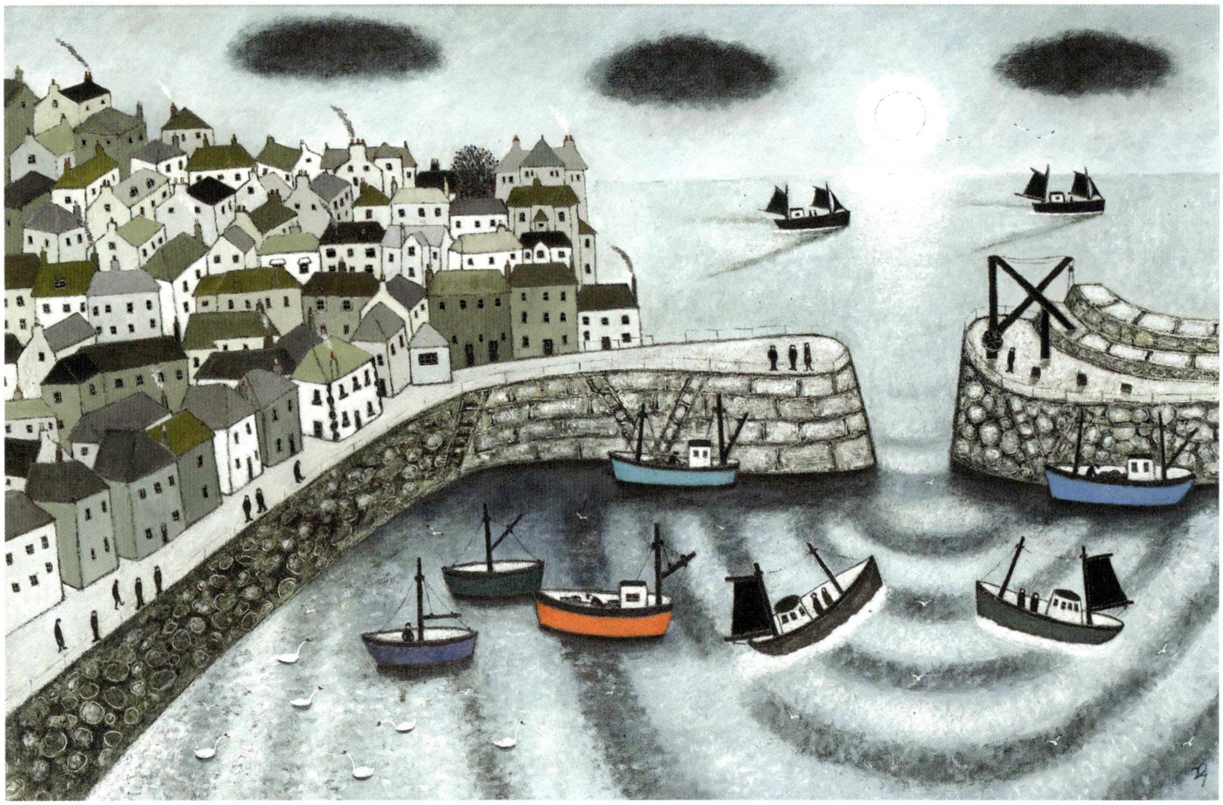

Dawn at Mousehole

This painting was one of the major exhibits in the solo show and one of her earliest scenes to feature characters so synonymous with Joan's later works.

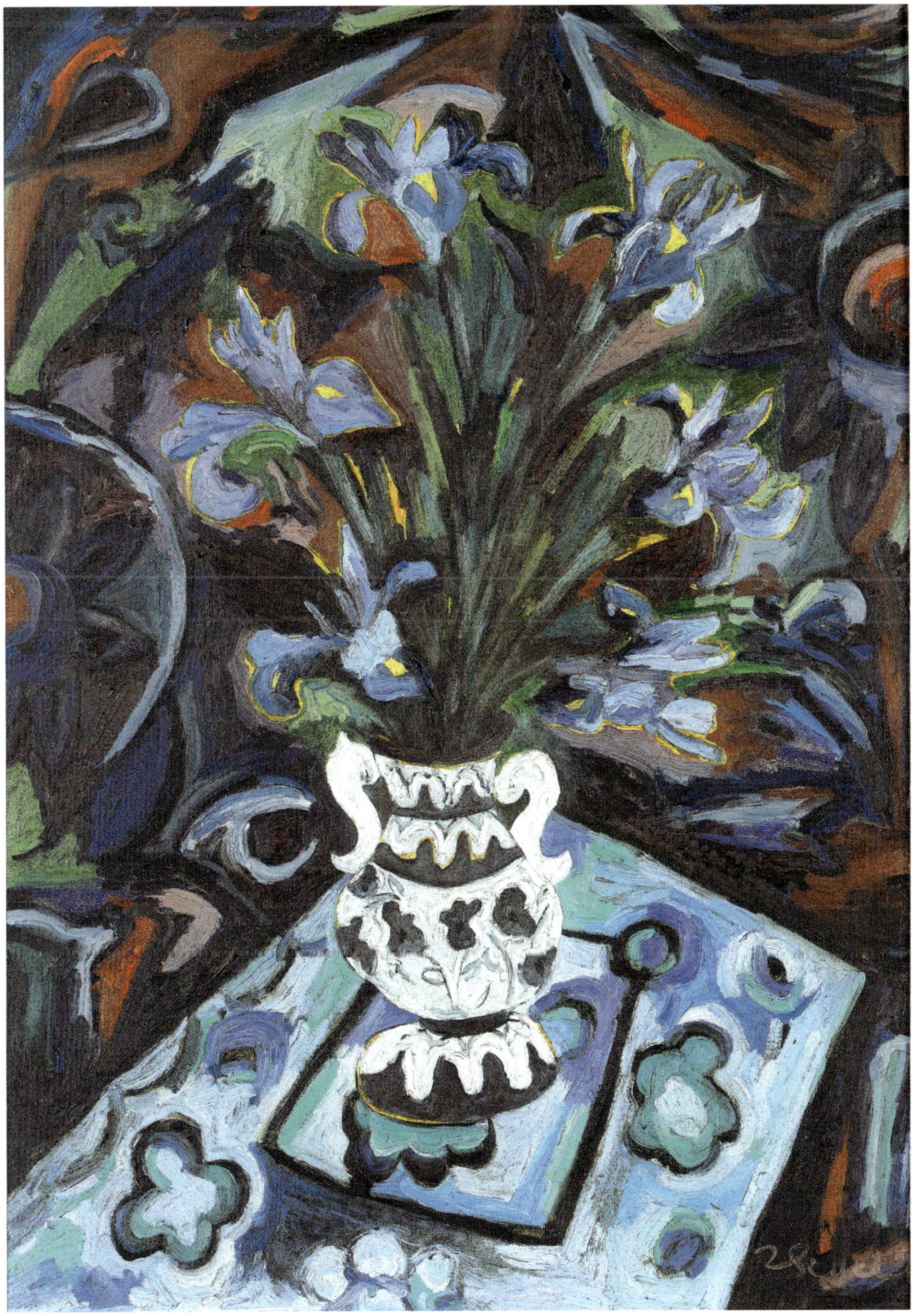

Still Life with Iris, another exhibit from first Solo Show, Plymouth Art Gallery 1969

Chapter 4 The Penwith Peninsula

Cornwall's Penwith Peninsula is an area of rich and exciting contrasts. In this chapter we follow Joan's painting excursions from the lovely Godrevy Point with its impressive lighthouse, past St. Ives, down the Atlantic coast and around Land's End. Once past Gwennap Head we enter the sheltered south coast of the peninsula. Along this coast are found the important harbours and towns of Mousehole, Newlyn and Penzance before reaching Marazion with its impressive views of St. Michael's Mount. Between the coasts lie the historic villages of St. Just, St. Buryan, Zennor, Madron and Morvah.

From the moment Joan moved to Cornwall she was fascinated by the people and places along this peninsula. She became absorbed in the day to day lives of the fishermen and their families sharing with them the anguish and uncertainties as the great Cornish fishing industry declined.

She found inspiration from a landscape dotted everywhere with tin mines and their engine houses as one by one they closed and were left to become ruins, standing proudly on the moors and headlands. The area is rich in Cornish legend with numerous pre-historic monuments and ancient sites, all providing Joan with dramatic backcloths for her paintings.

Throughout the area's history, farming has played an important part. The land is of variable quality and the working of it a demanding occupation. The fields tend to be small and over the last hundred years the keeping of livestock has given way more and more to the development of the market garden industry and in particular to the growing of flowers. Fields of violets, daffodils and narcissi abound in early Spring. Joan had many friends amongst the farmers and growers and often featured them in her paintings.

As we travel along the coast it would seem that around every corner we come upon a dramatic cove nestled between two massive rock faces or a beautiful white sandy beach. There are dozens of small harbours which once had their own fishermen with their small boats so necessary for the survival of the village or hamlet. Now these are the haunts of the thousands of holiday makers who each year descend upon west Cornwall to enjoy the stunning scenery and the mild climate.

This then was Joan's stage. She toured the region sketch book always to hand to provide us with wonderful pictures full of history, sometimes sad but so often humorous and warm.

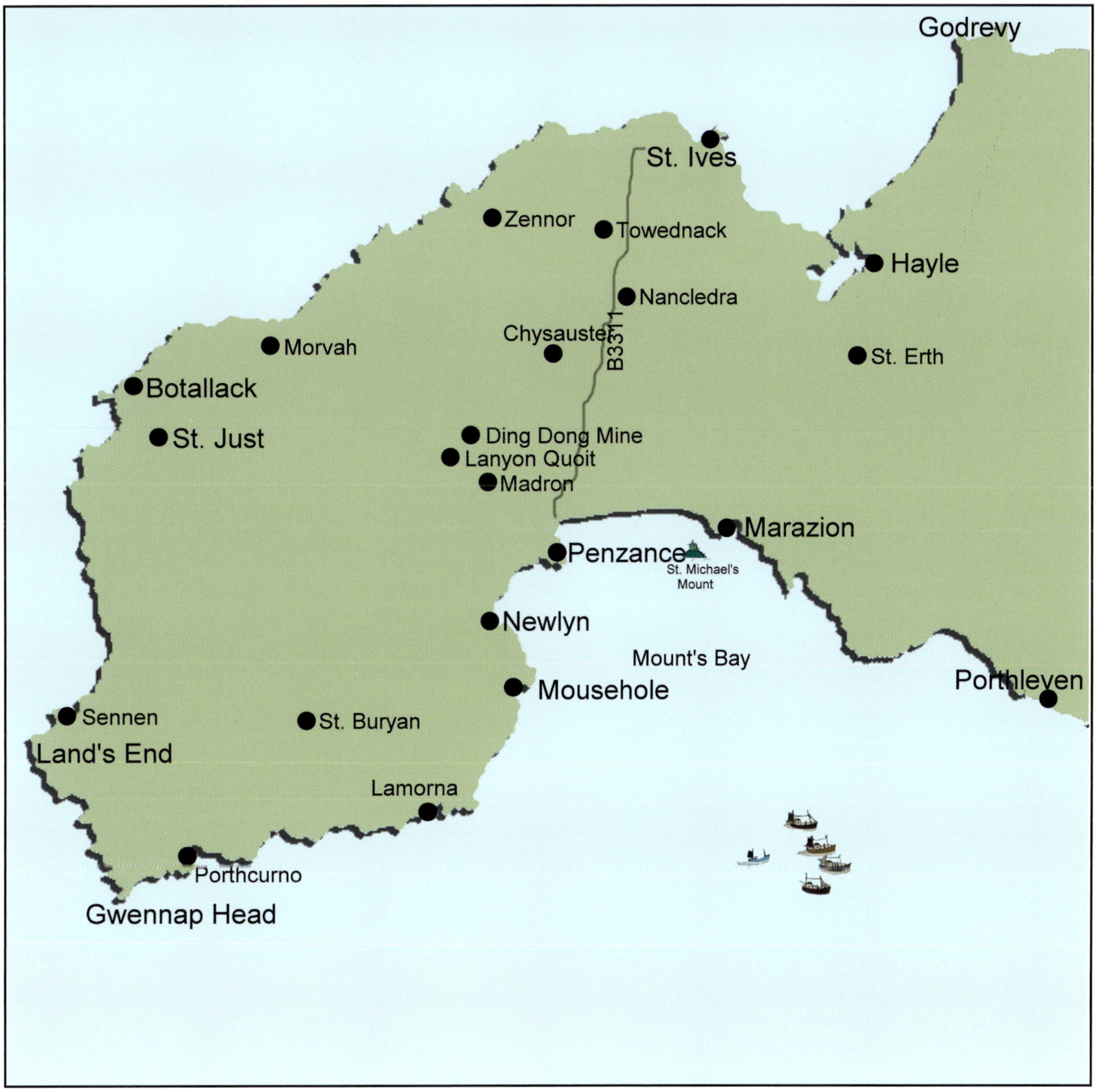
Godrevy
St. Ives
Zennor
Towednack
Hayle
Nancledra
Chysauster
B3311
Morvah
St. Erth
Botallack
St. Just
Ding Dong Mine
Lanyon Quoit
Madron
Marazion
Penzance
St. Michael's Mount
Newlyn
Mount's Bay
Mousehole
Porthleven
Sennen
St. Buryan
Land's End
Lamorna
Porthcurno
Gwennap Head

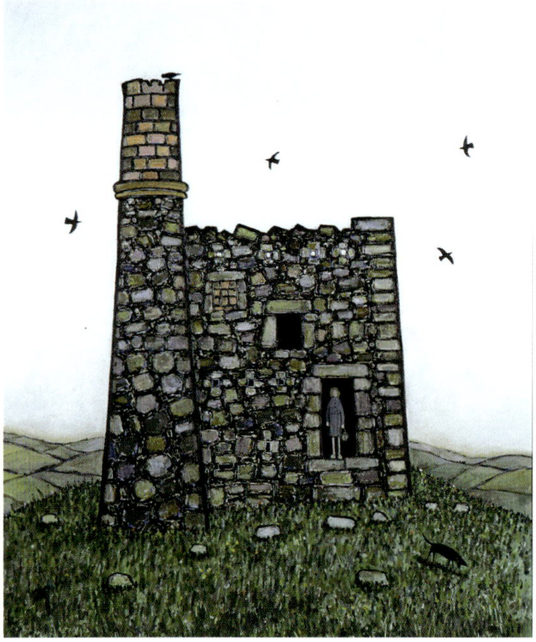

Ding Dong Mine

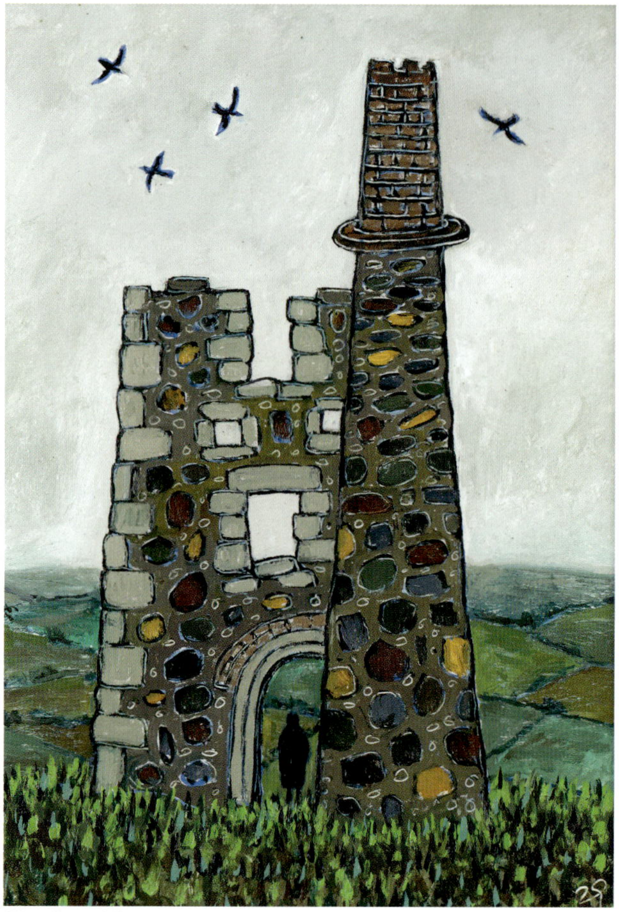

Ding Dong Mine

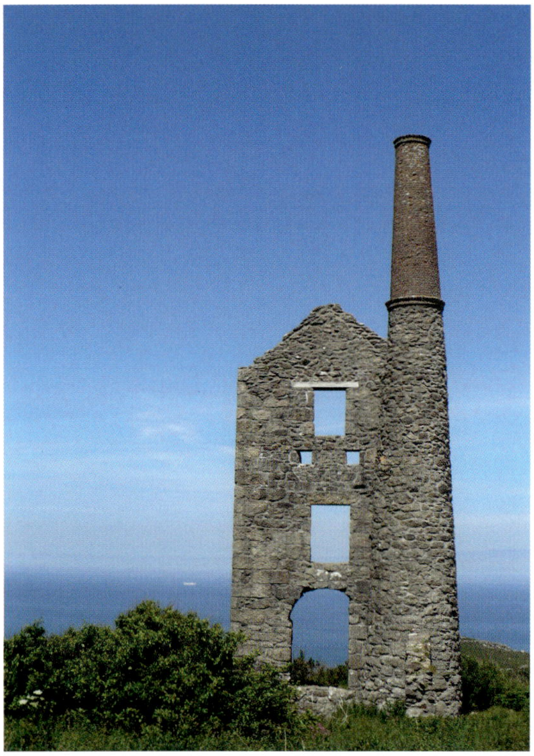

Carn Garver 2008

Tin Mines and Engine Houses

Ding Dong Mine

Lying in the heart of the moors of West Penwith, Ding Dong Mine is reputed to be one of the oldest tin mines in Cornwall. It ceased to operate at the end of the nineteenth century, but remains a prominent landmark.

Botallack Mine

Botallack mine lies in the St. Just mining area close to Land's End. It is one of the most ancient tin and copper mining districts in Cornwall. The mines are famous for the magnificent granite and stone engine houses which stand perched on the cliff edge, 30ft above the Atlantic Ocean.

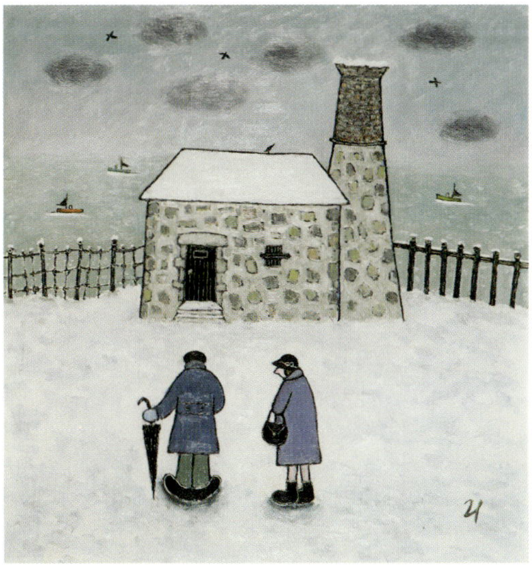

Old Engine House, Botallack, Wintertime

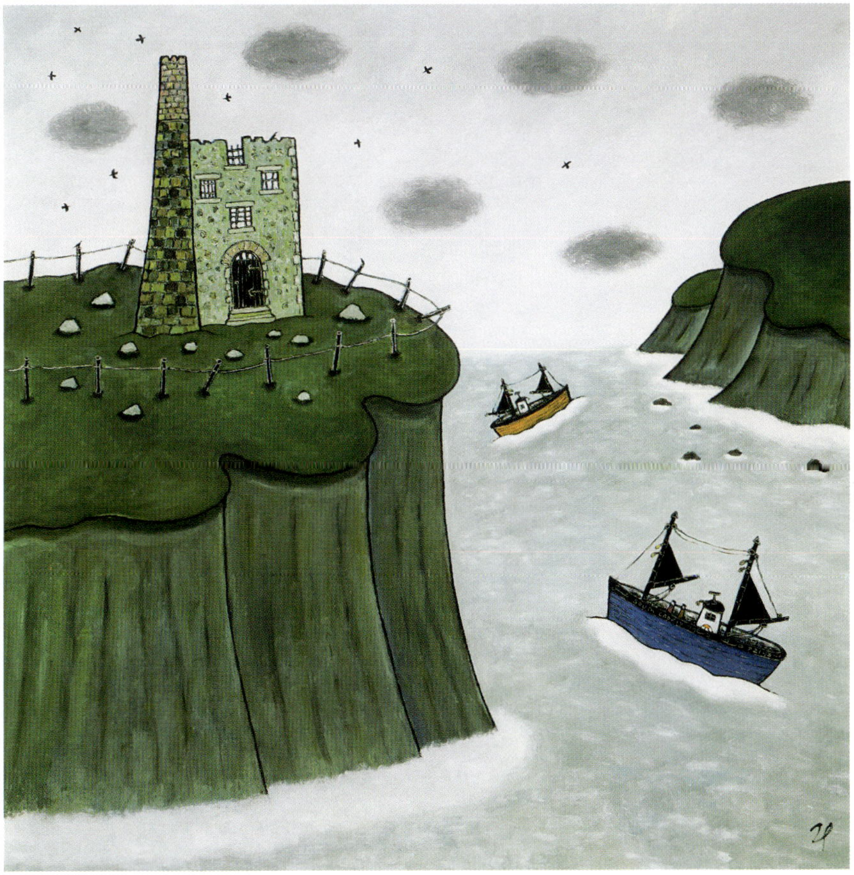

Fishing Boats Passing Tin Mine at Botallack Head

Lanyon Quoit

Lanyon Quoit is the best known of the Cornish quoits and is thought to date back to the New Stone Age. It stands just off the road leading from Madron to Morvah and is believed to be the remains of a long barrow or chambered tomb.

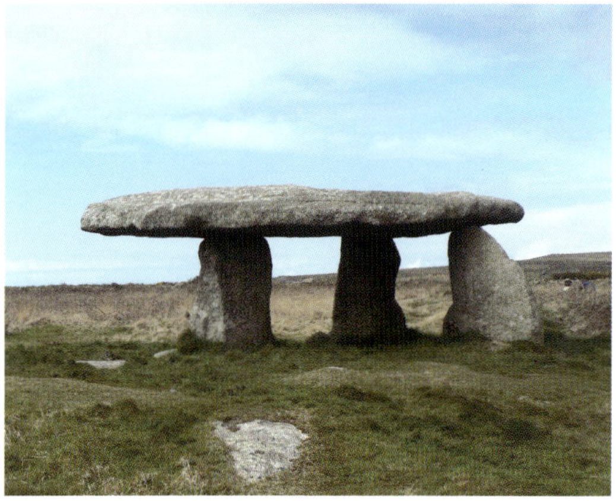

Lanyon Quoit 2008

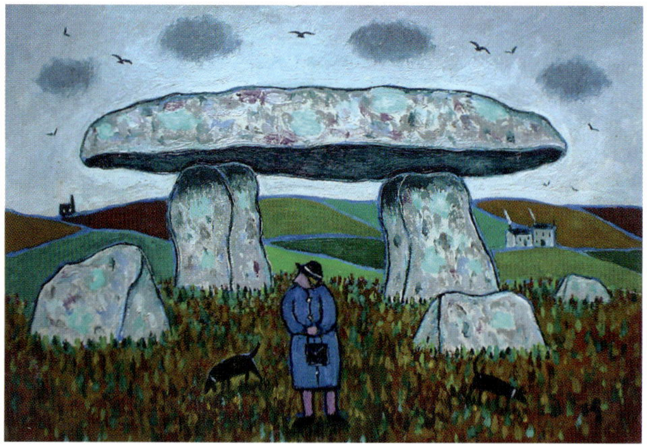

Lanyon Quoit

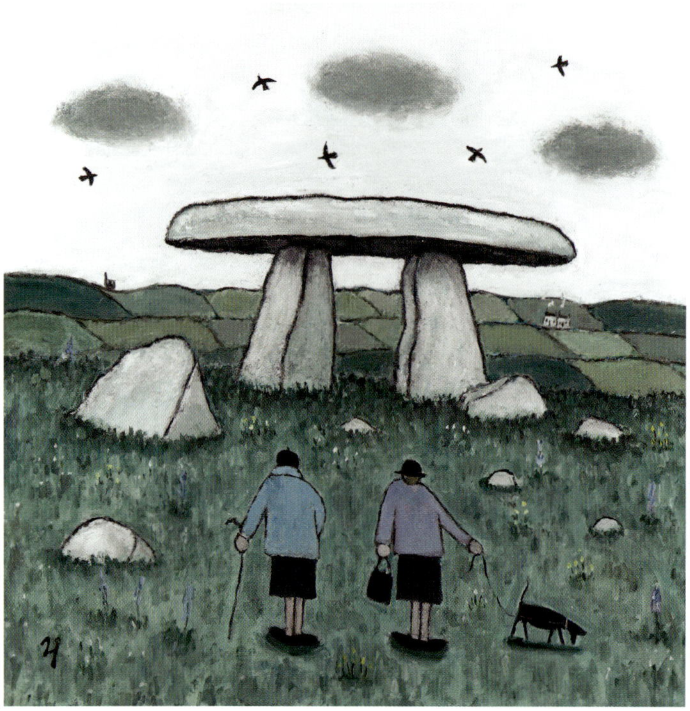

Visiting Lanyon Quoit

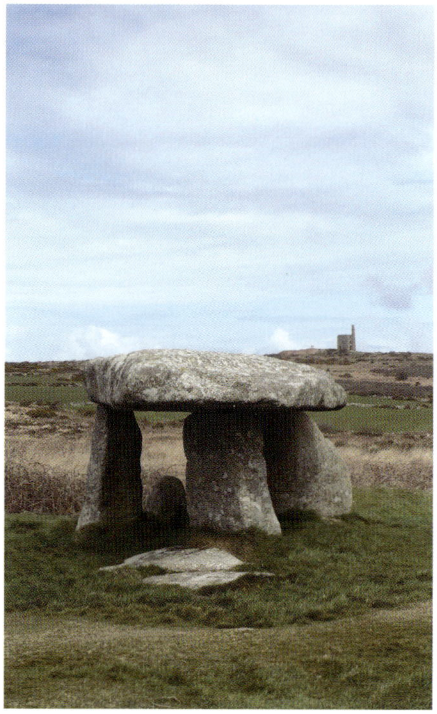

Lanyon Quoit, Ding Dong Mine on horizon 2008

Land's End and Longships

Joan was painting the dramatic scenery around Land's End long before it turned into today's Theme Park.

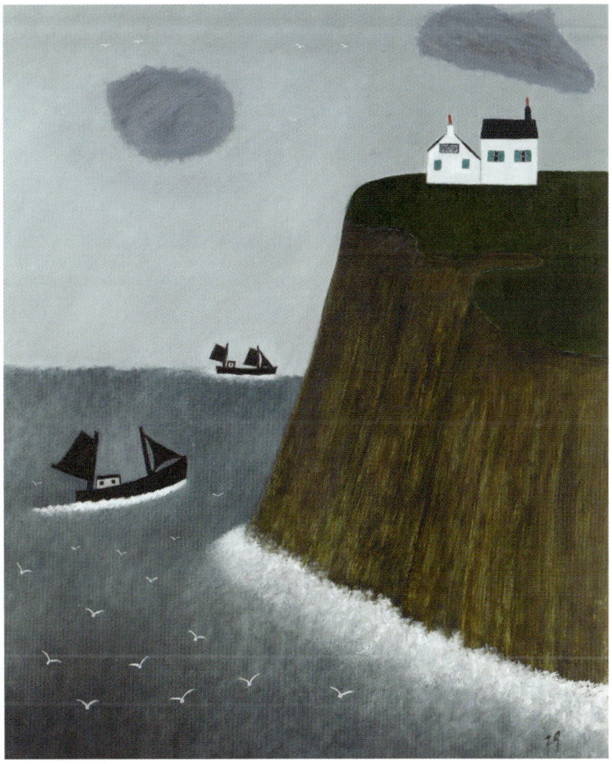

Land's End

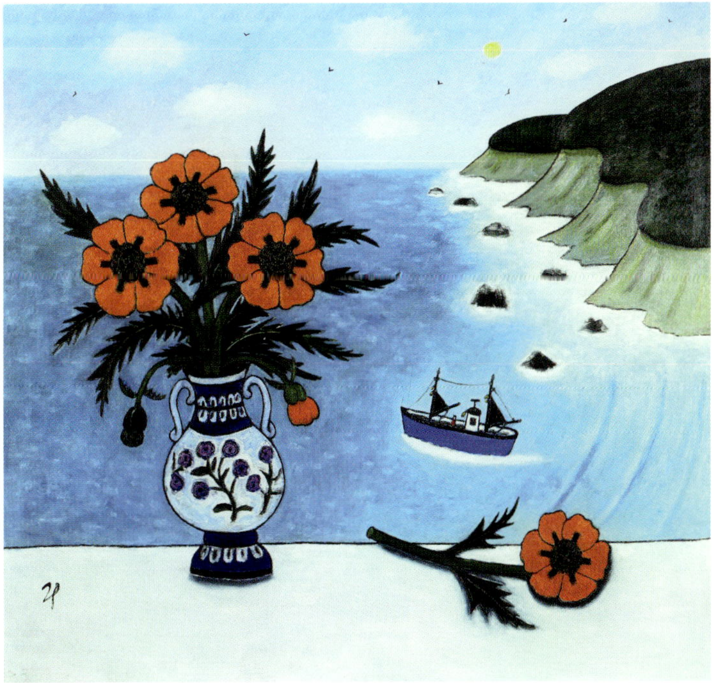

View of Land's End with Poppies

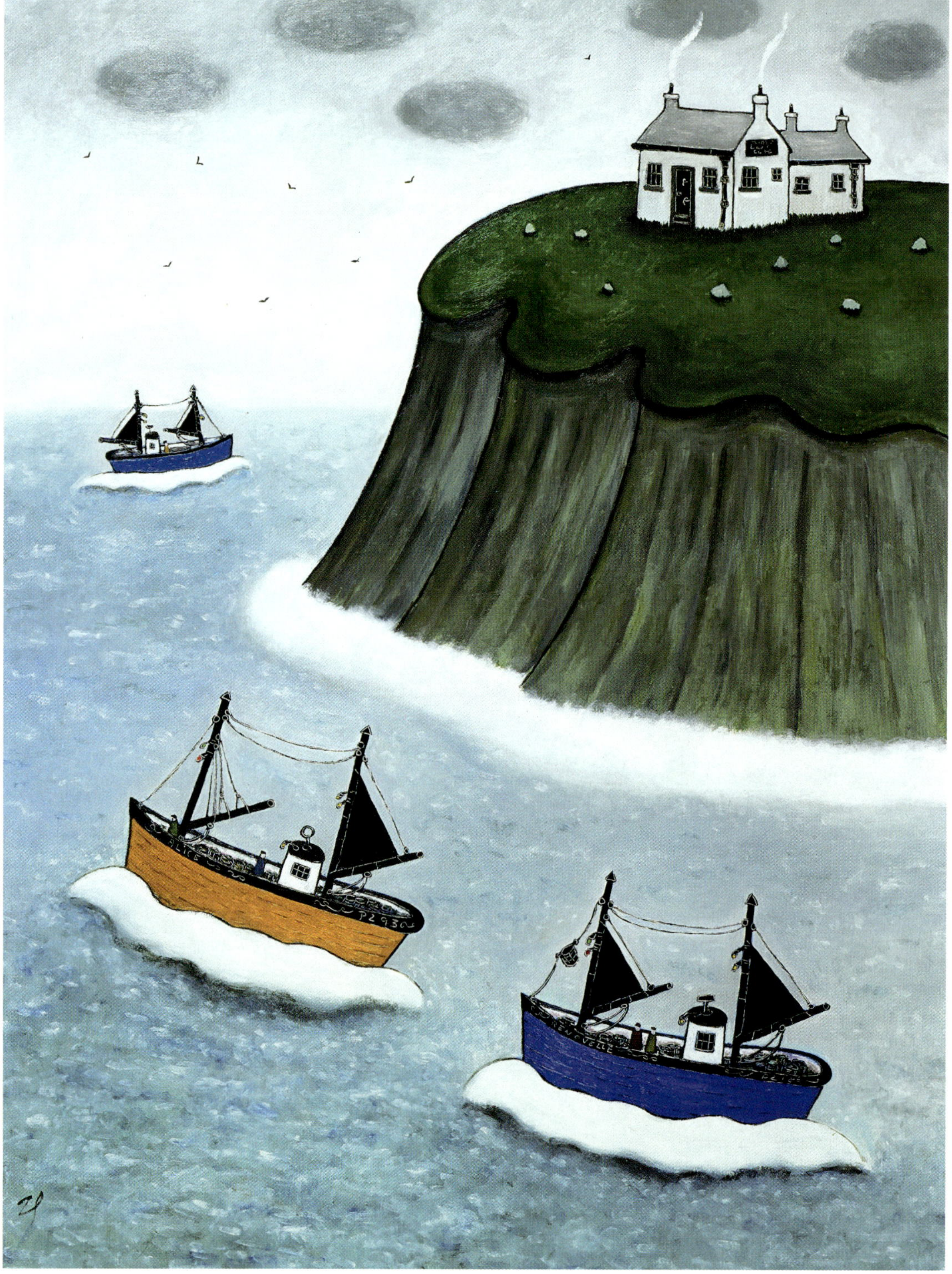

Going Fishing past the 'First and Last' House in England

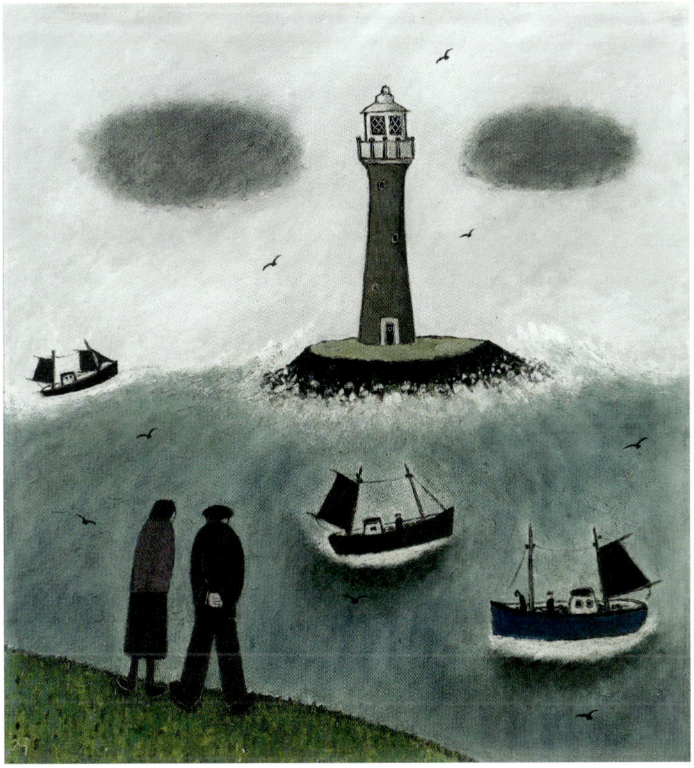

Longships Lighthouse

Longships is a group of rocks to the west of Land's End. A lighthouse was first built here in 1795 but the taller tower was built by 1873. It is now unmanned and automatically operated.

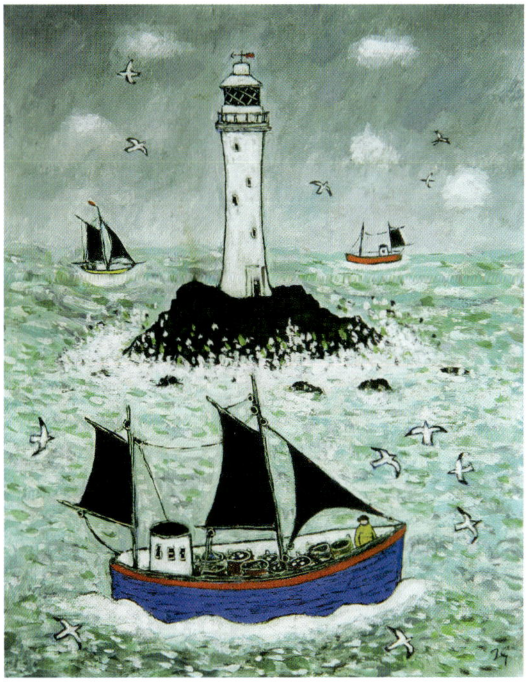

Sailing Past Longships

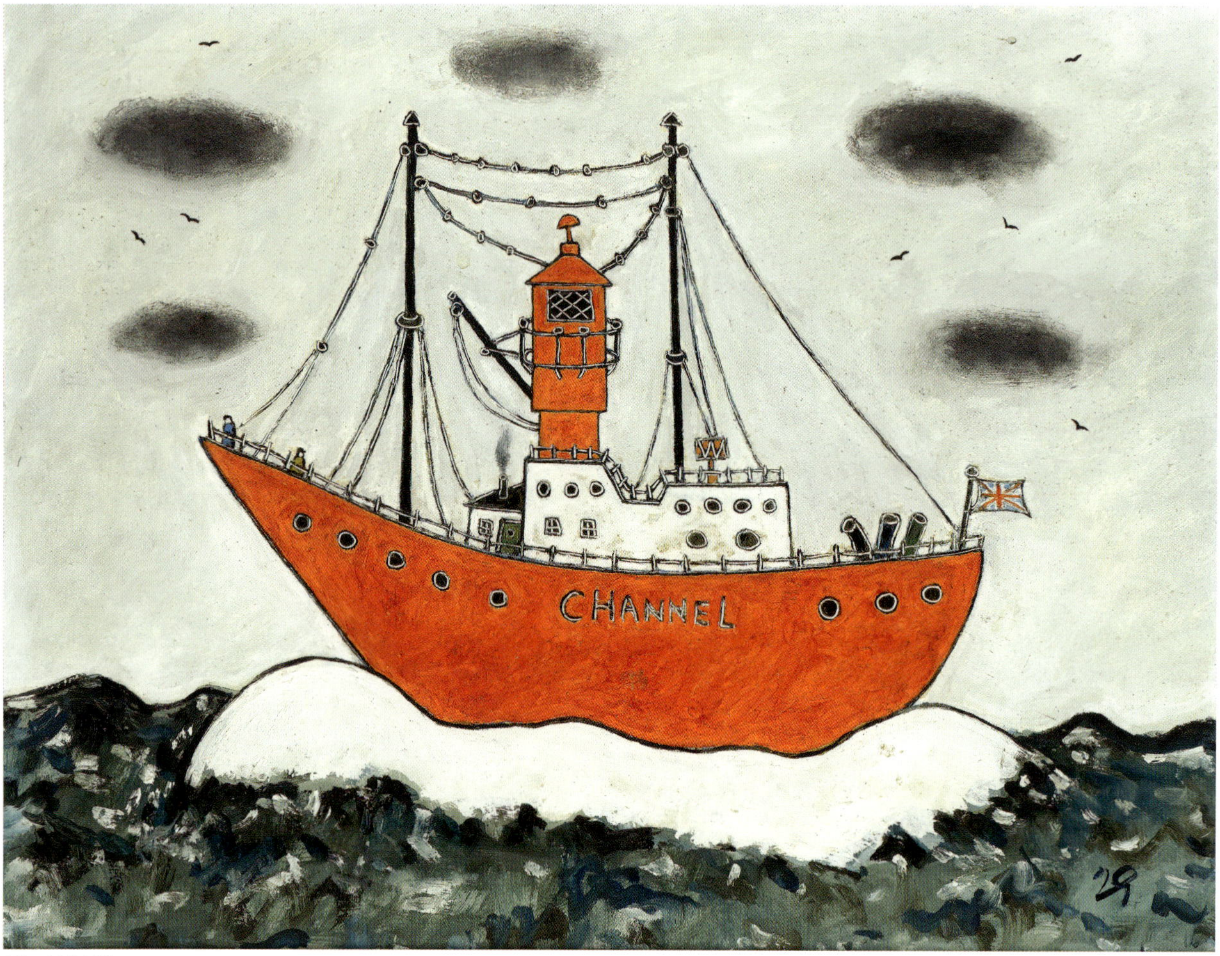

The Lightship

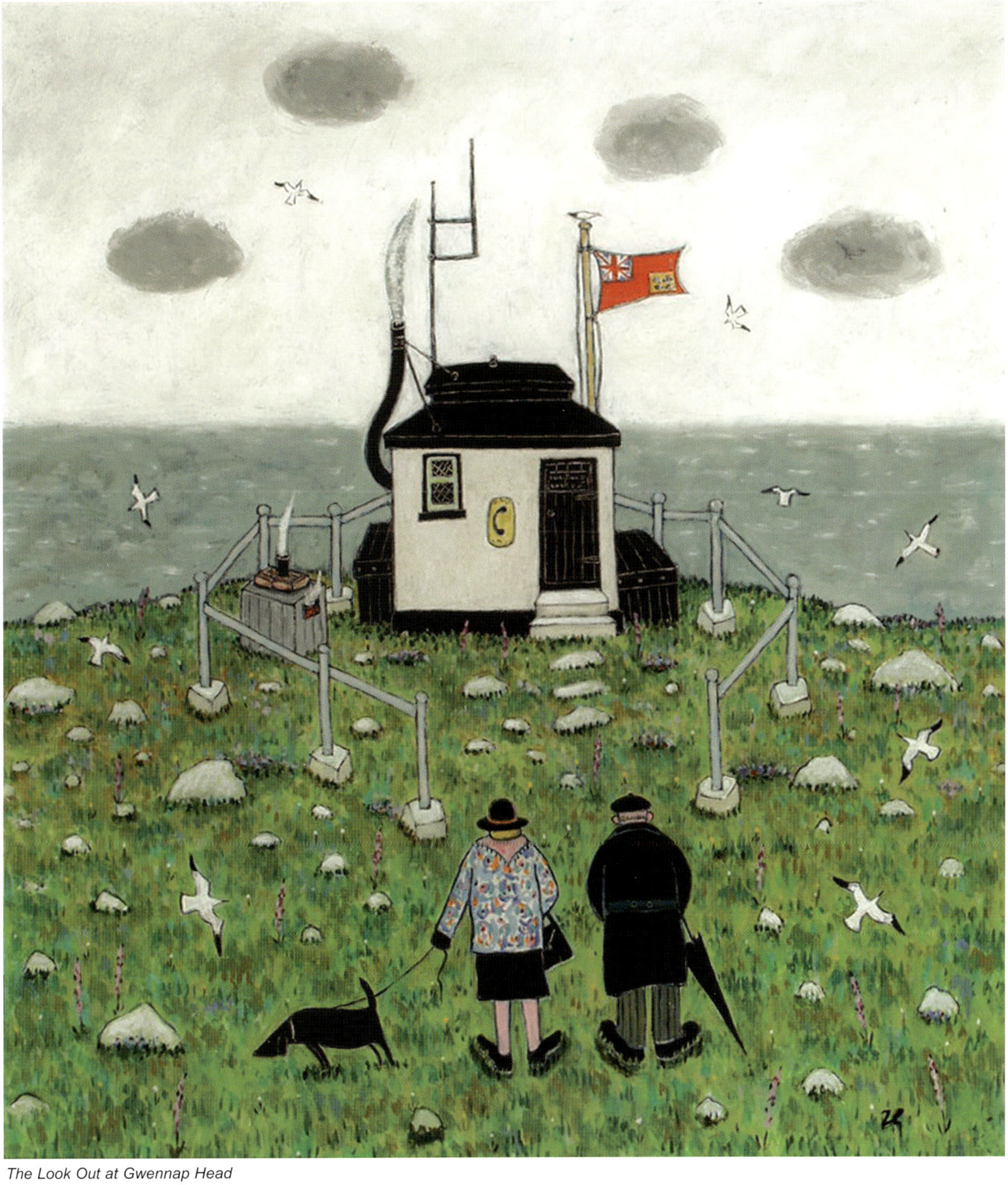

The Look Out at Gwennap Head

Beaches and Coves

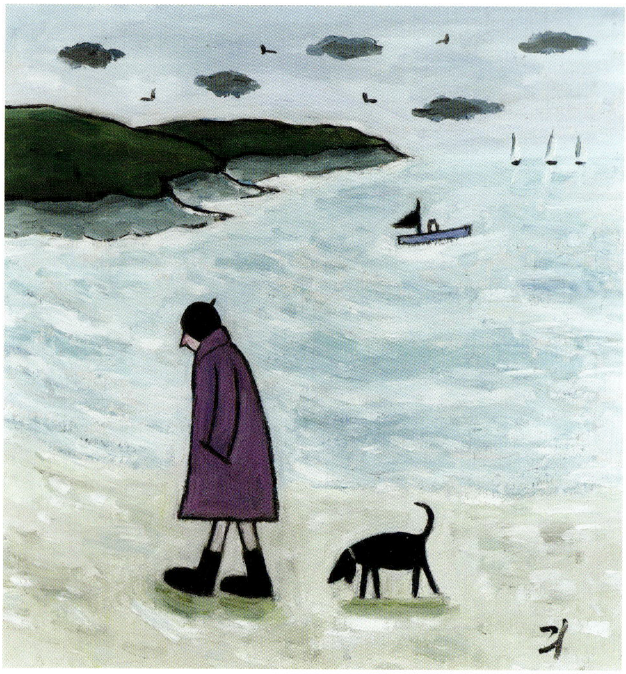
Walking the Dog on Sennen Beach

Sennen

A wonderful stretch of sand loved by holidaymakers but the cove still retains the atmosphere of an old fishing village.

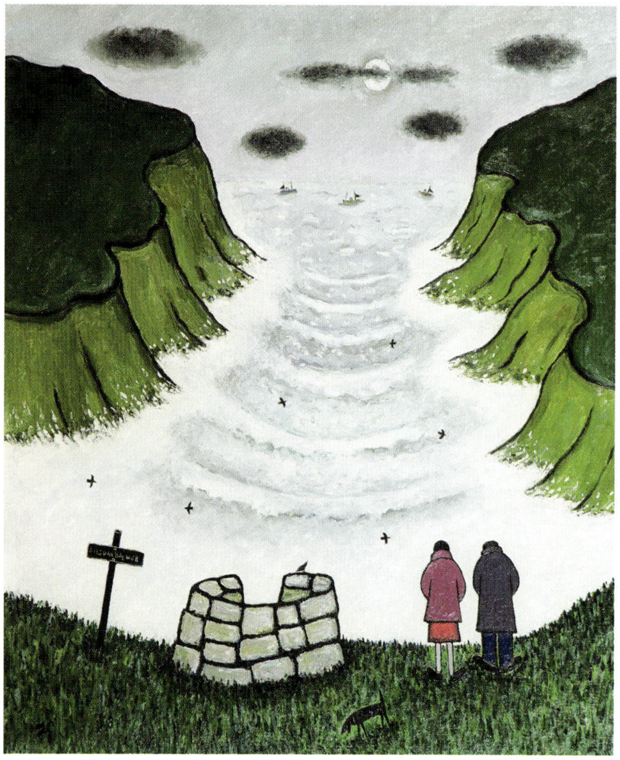
The Wishing Well at Pordenack Point

Pordenack Point

The first major headland from Land's End.

Porthcurno

Joan much admired Rowena Cade, who from 1931 until she died in 1983 planned, built and financed the Minack Theatre which is located on the cliffs just west of Porthcurno. It is said that she had converted this cave on Porthcurno Beach as a hideaway from her dominant mother. Nobody could reach her when the tide was in.

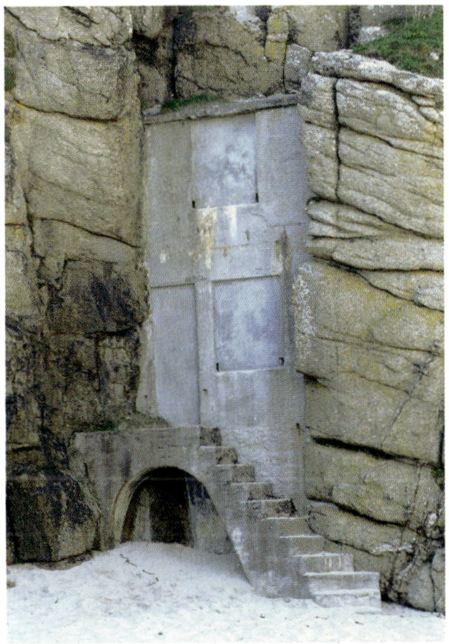

Rowena Cade's Cottage at Porthcurno 2008

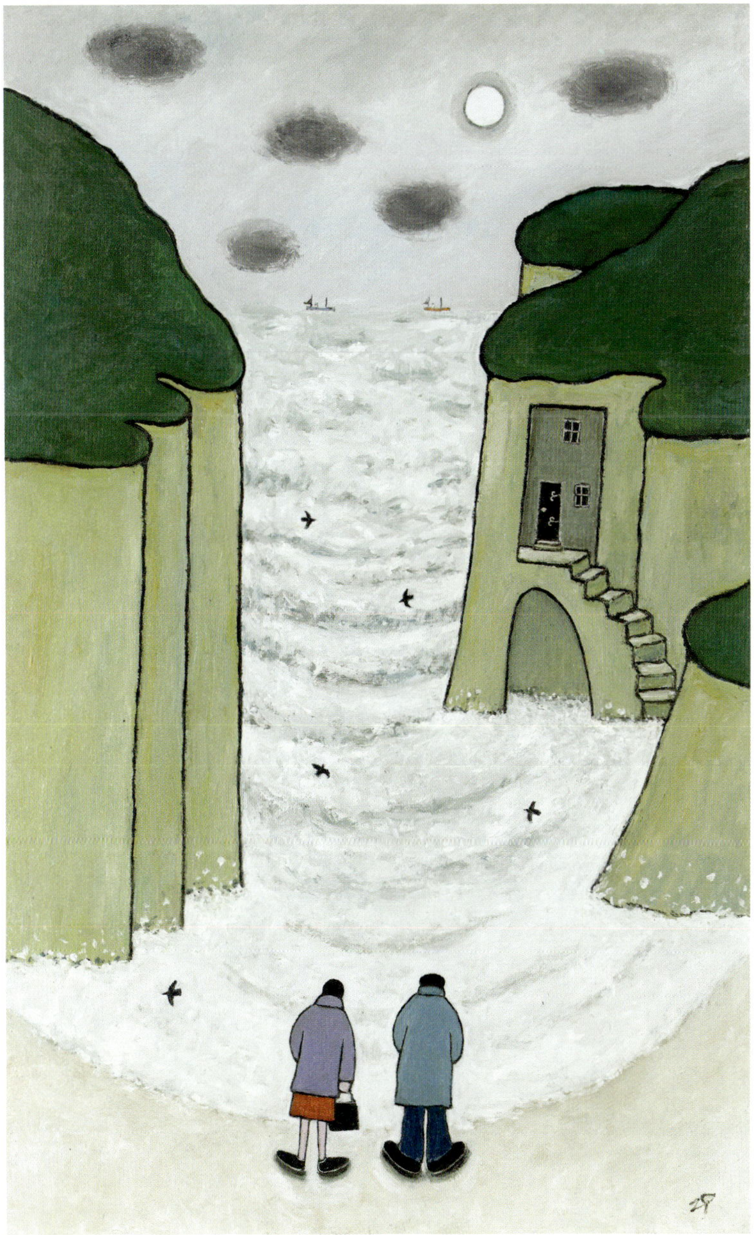

Rowena Cade's Cottage at Porthcurno

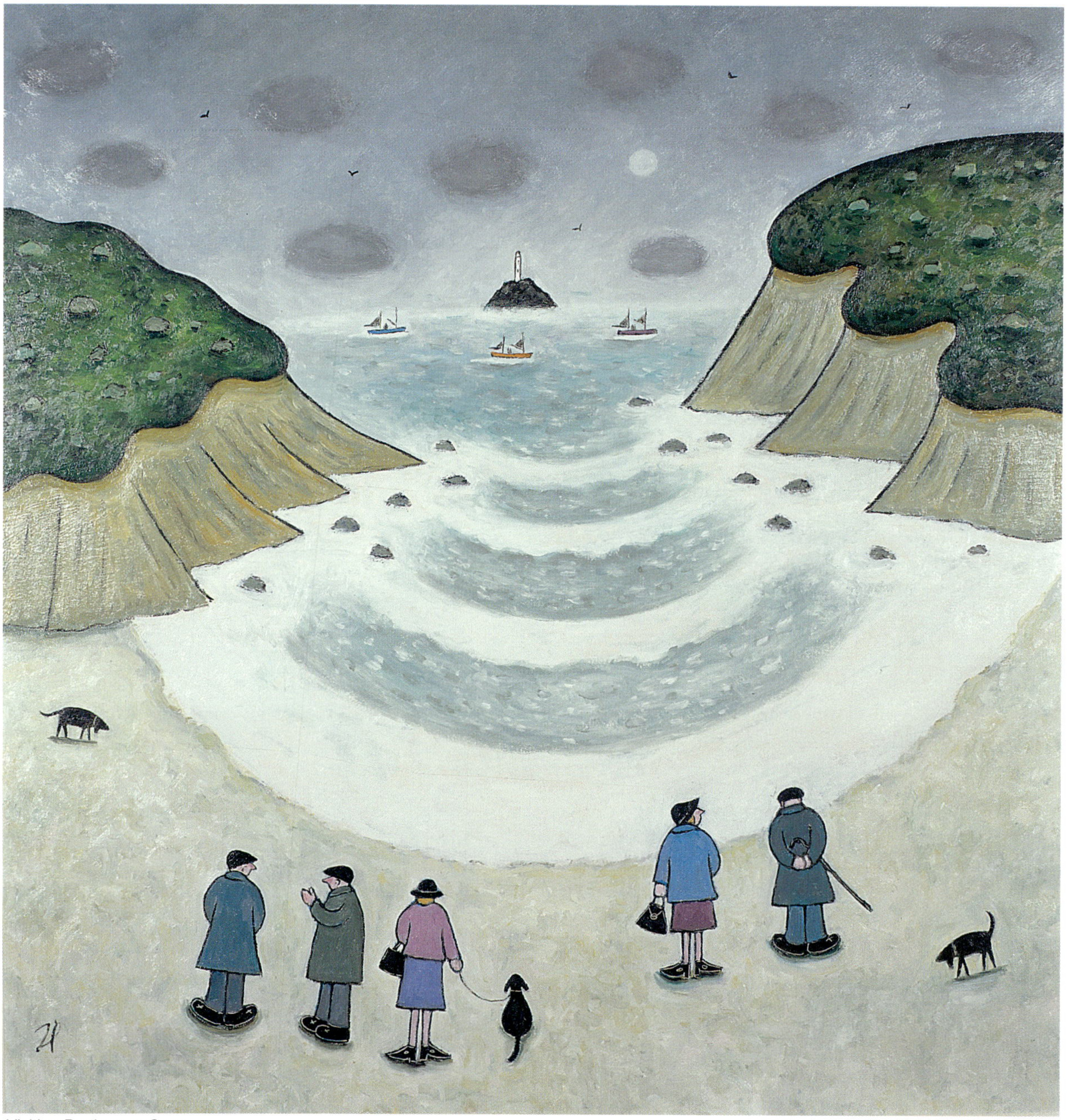

Visiting Porthcurno Cove

Lamorna

A beautiful cove just a few minutes drive or a spectacular cliff top walk from Mousehole is remembered for the Post-Impressionist colony of artists who lived here in the early part of the twentieth century. Amongst the most famous were Laura Knight, Samuel John Lamorna Birch, Harold Knight and Alfred Munnings. Augustus John was a frequent visitor. It is an artists' paradise.

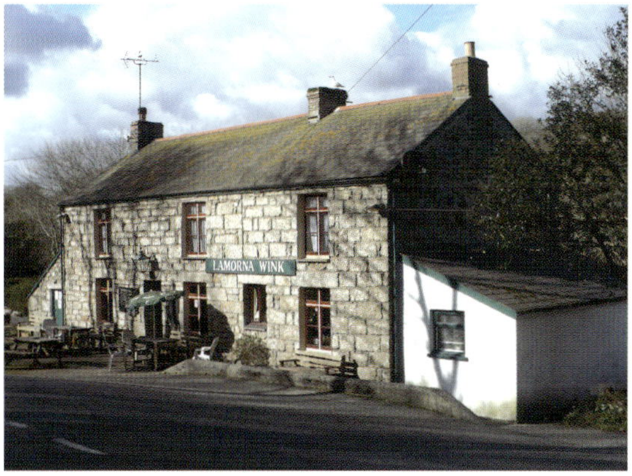

The Wink 2008

Conveniently situated on the lane leading down to the cove is "The Wink" frequented now just as it was in Laura Knight's day by artists and holidaymakers alike.

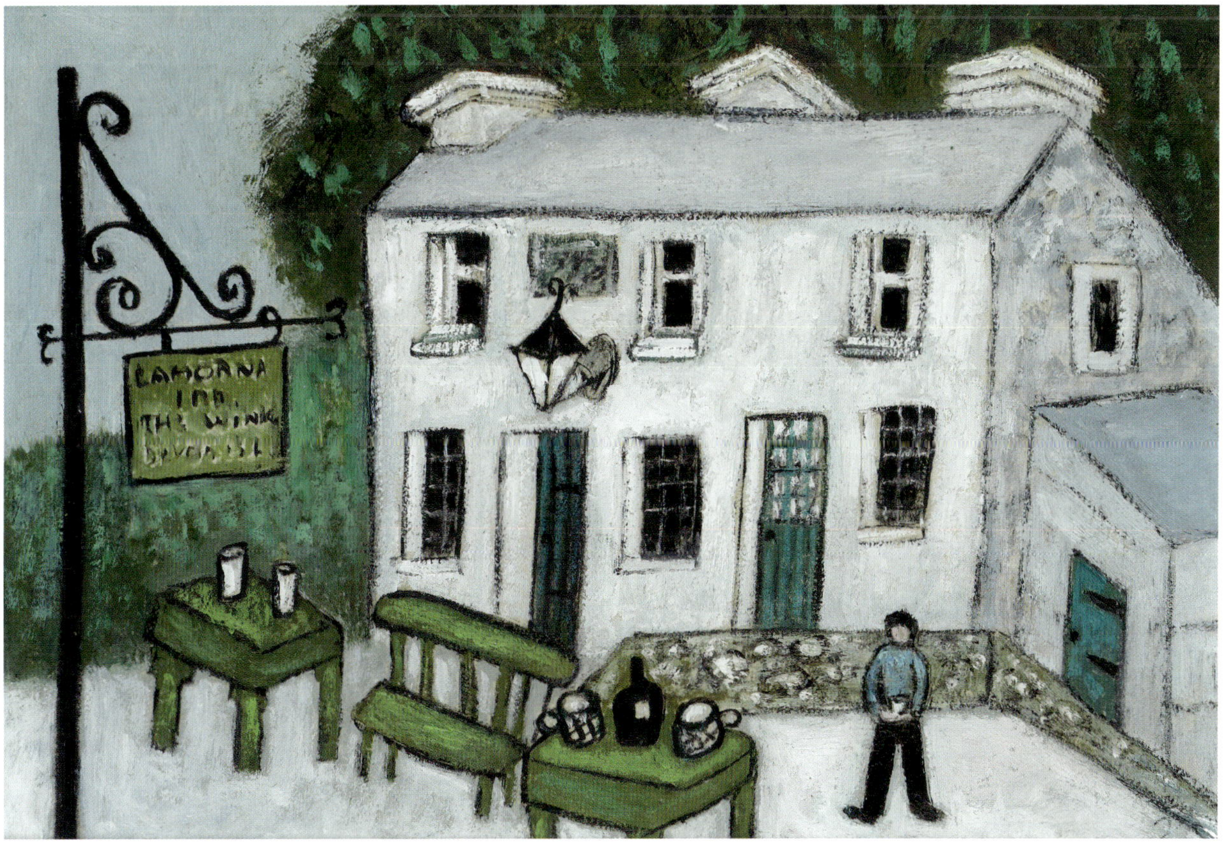

The Wink

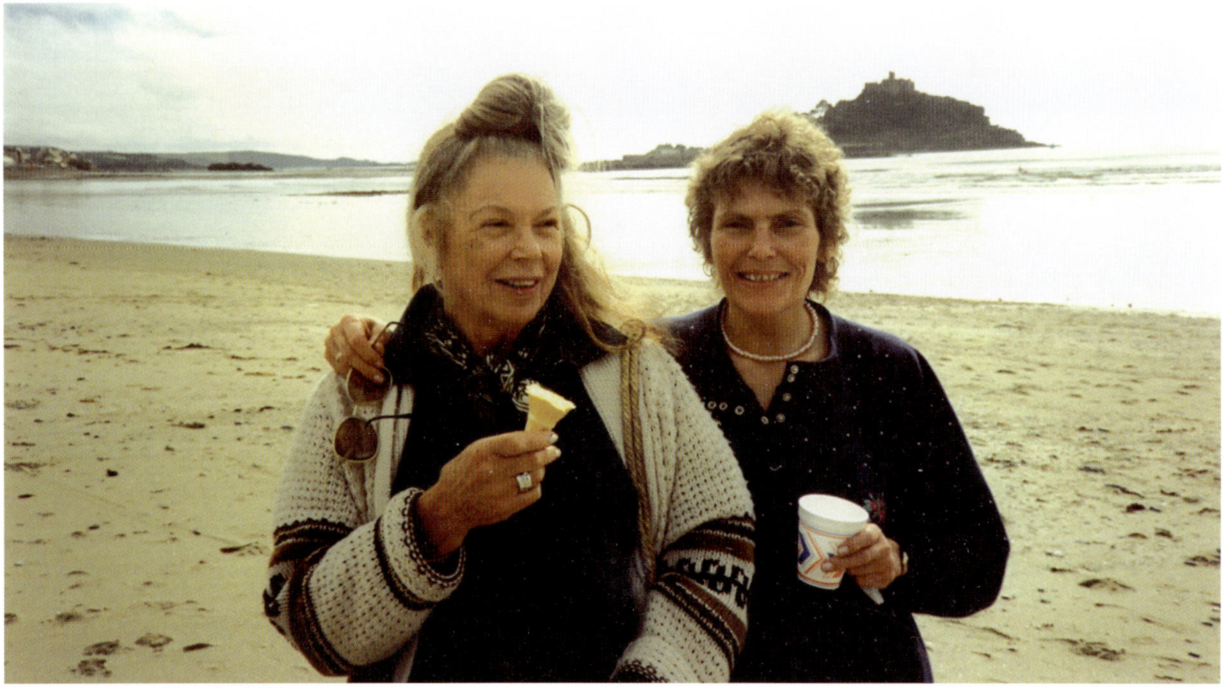

Joan with Mara at Marazion 1985

Marazion

The old town of Marazion is a popular destination for beach holidays and water sports. It is perhaps best known for St. Michael's Mount the island and castle reached by a causeway at low tide.

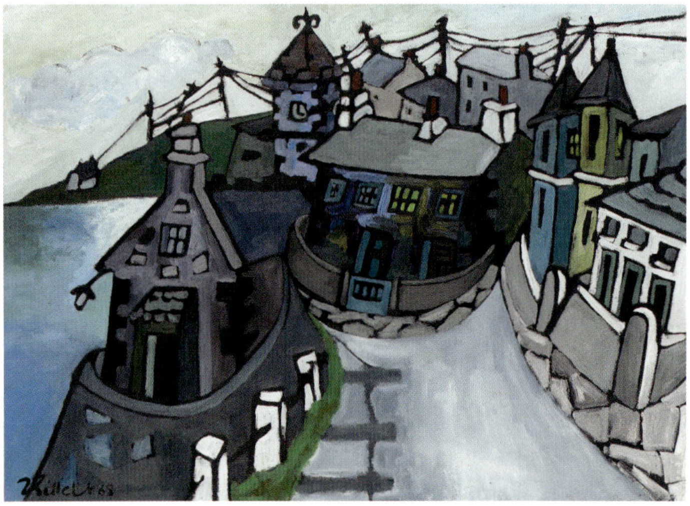

Marazion 1968

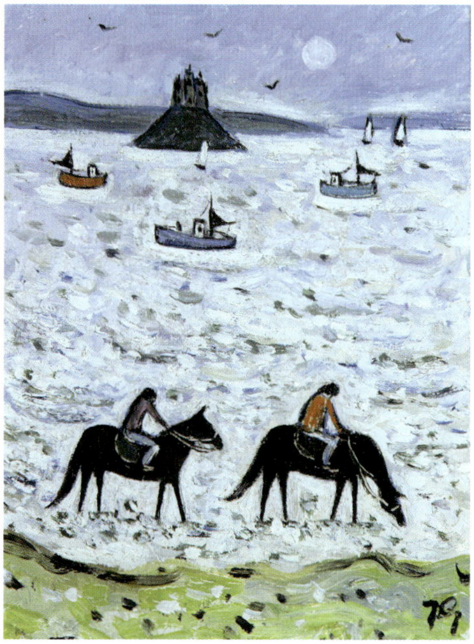

Riding at Marazion

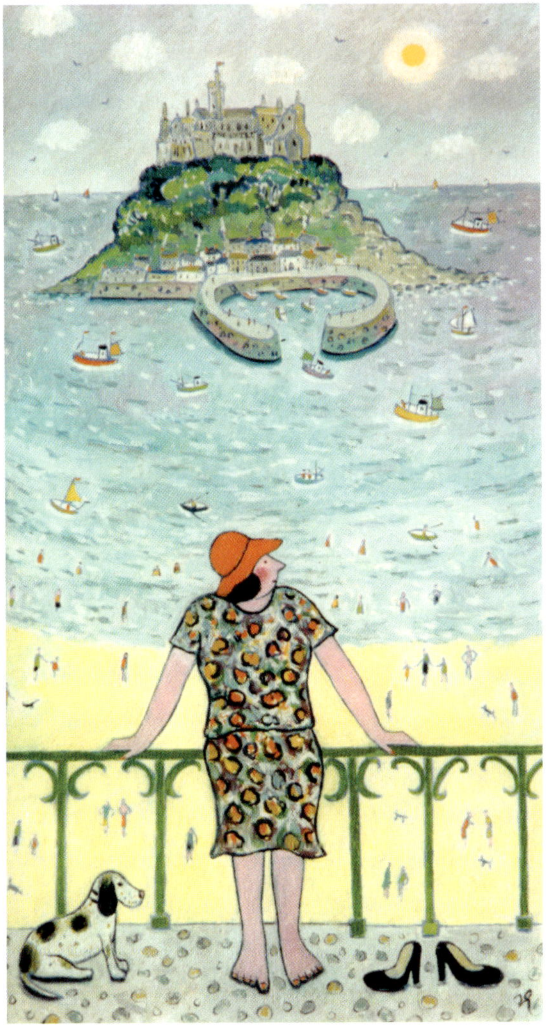

My Feet Hurt

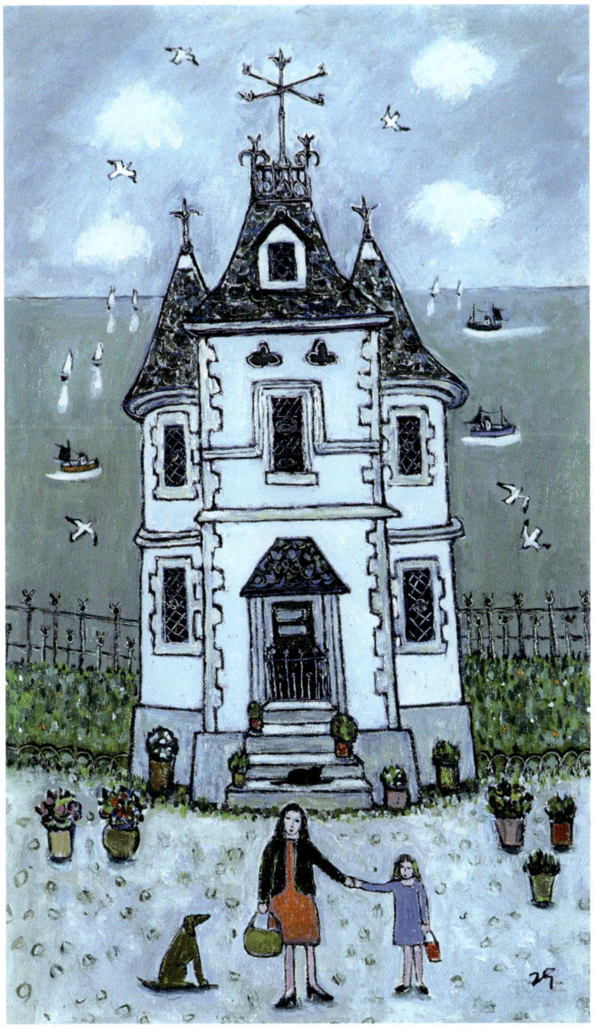

Staying at 'Seaview' Marazion

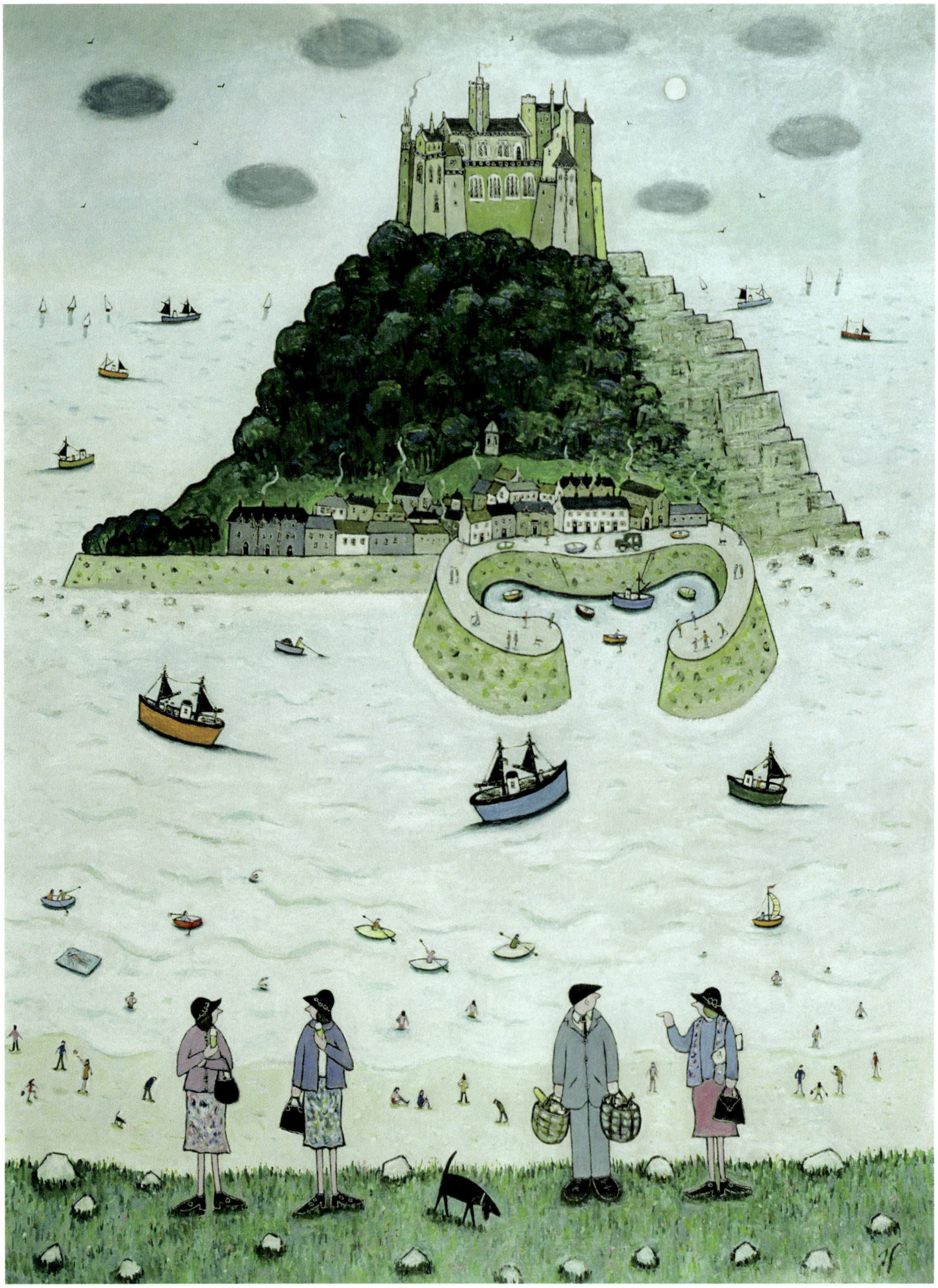

St. Michael's Mount

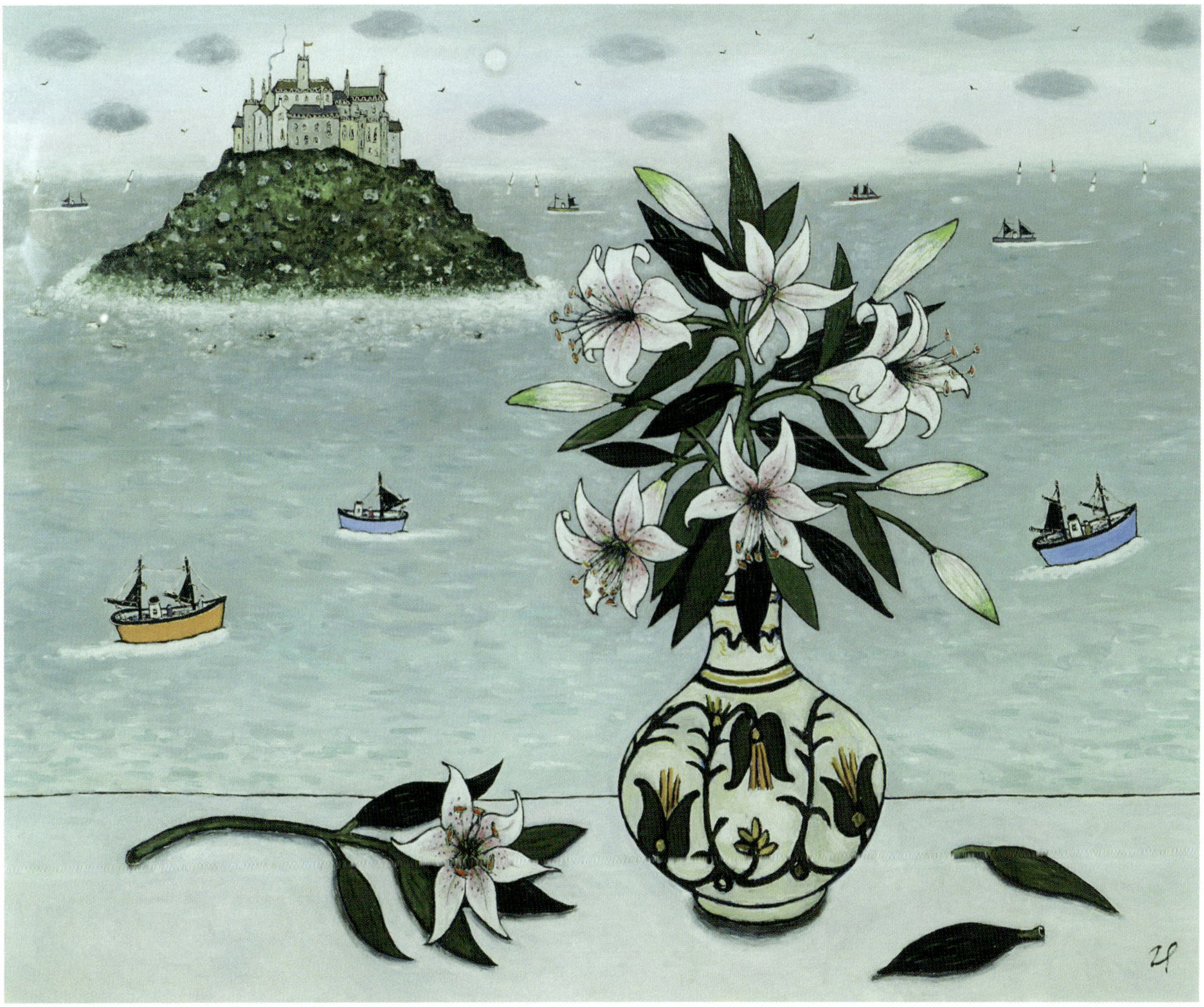
St. Michael's Mount with Lilies

Porthleven

Porthleven faces southwest directly into the prevailing wind and its development as a port was always constrained by its position. The growth in the number of merchant ships sailing around Mount's Bay from the early nineteenth century gave rise for a need, in times of distress, for a safe refuge along this coast line. Thus Porthleven grew from a small fishing inlet to a large harbour. The construction of this harbour was completed in 1825.

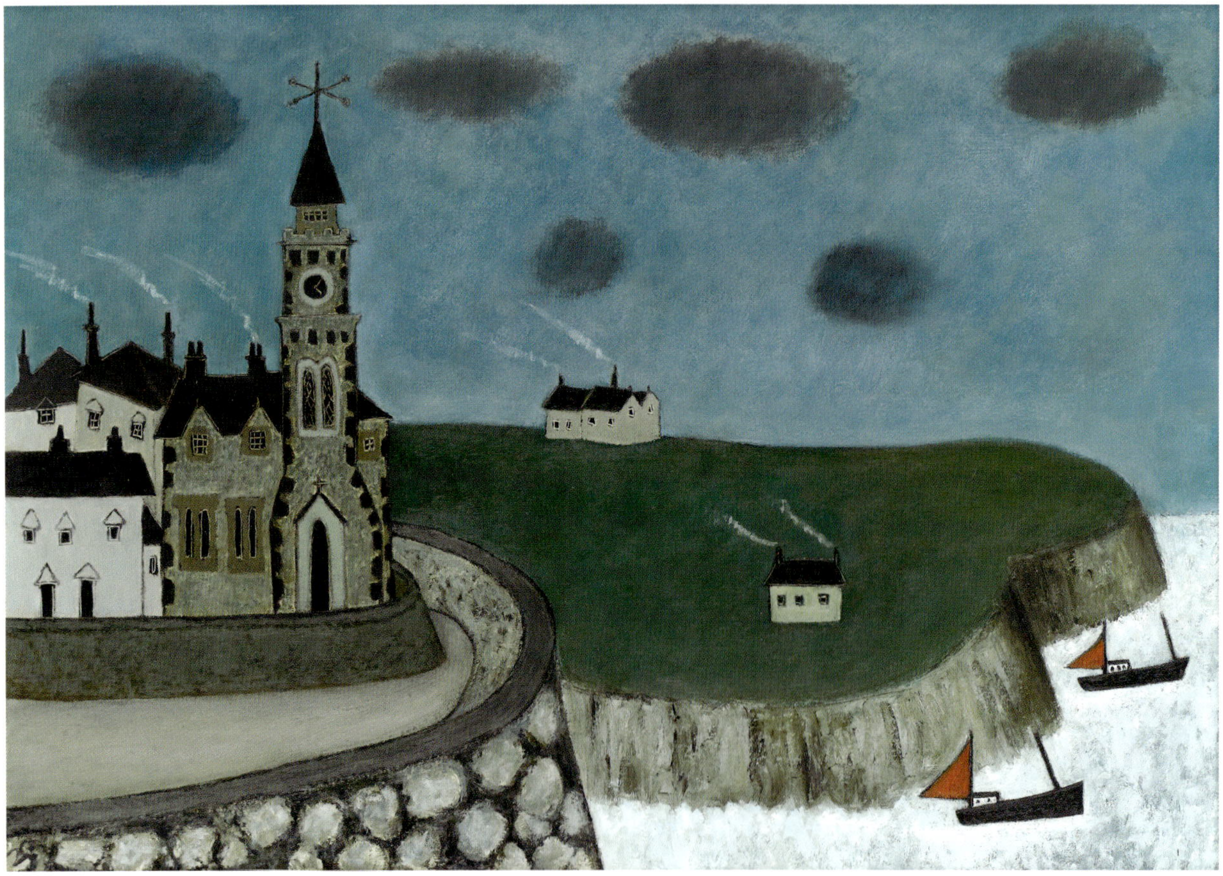

Porthleven

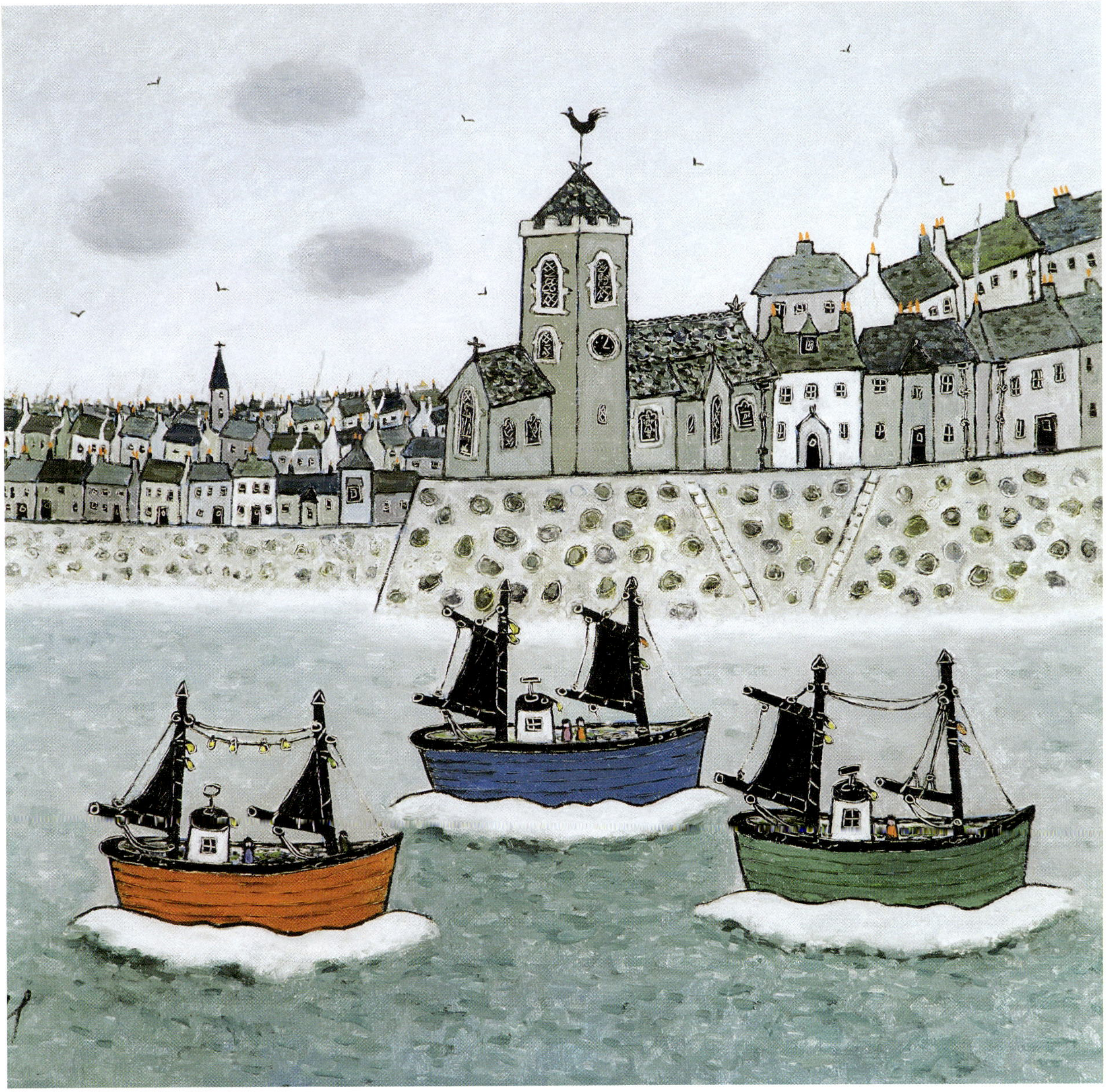
Returning Home to Porthleven

Farming and Village Life

Farmers and Growers

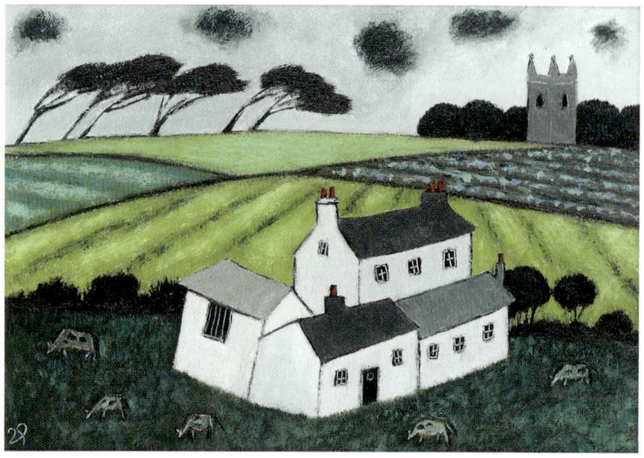
Trevithal Farm above Paul

Trevithal Farm is situated between Paul and Mousehole. This was one of Joan's favourite walks, usually ending up at the King's Arms in Paul.

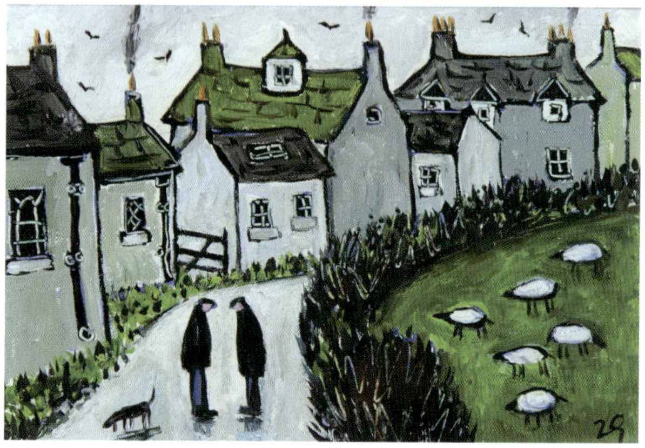
Harvey's Farm

Harvey's Farm was on top of Raginnis Hill. It was farmed by the three Harvey brothers who were all friends of Joan's.

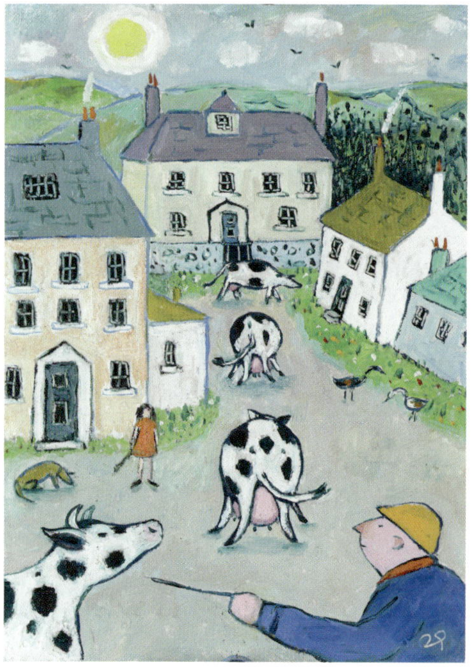
Taking the Cows Home

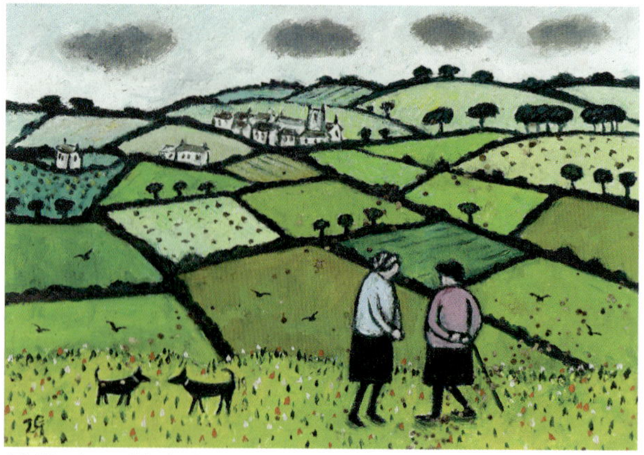
Fields above St. Just

The land that stretches above the beaches and harbours is a patchwork of small fields and market gardens.

Joan's great friend Edgar Wallace farmed the fields around Mousehole leading to the Coastguards. His main crop was violets which were picked daily during the season and transported on the 5.00am train from Penzance to reach Covent Garden that morning.

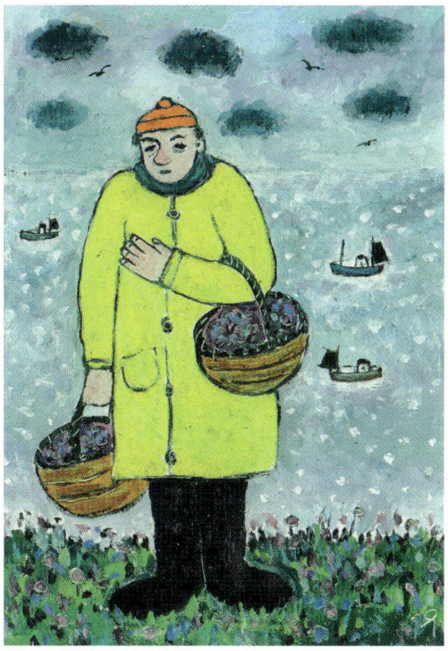

Edgar Wallace

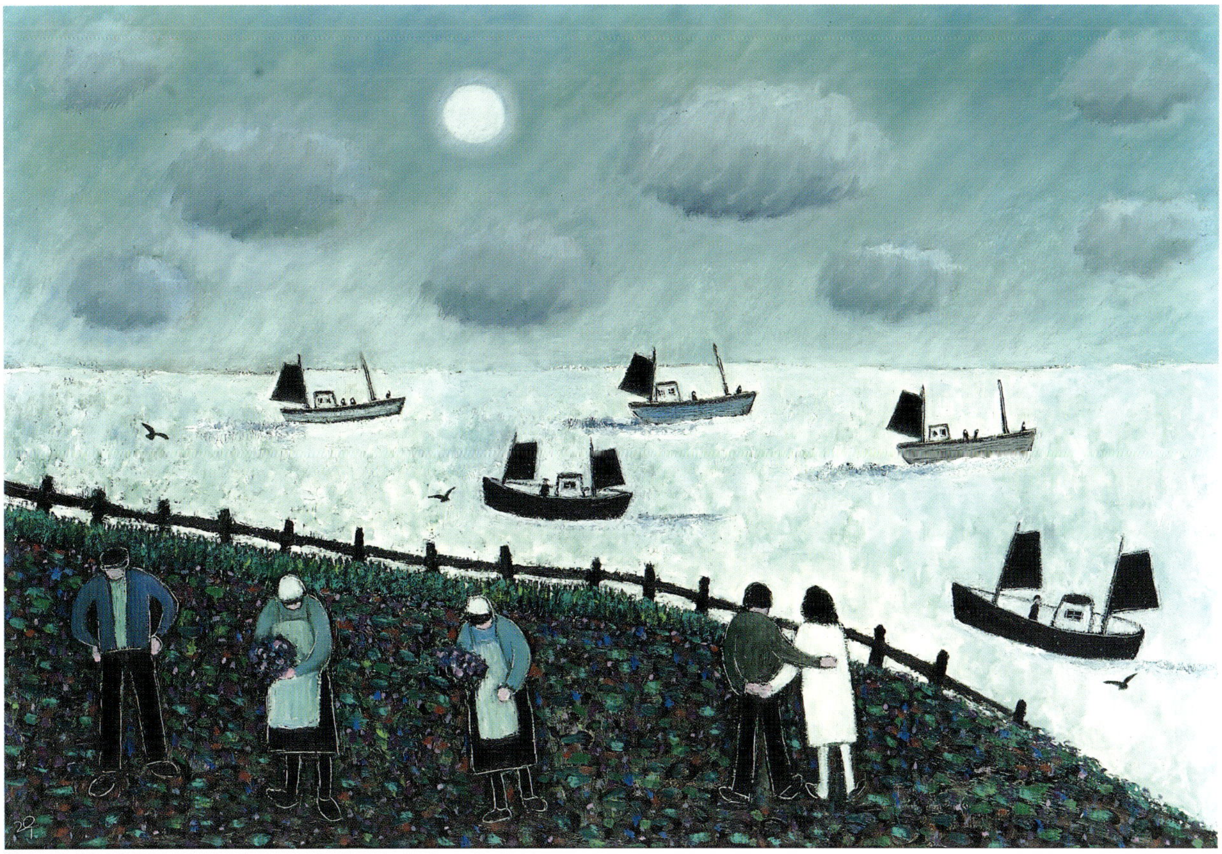

Edgar's Violet Farm

Village Scenes

St. Just was once the centre of the West Cornwall mining industry and disused engine houses are scattered around the immediate countryside.

There is a lovely 15th century church and a most impressive war memorial in the village square.

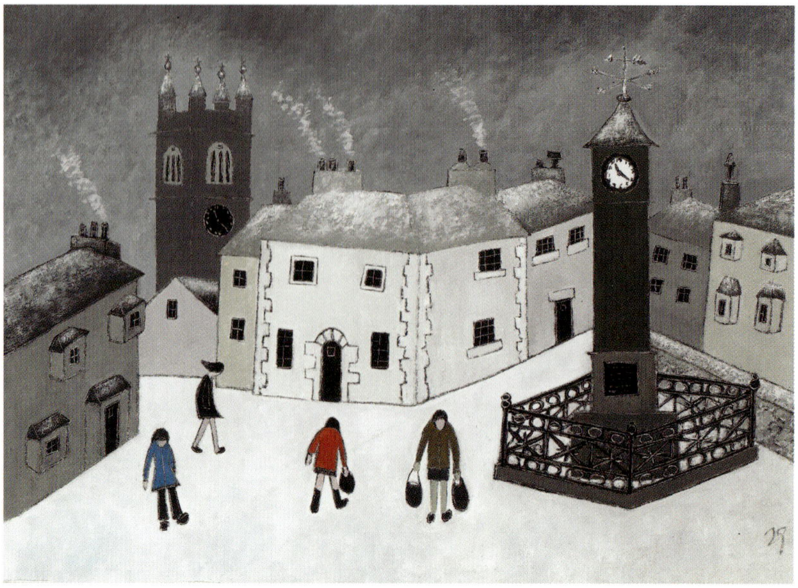

The War Memorial at St. Just

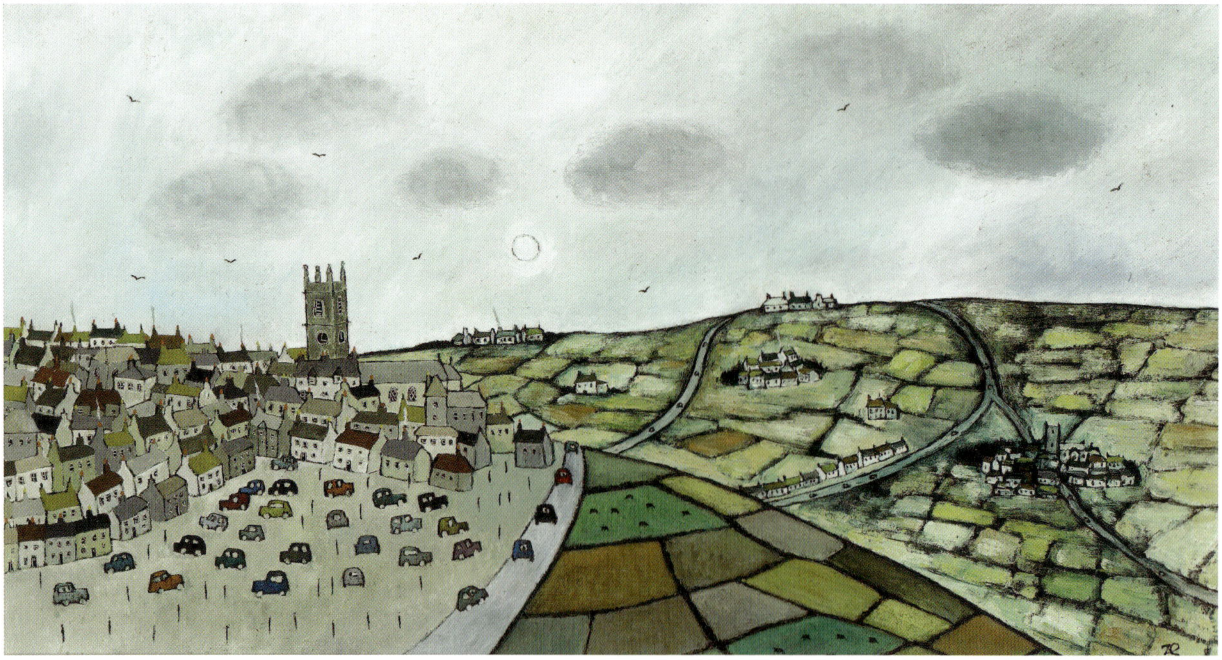

St. Just

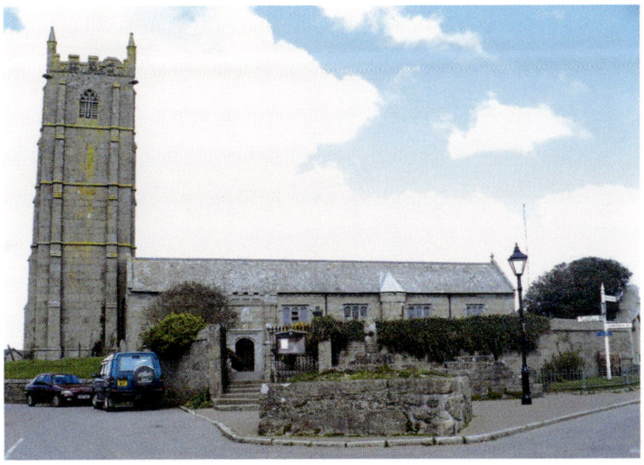

St. Buryan Church 2008

St. Buryan's 14th century church is a distinctive landmark for miles around. It has a circular graveyard surrounded by granite built cottages.

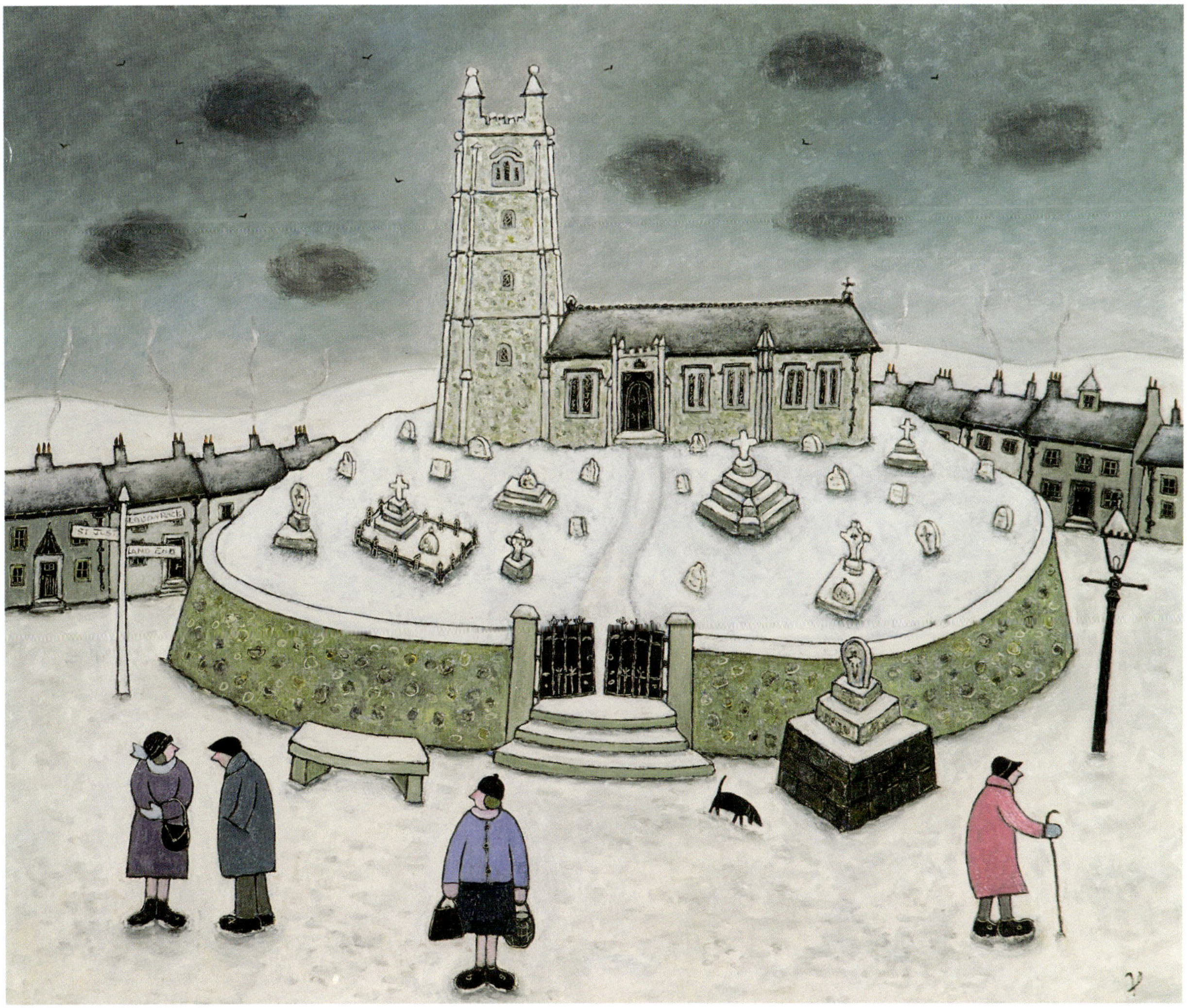

St. Buryan Church, Wintertime

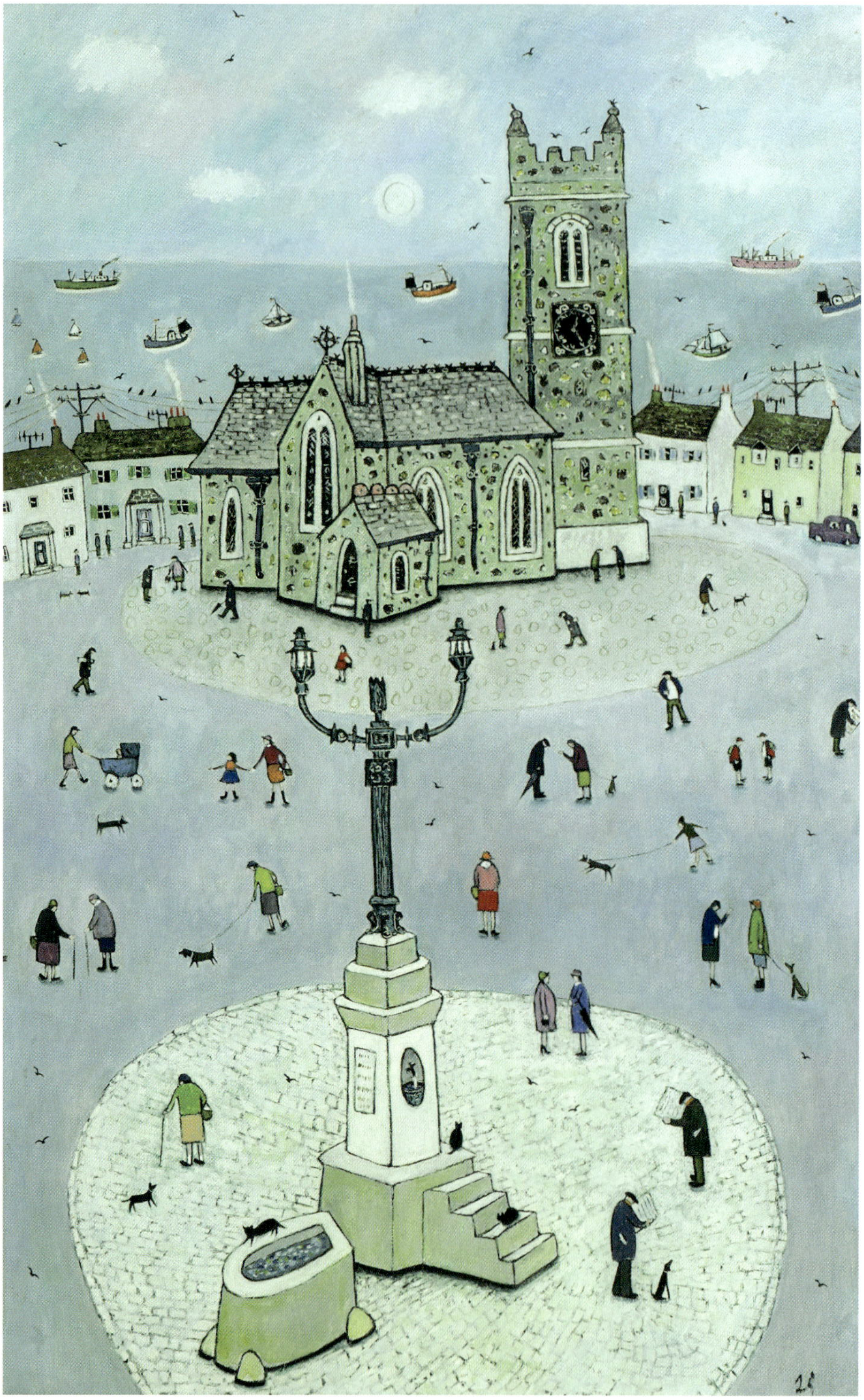

Village Life

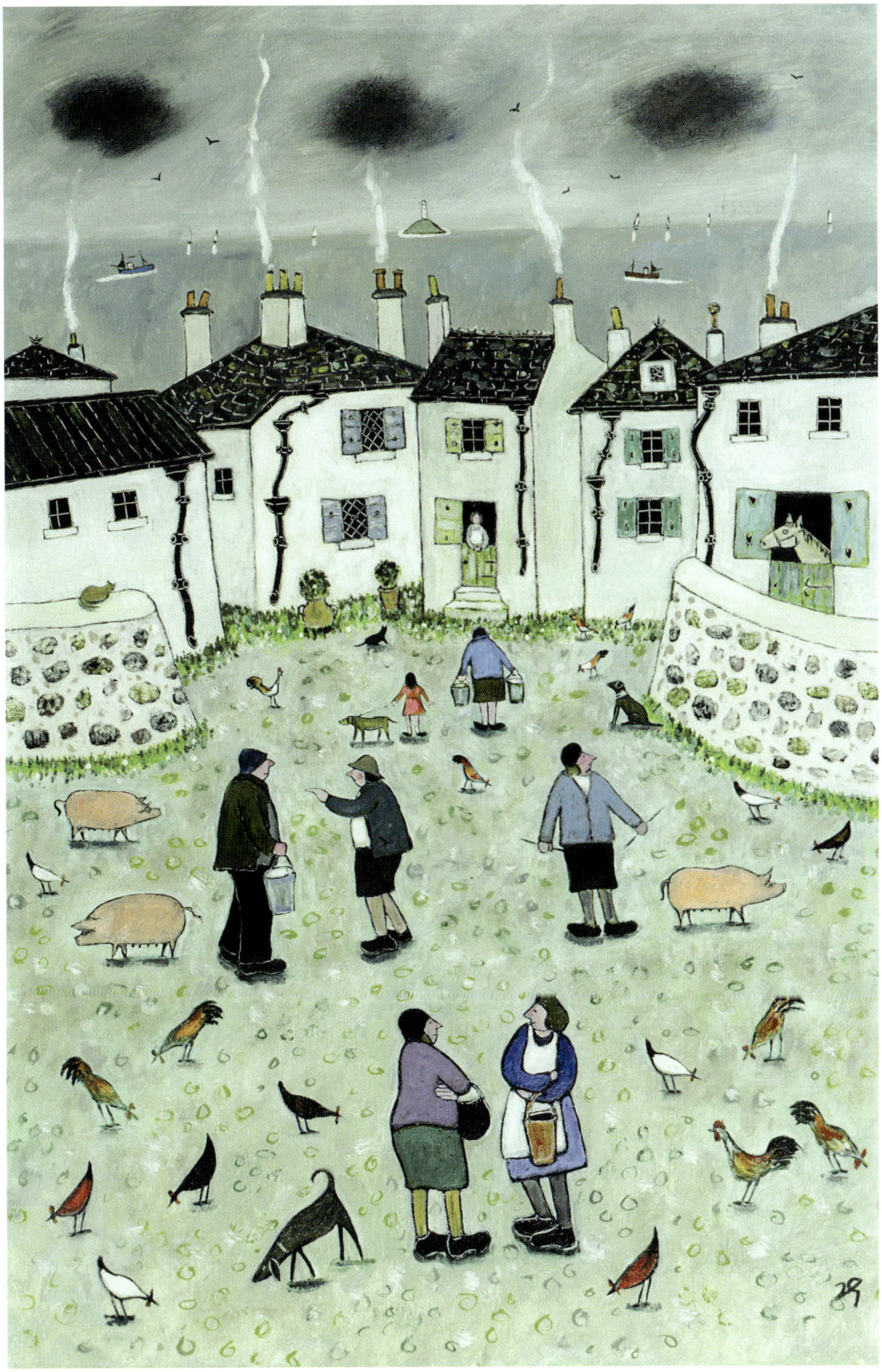

Early One Morning

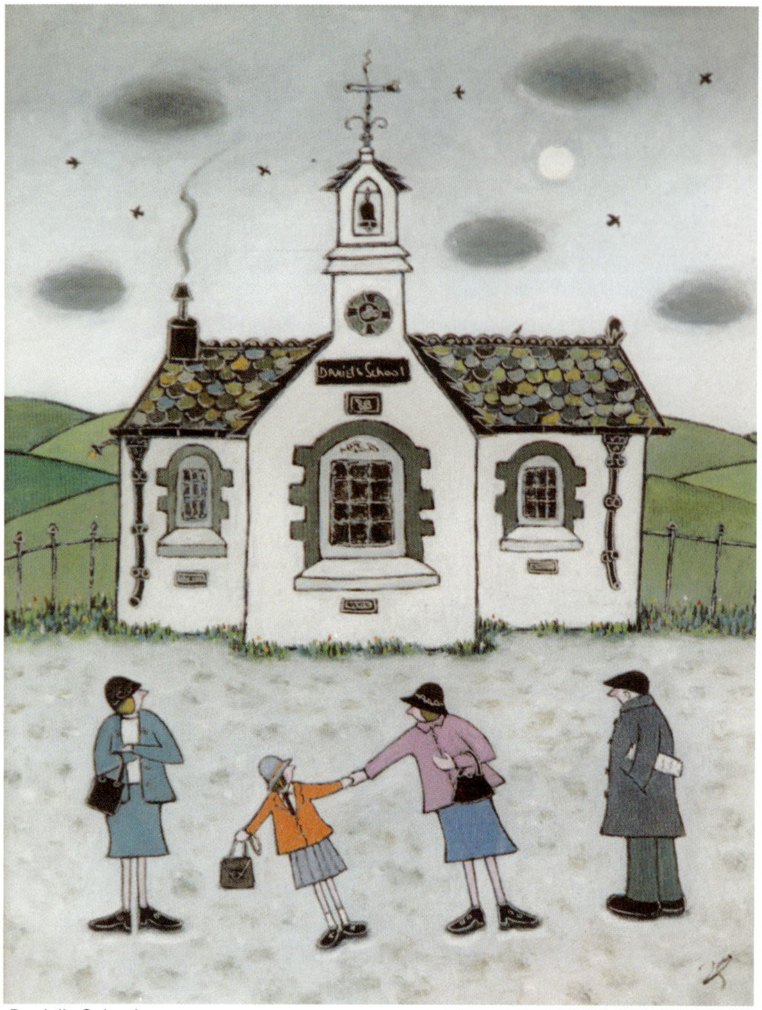

Daniel's School

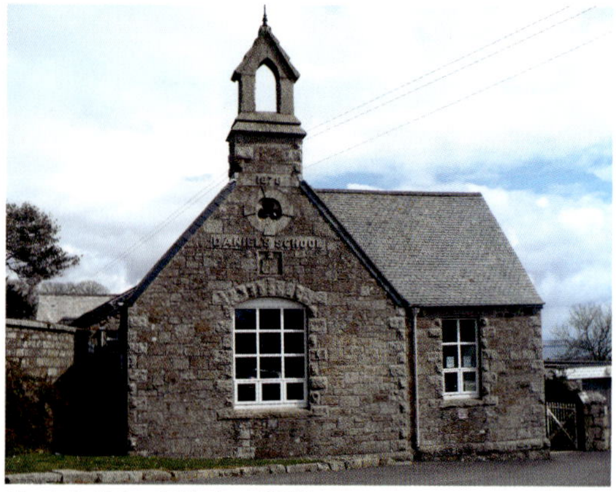

Daniel's School, Madron 2008

Madron charity school was founded by George Daniel in 1710 for the poor children of the village. The present school building dates from 1878.

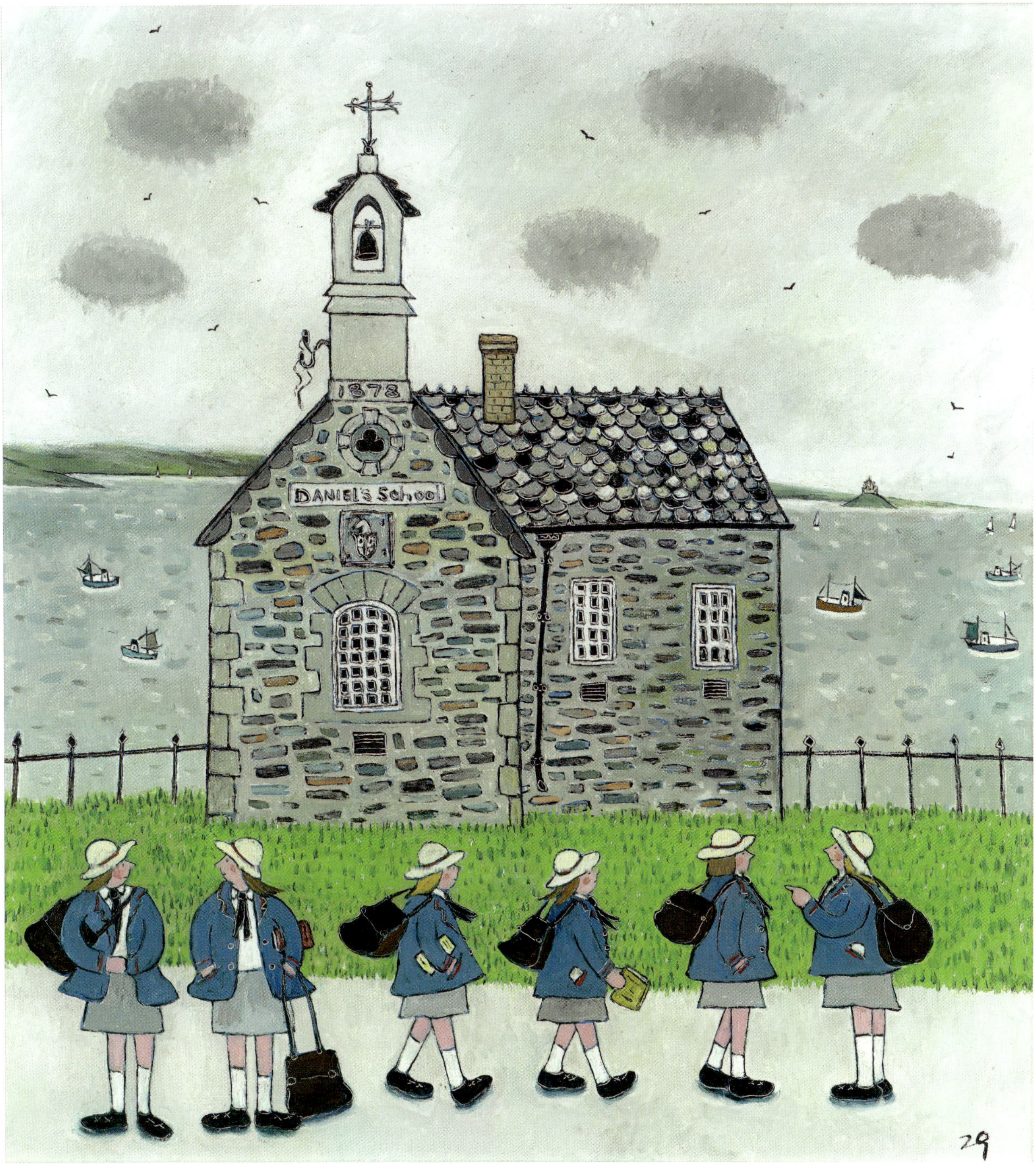

The New Girls, Daniel's School, Madron

Chapter 5 Newlyn

The small fishing town of Newlyn has been a major influence on Joan's work.

When the railway reached West Cornwall in 1877 St. Ives and Newlyn began to attract artists drawn to the wonderful scenery, the quality of light and the day to day lives of the fishermen and their families.

The group of artists known as the Newlyn School, began to settle from 1882. The first to arrive was Walter Langley closely followed by Stanhope Forbes and many others. From that time to the present day many artists have come to Newlyn thus ensuring that its rich artistic tradition lives on.

Being little more than a mile from Joan's home in Mousehole, Newlyn has provided her with such rich subject matter.

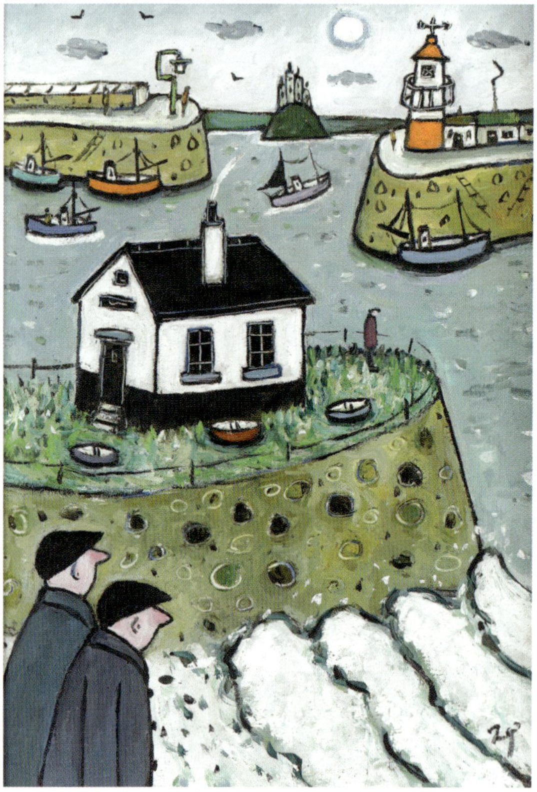

"Just Looking", View of Newlyn Harbour

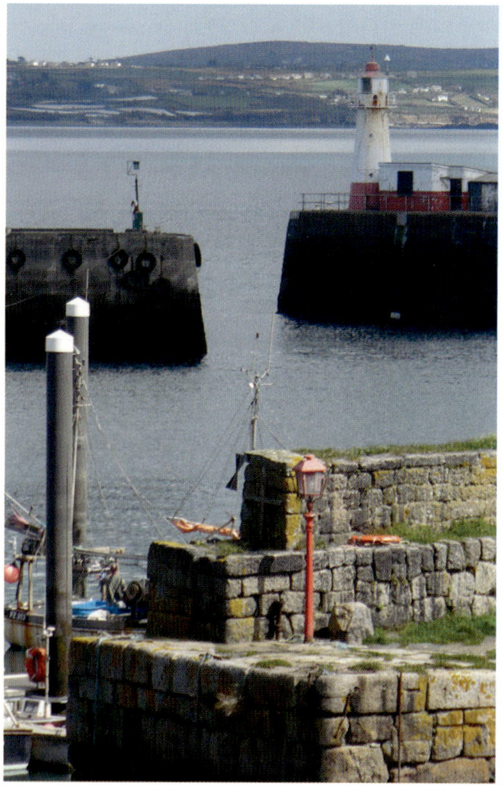

Old Newlyn Harbour 2008

The Old Harbour much painted by the Newlyn School Artists of the 1880's can still be seen today.

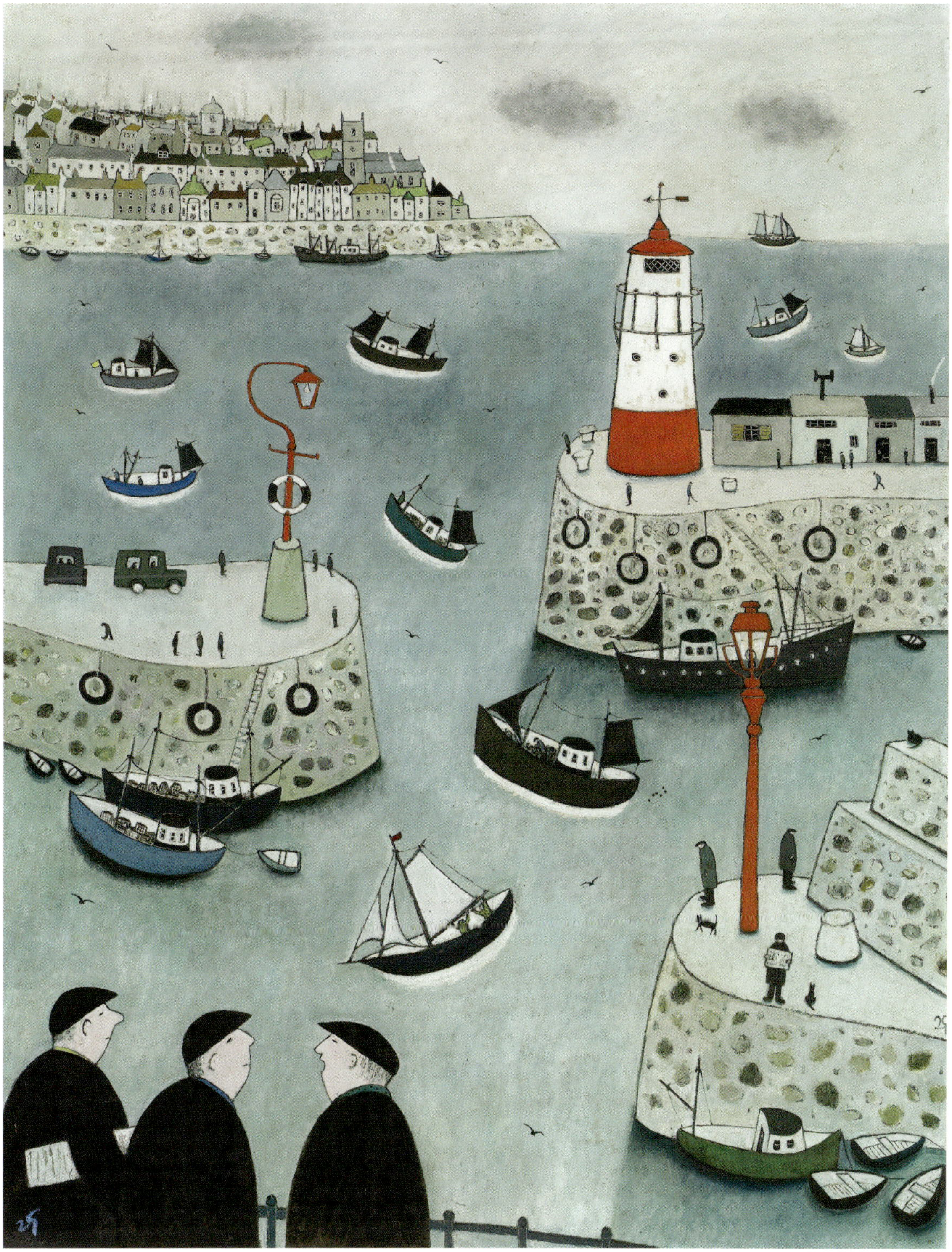

"I wish I was still fishing today"

The Newlyn Fishing Fleet

Newlyn once the home to dozens of trawlers is now struggling to maintain its role as one of the UK's major Fishing Ports. Joan shared the happiness, the sadness, the hardships and the hopes of the Newlyn fisherfolk fighting to keep their boats at sea and thus protect their livelihood.

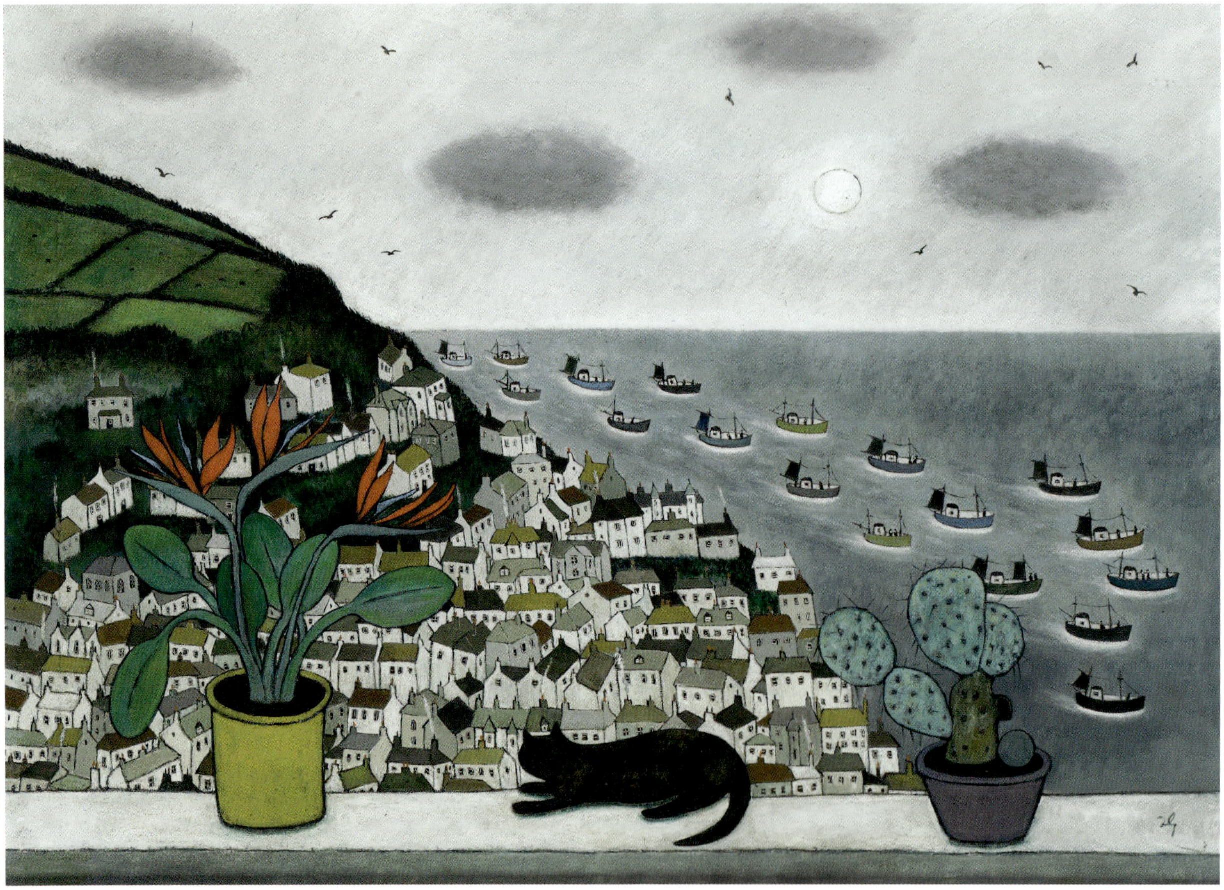

Fishing Fleet Leaving Newlyn c. 1975

In the 1970's hand lining for mackerel was the major fishing industry for Newlyn, and every day some two hundred boats would leave the harbour.

The Red Lamp

Joan and her friends fought long and hard to persuade Trinity House to keep this Red Lamp at the end of the Old Newlyn Quay.

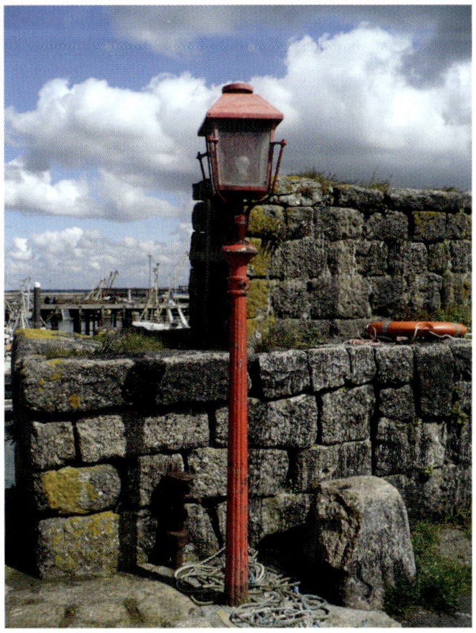

The Red Lamp 2008

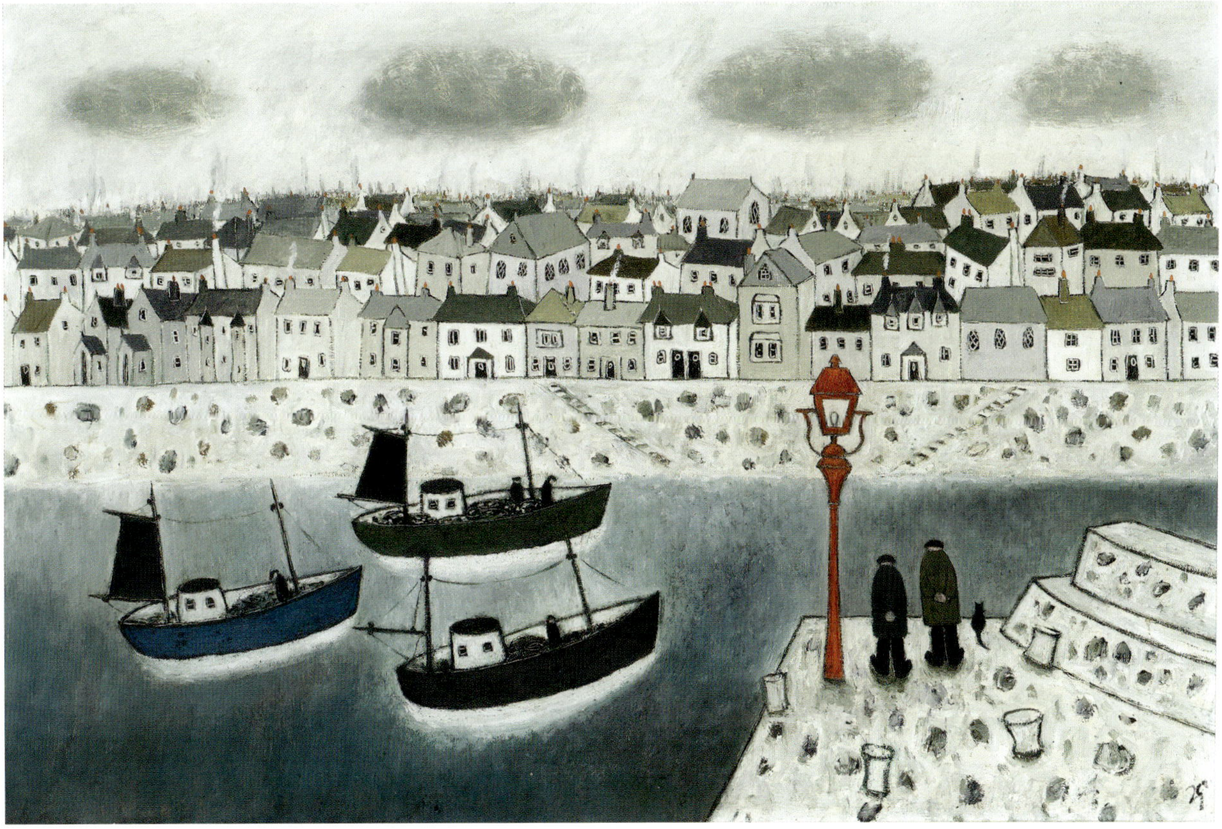

Crabbers Leaving Newlyn

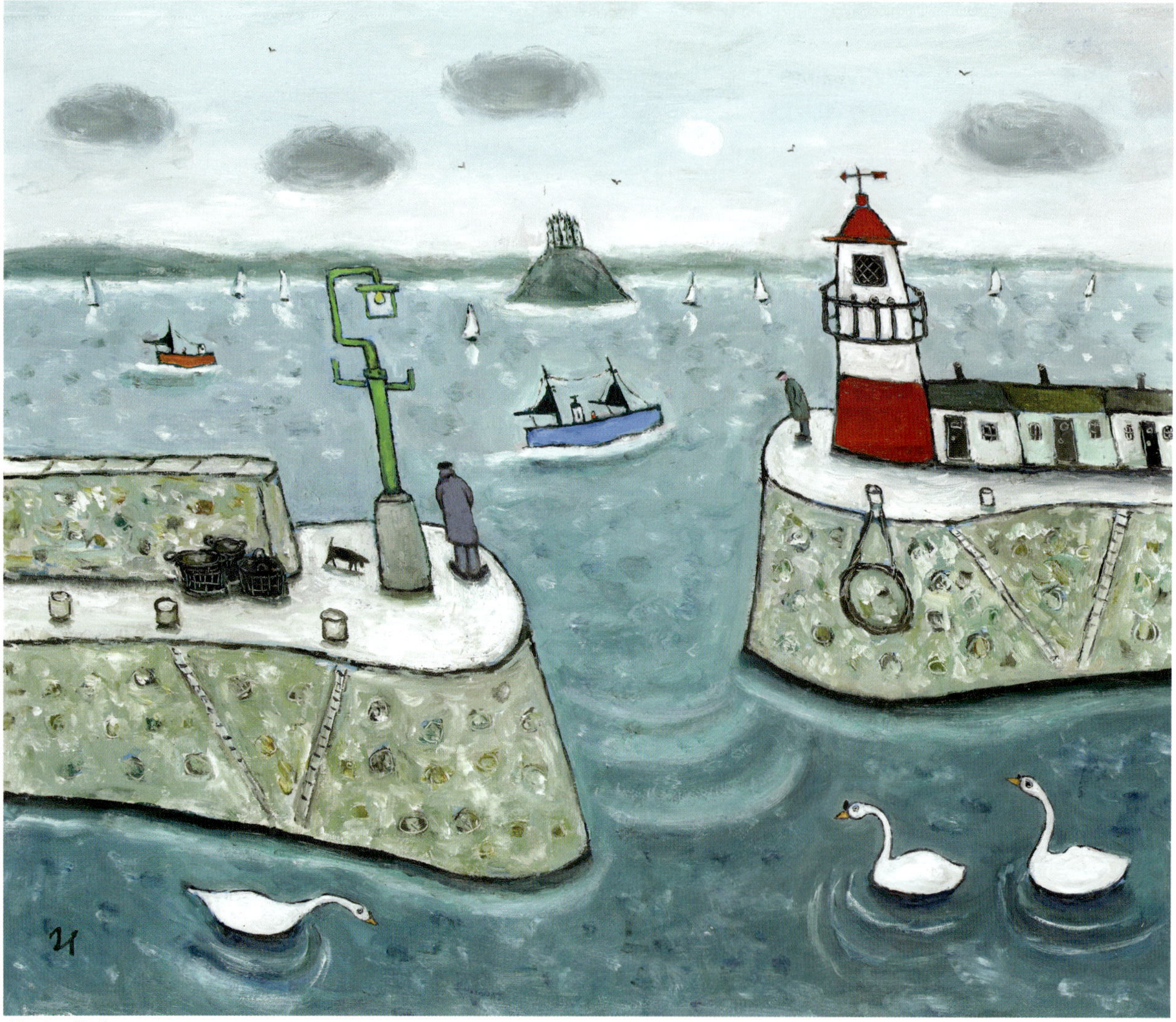

Newlyn Harbour

Blessing the Fleet

The Newlyn Fish Festival is celebrated each year, usually on August Bank Holiday. The Blessing of the fleet is a traditional ceremony held in aid of the fishing fleet and the safety of the men who work with the boats and their families. Church of England and Roman Catholic Bishops from the Cornish Dioceses often attend these ceremonies.

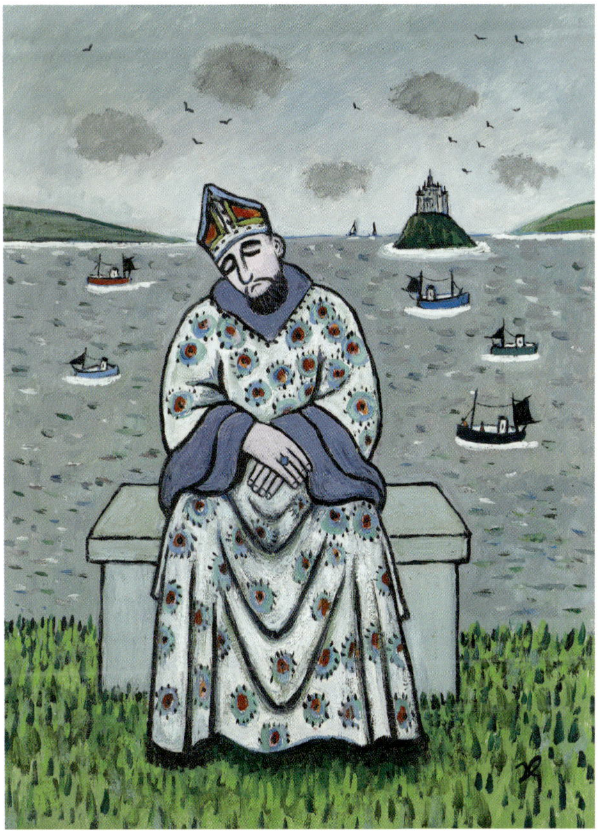

The Sleeping Bishop

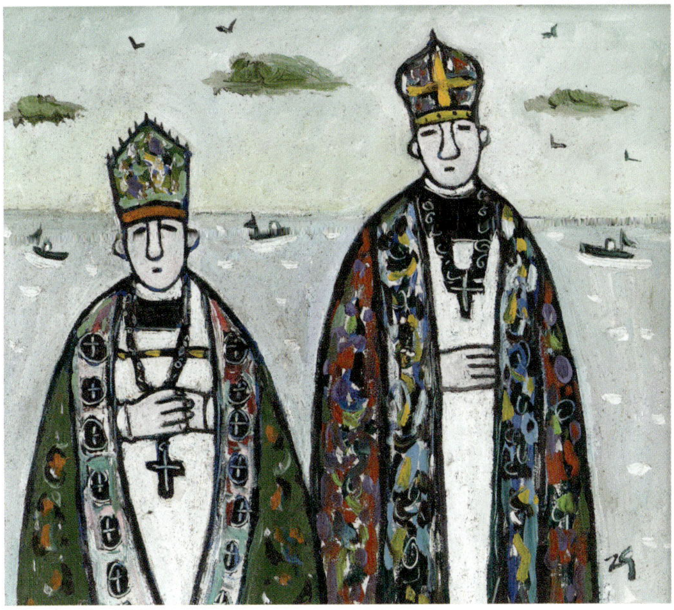

Blessing the Fish

Joan's humorous view of the participants of the Blessing the Fleet services.

The Newlyn Art Gallery

John Halkes who kept the Orion Gallery in Penzance greatly encouraged Joan and started showing her work. When it amalgamated with the Newlyn Gallery to become the Newlyn Orion in 1974 Halkes became its Director, thus starting Joan's long association with the Newlyn Orion. The Gallery owns this wonderful work titled:- "The Newlyn Exhibition 1979".

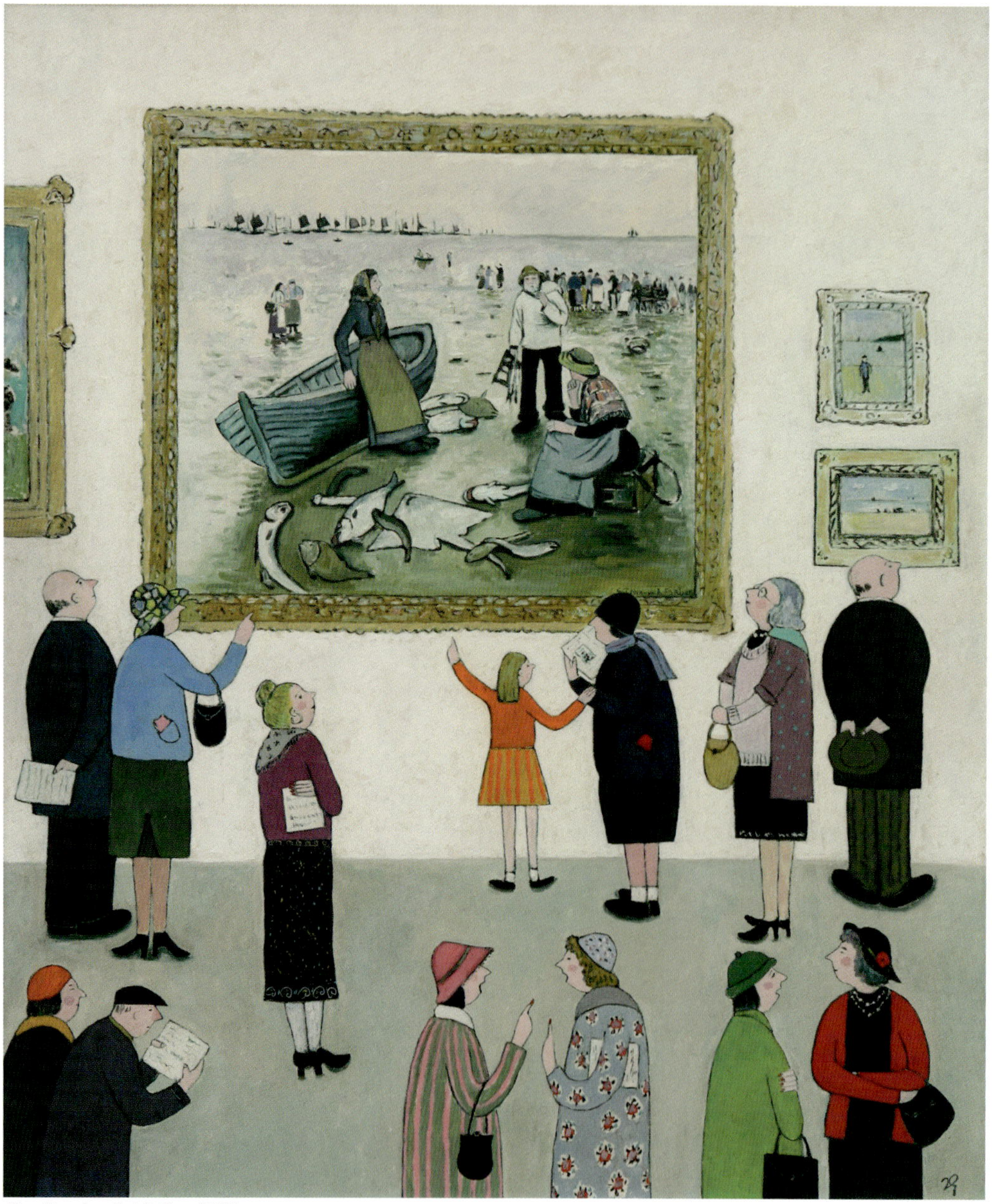

The Newlyn Exhibition 1979

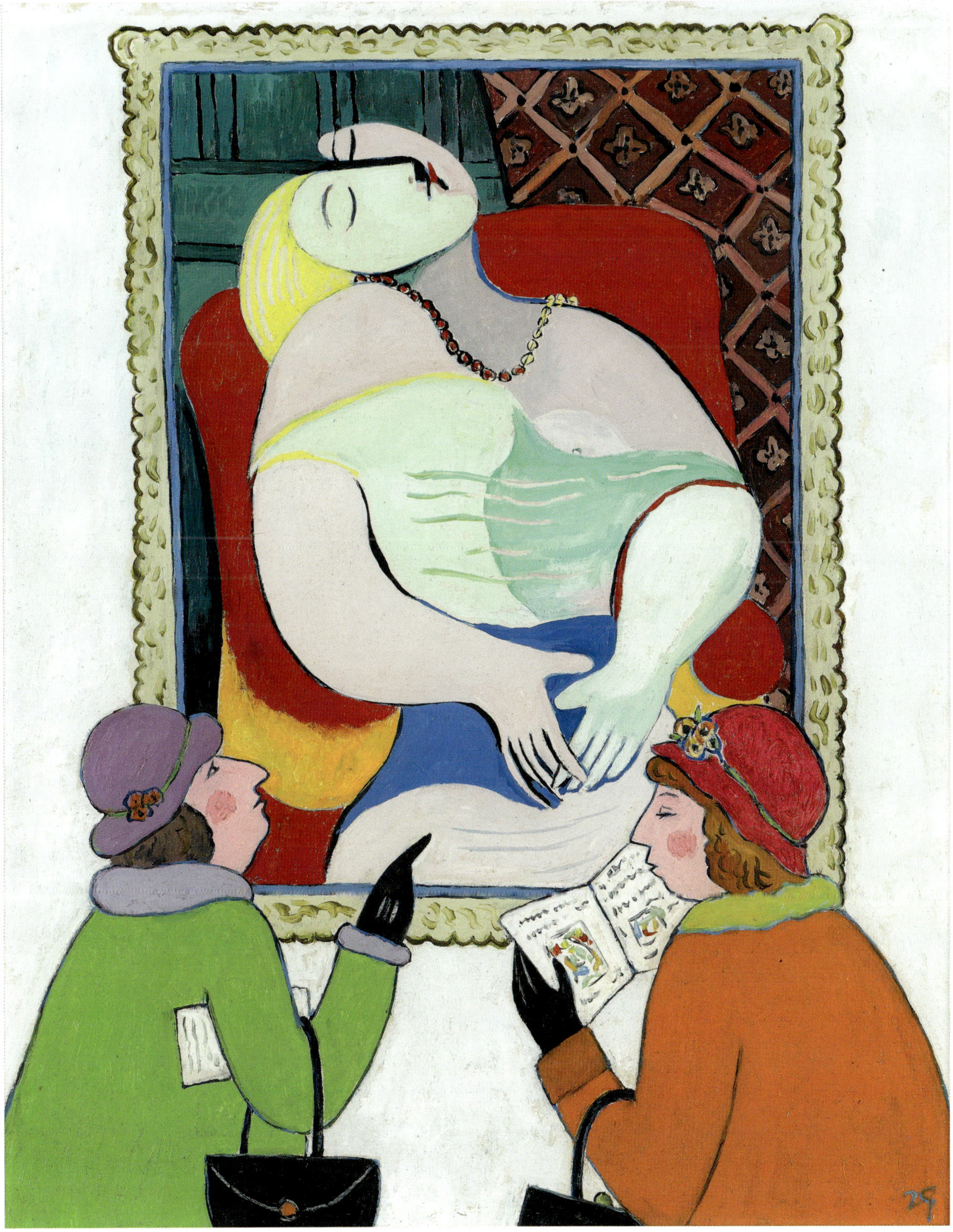

"It's by someone called Picasso"

Chapter 6 Penzance

Prior to the sixteenth century Mousehole was the principal harbour in Mount's Bay, Penzance was only a small settlement. Due to the growth of the tin industry and the westward movement of mining activity Charles II made Penzance the coinage town for tin removing the privilege from Bodmin and Lostwithiel. From this point on Penzance developed rapidly. Its maritime trade grew in all directions and the town became a market for all Cornwall.

In 1852 a railway from Penzance to Redruth was opened which was later extended to London. This made it even easier to transport tin and fish from Penzance to the capital.

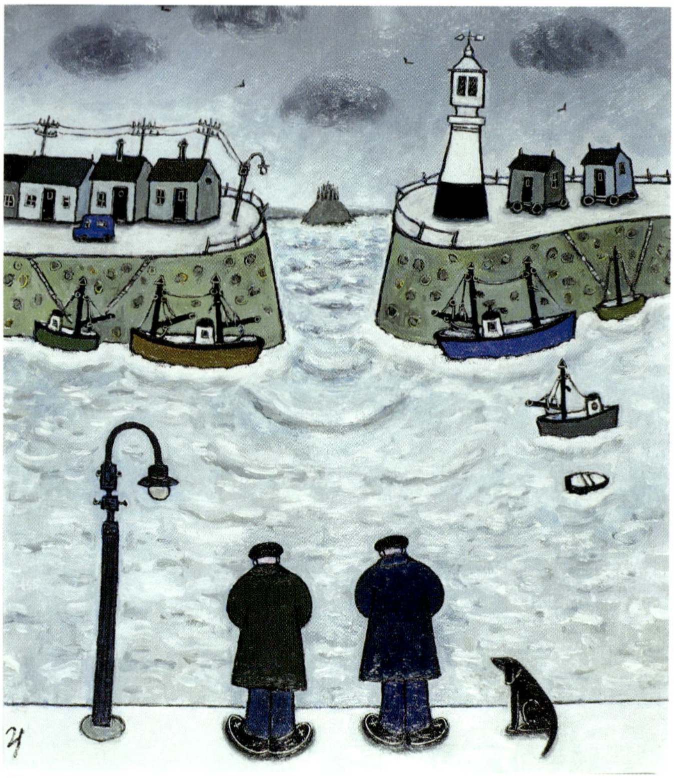

Bill and Ted at Penzance

The Harbour

Once a thriving fishing port, today the harbour provides both a commercial and recreational service. Joan was worried that all the developments in Penzance would mean that the famous lighthouse would disappear.

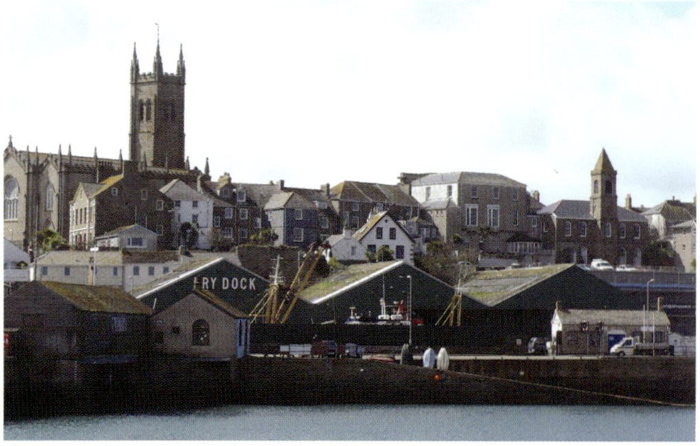

Penzance Town from the Harbour 2008

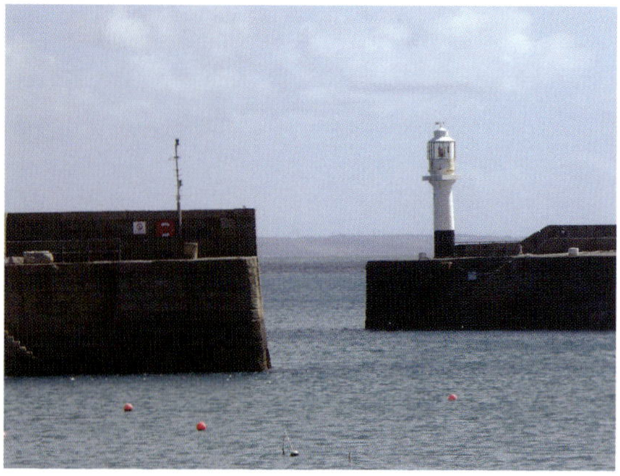

Penzance Harbour 2008

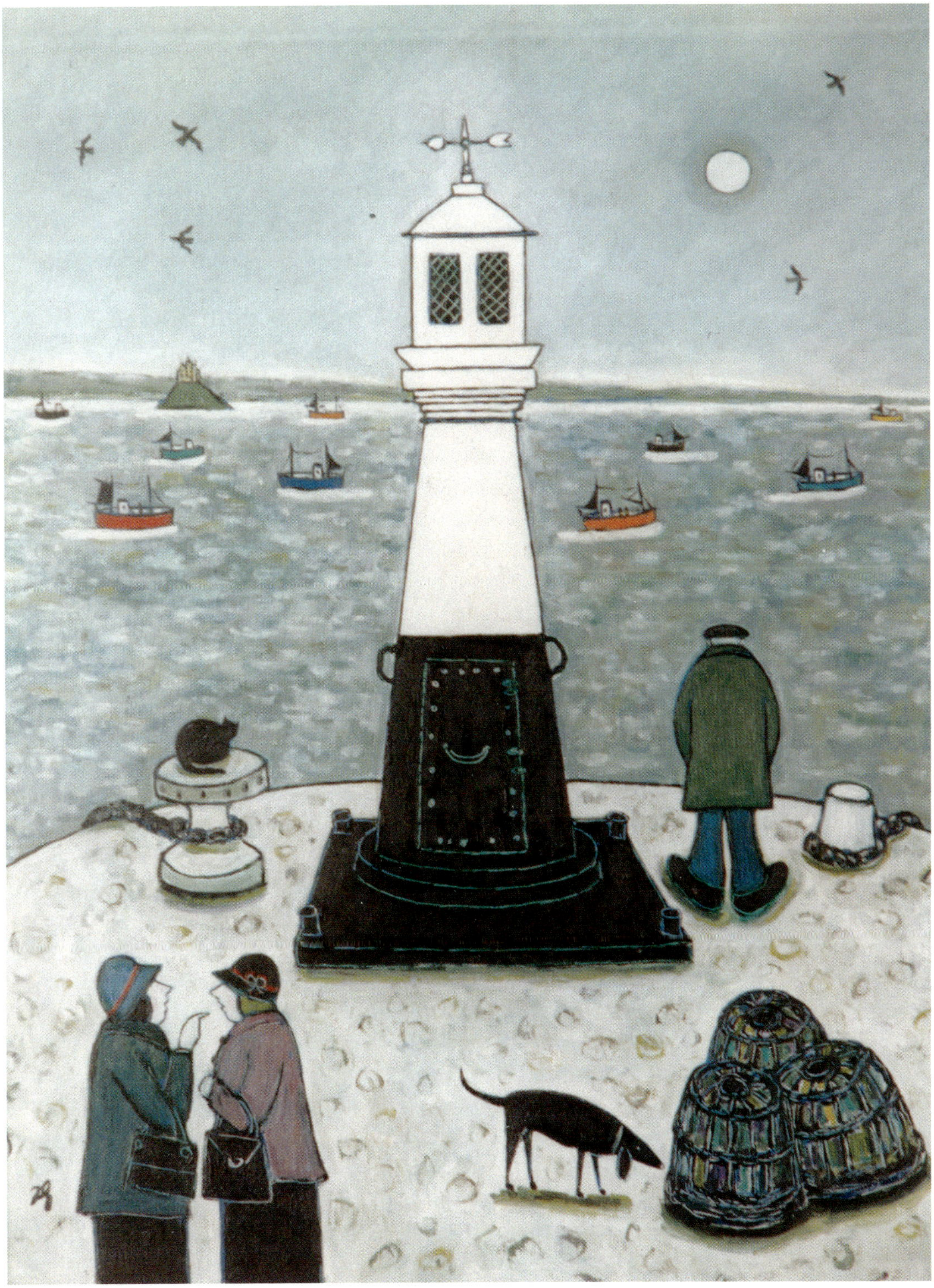

Waiting for the "Scillonian"

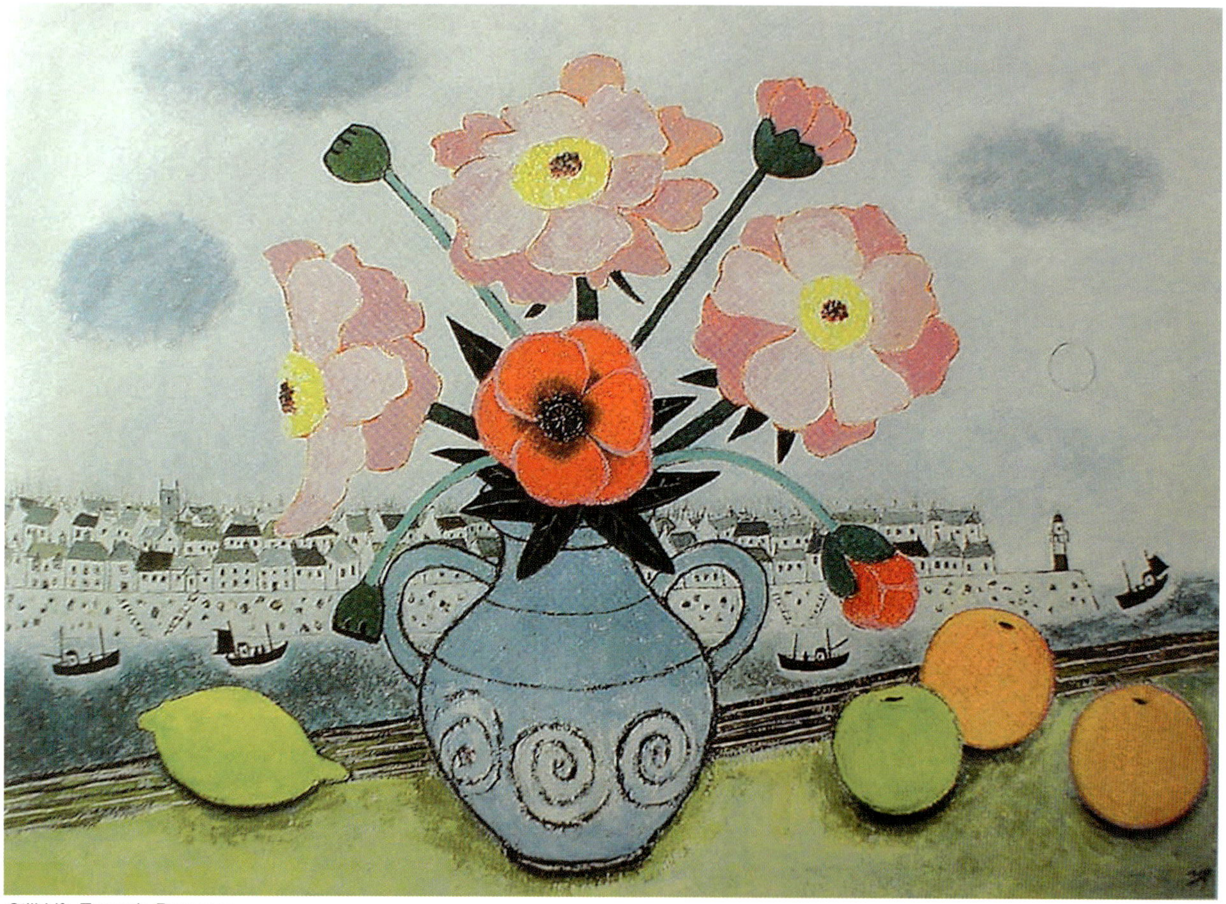

Still Life Towards Penzance

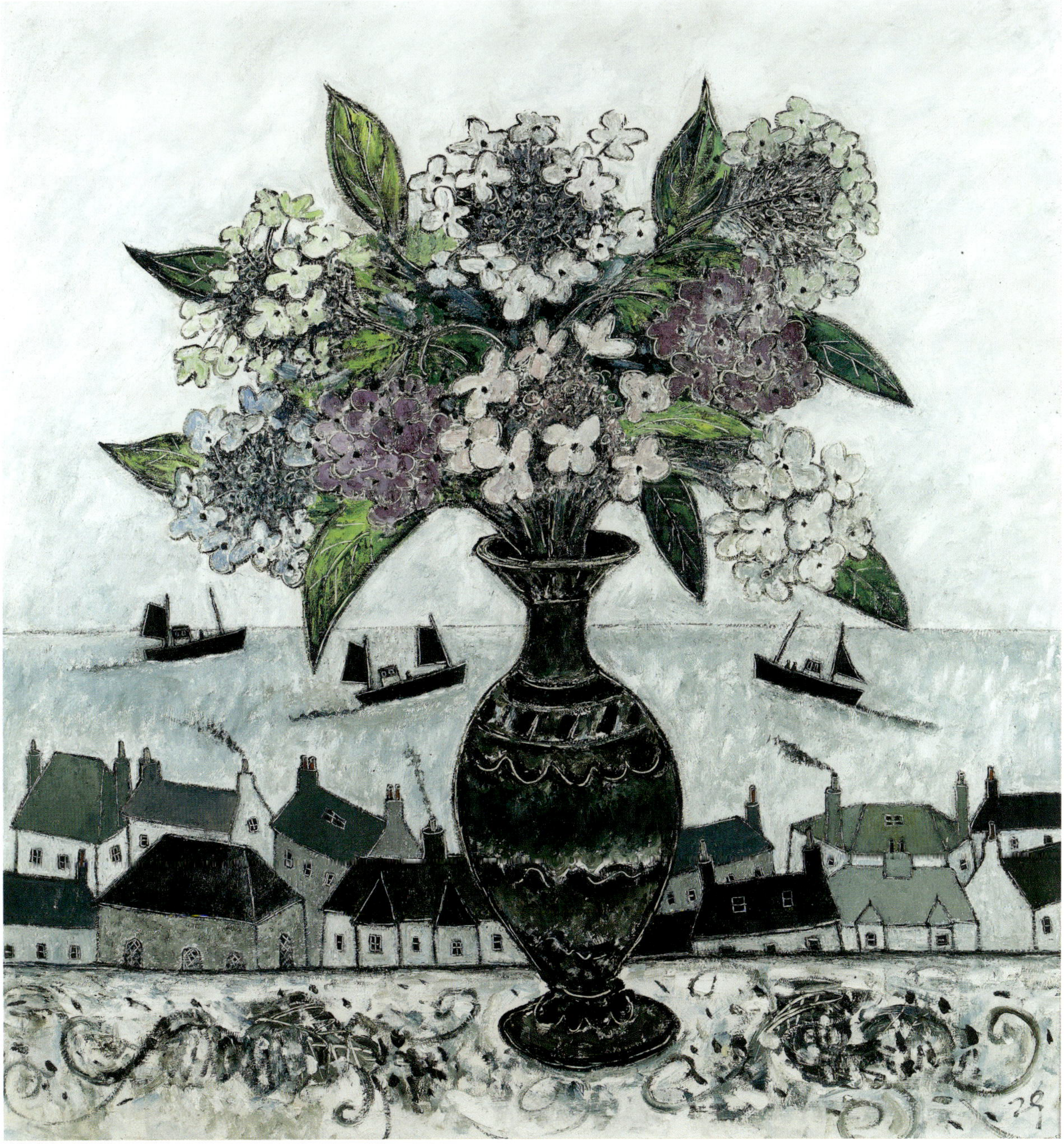
Still Life with Hydrangea

Morrab Gardens

One of Joan's favourite places to sit and sketch was Morrab Gardens. A Victorian garden designed by Reginald Upcher which became a public park in 1888. It has a fine bandstand and fountain.

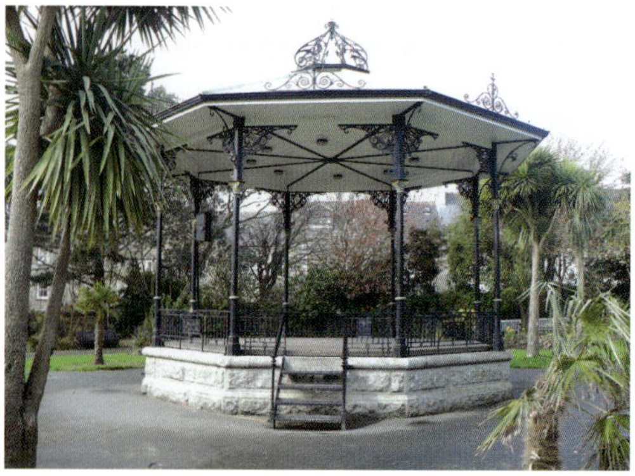

The Bandstand in Morrab Gardens 2008

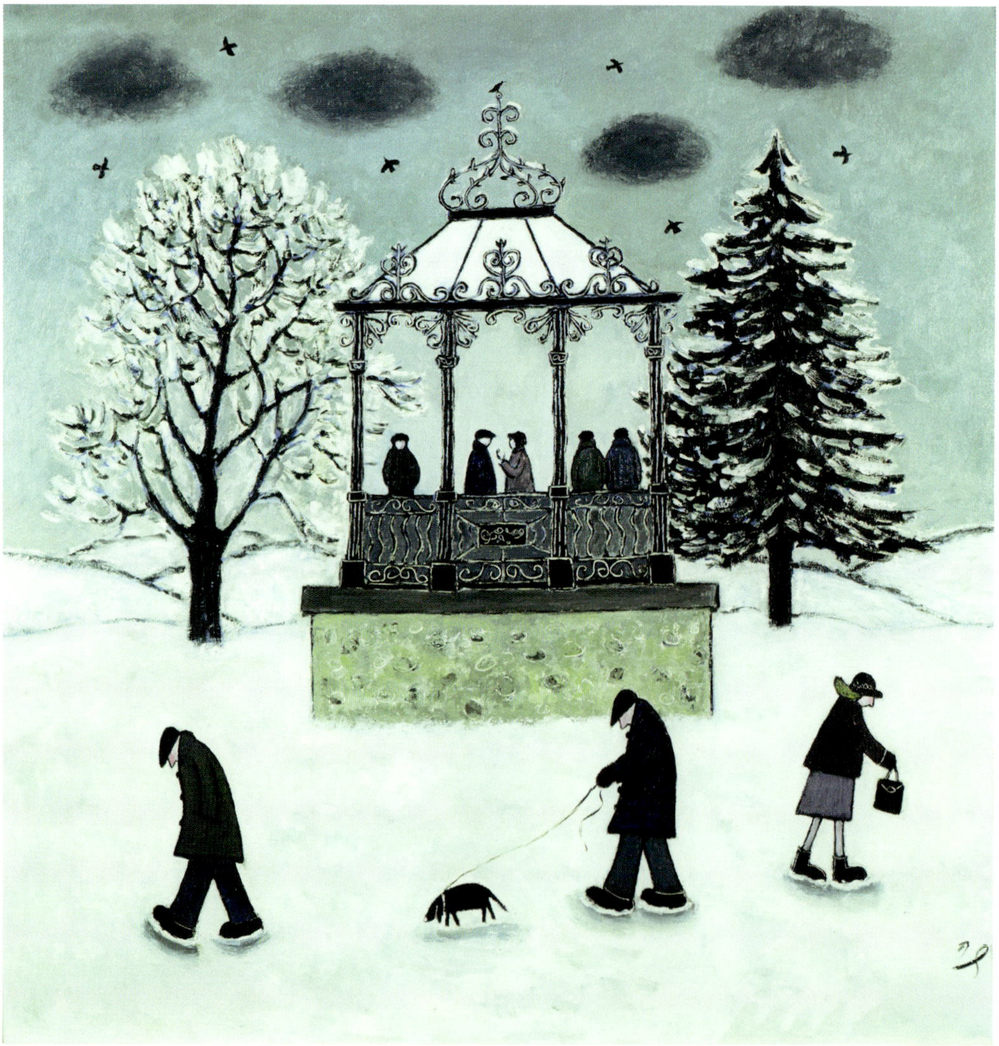

The Bandstand, Morrab Gardens, Penzance

The Penlee Bowls Club

The Penlee Bowls Club located on the seafront between Penzance and Newlyn is still going strong today.

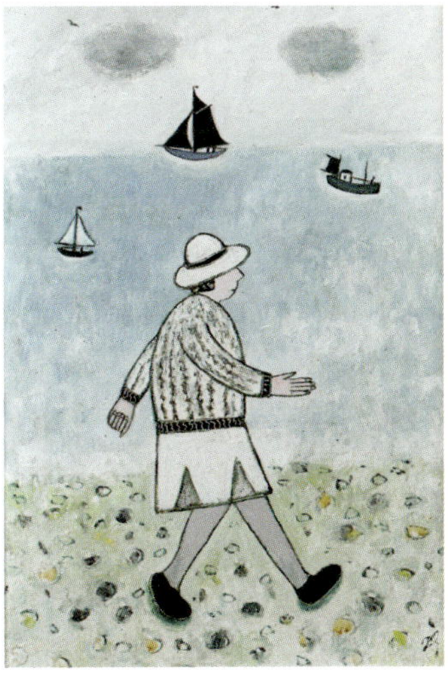

"I'm Late"

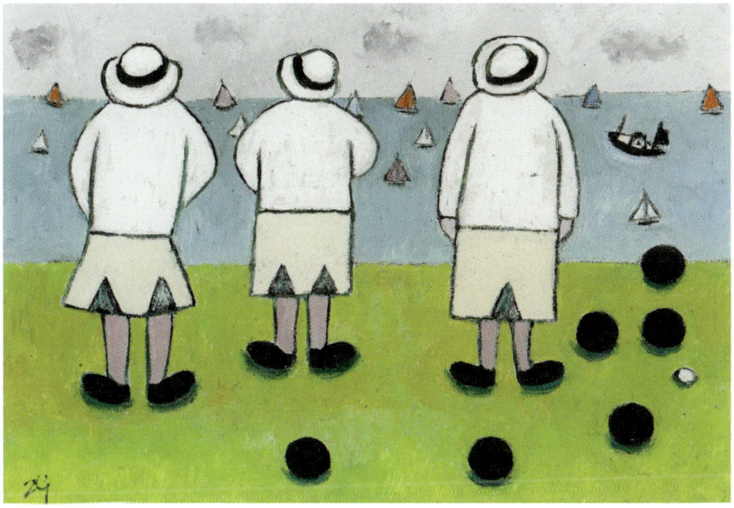

A Most Important Match

Queen's Hotel

A large hotel situated on the promenade with breathtaking views of Mount's Bay. Much used by Joan as a setting for her paintings.

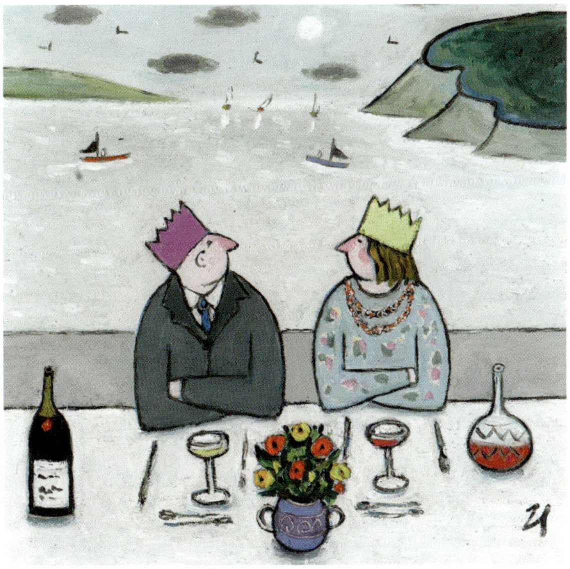

Christmas Party at the Queen's

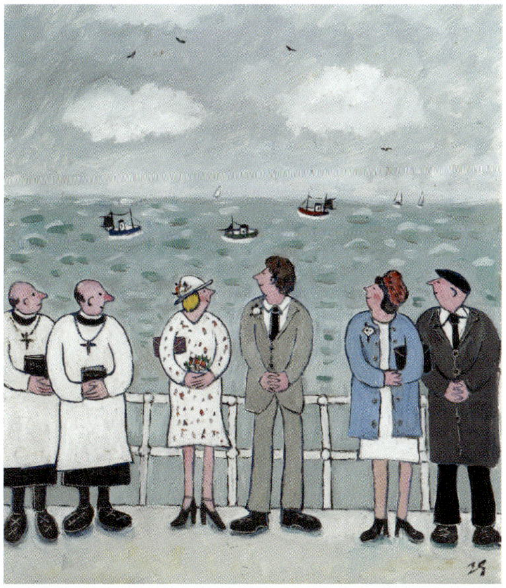

Wedding Reception outside the Queen's

Chapter 7 St. Ives and Thereabouts

Joan loved St. Ives. Like so many artists before her she never failed to be inspired by the busy harbour, the steep cobbled streets, the maze of fishermen's cottages and the bustle of locals and holidaymakers alike.

The B3311, Penzance to St. Ives

Almost every week in all winds and weathers Joan's old Morris Minor would take the back road from Penzance to St. Ives for a day's sketching. This road itself provided her with so much material. She would sketch the old engine house preserved from the Giew Tin Mine, Chysauster Ancient Village or the lovely little church at Towednack.

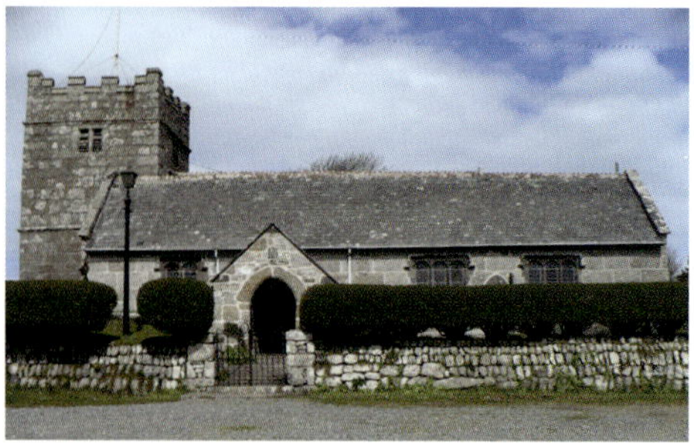

Towednack Church 2008

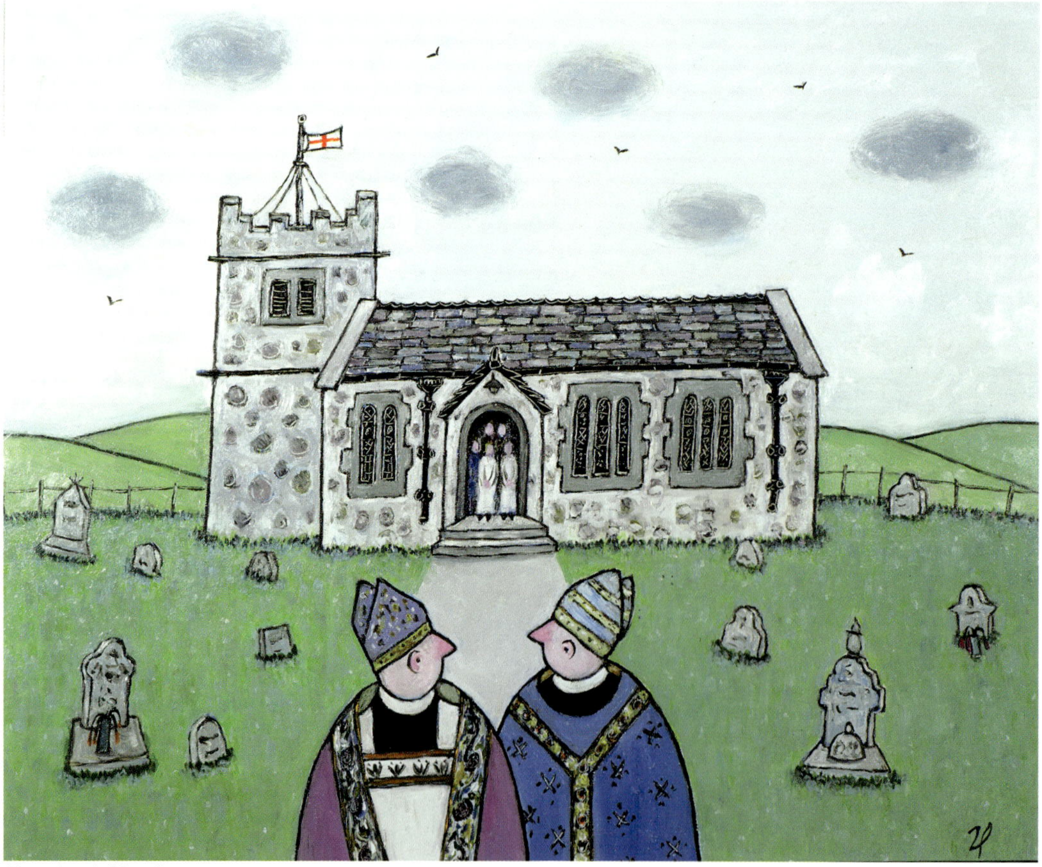

Towednack Church

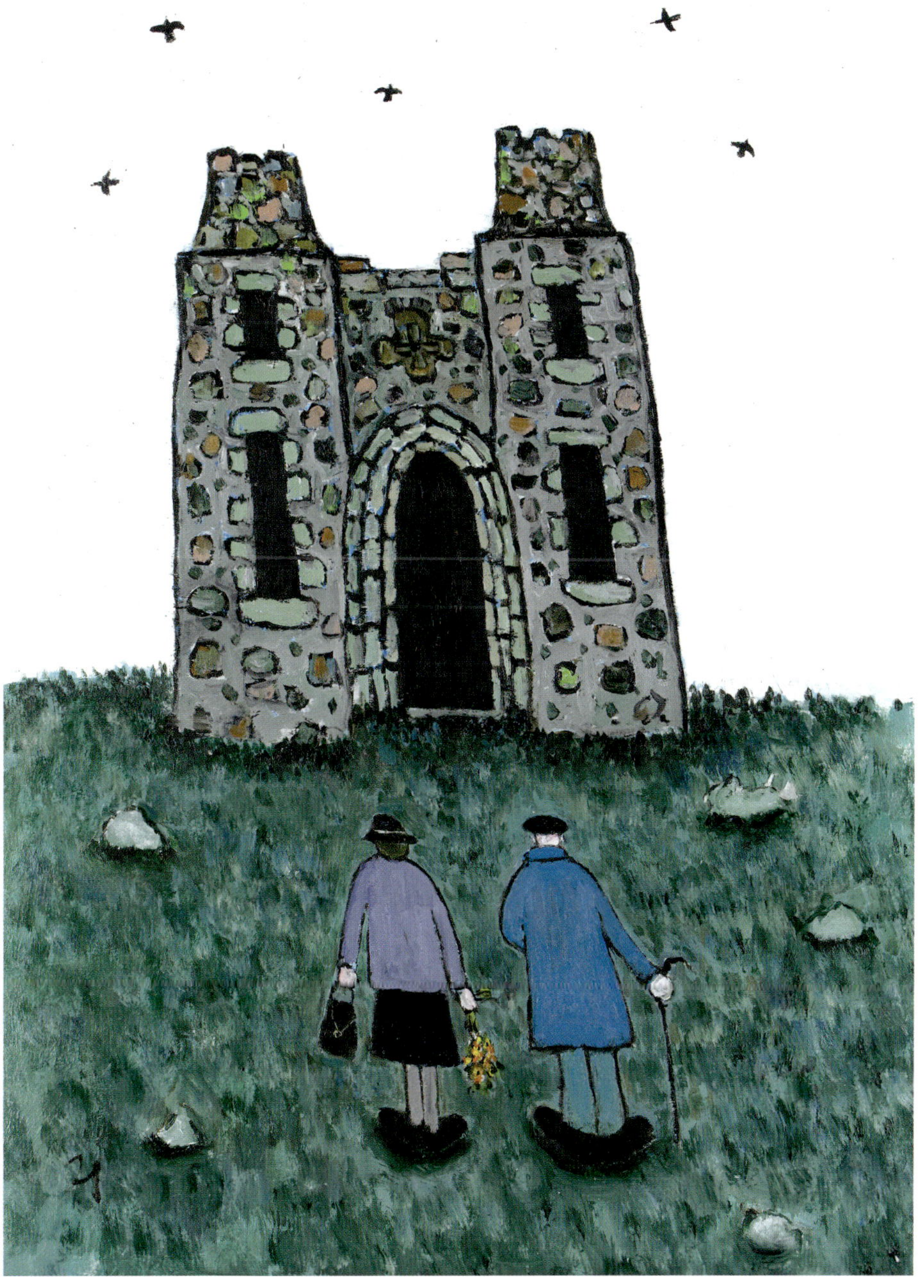

Roger's Folly

Just off the B3311, and difficult to find is Roger's Tower a tiny square folly built on the ramparts of an Iron age fort on the summit of Castle-an-Dinas.

The Harbour

With so much to paint, it has to be one of the most picturesque harbours in the world and Joan produced a wealth of marvellous paintings over the years.

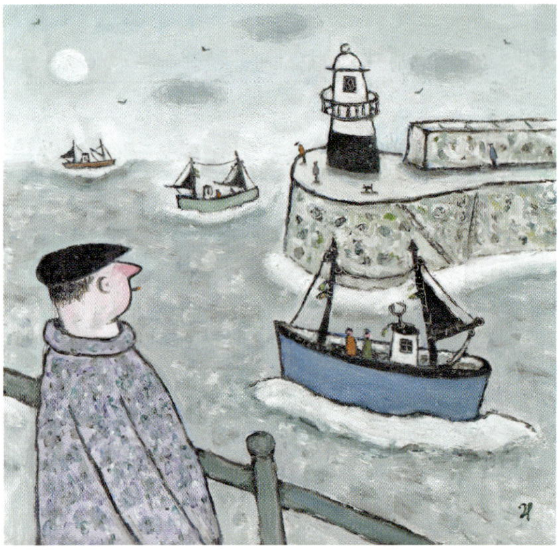

Watching the Fishing Boats at St. Ives

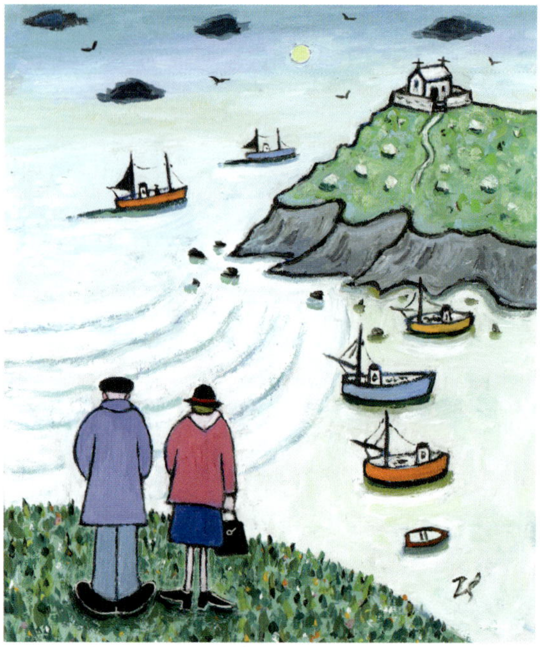

A Lovely Spring Morning at St. Ives

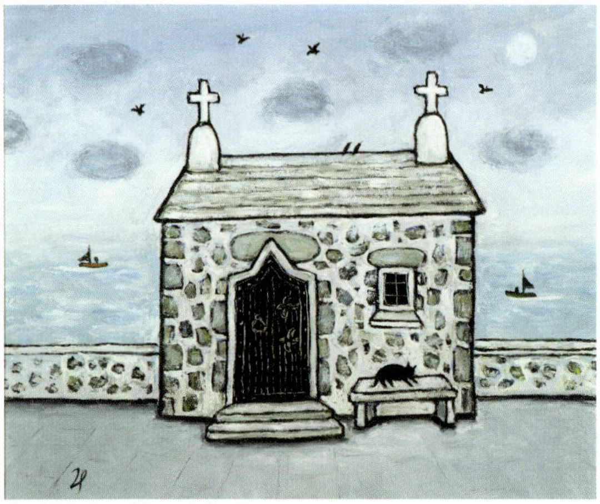

St. Nicholas Chapel, St. Ives

The Island

The island is a small hilly peninsula that separates Porthmeor and Porthminster beaches. The old chapel of St. Nicholas is on the island, the site dates from the fifteenth century and the present building from 1911.

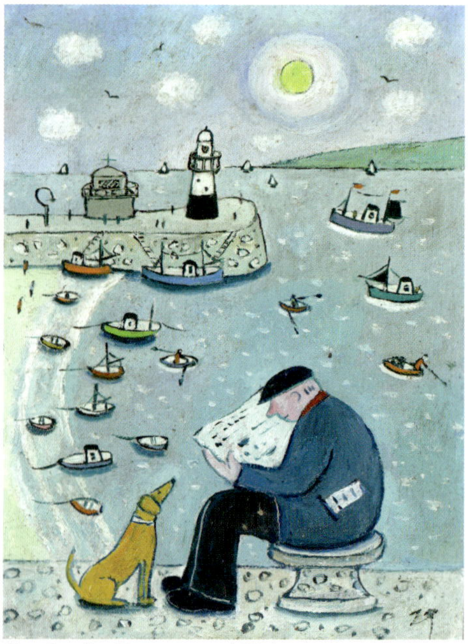

Reading the Newspaper at St. Ives

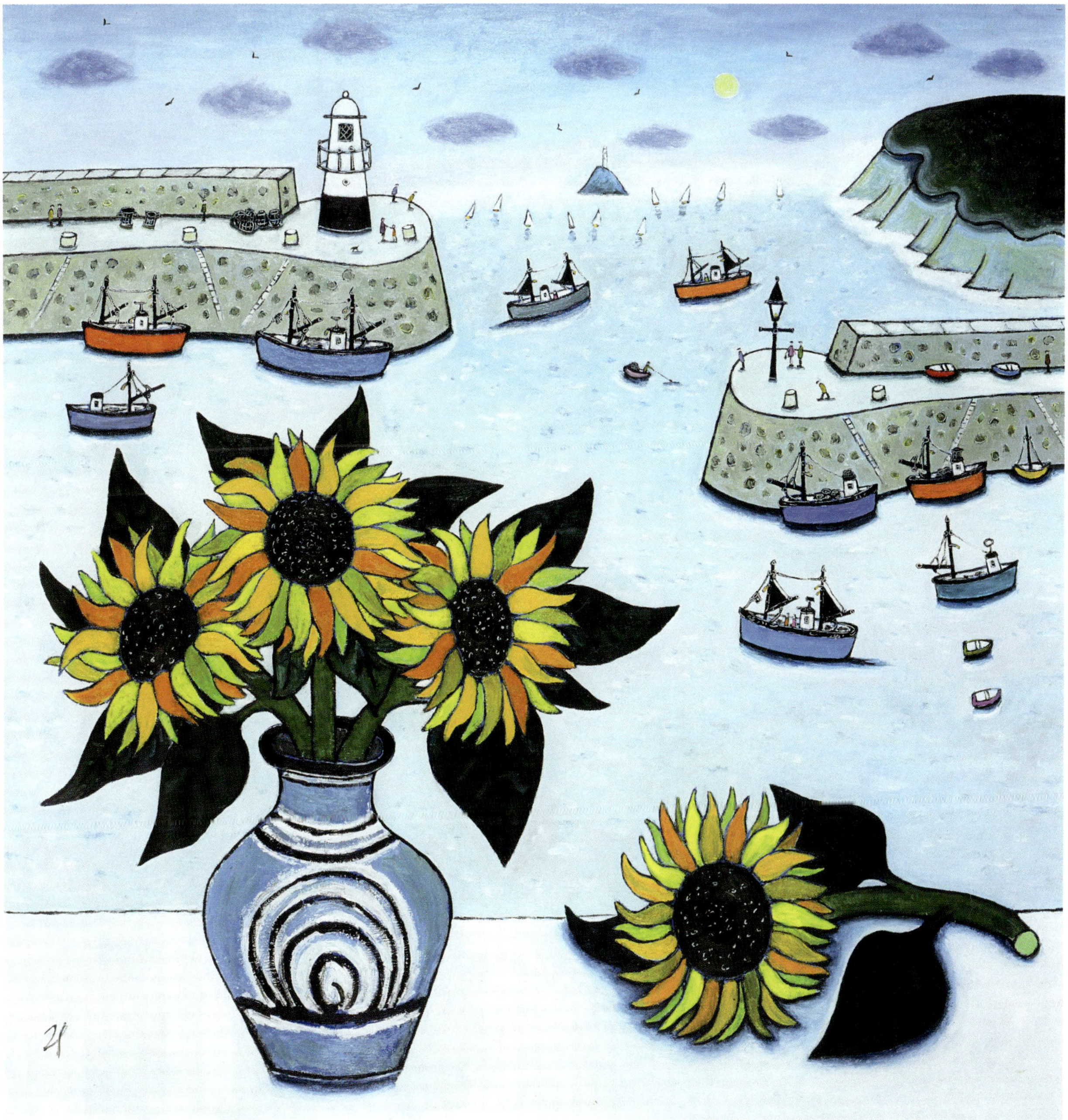

St. Ives Harbour with Sunflowers

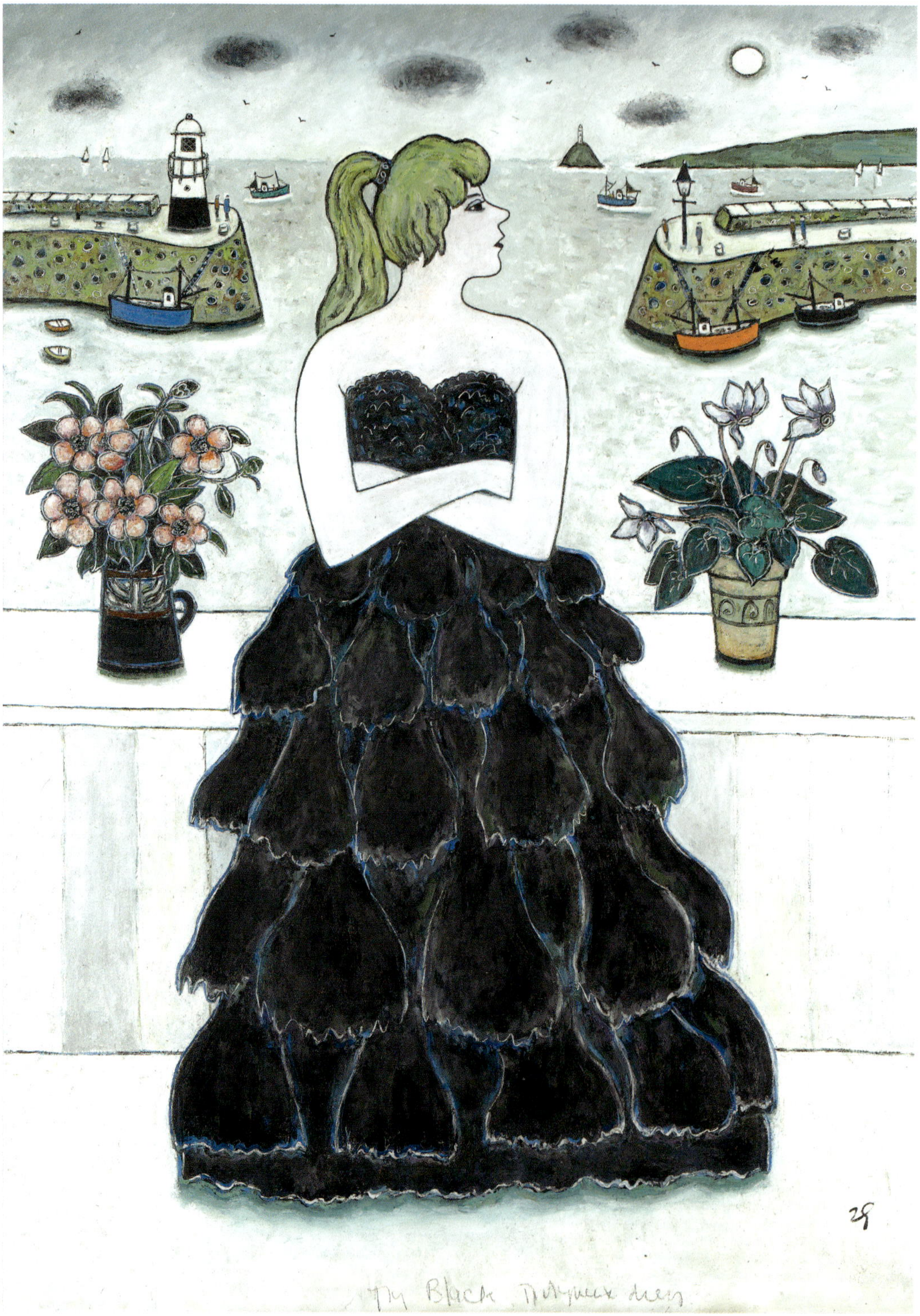

Wearing My Black Molyneaux Dress at St. Ives

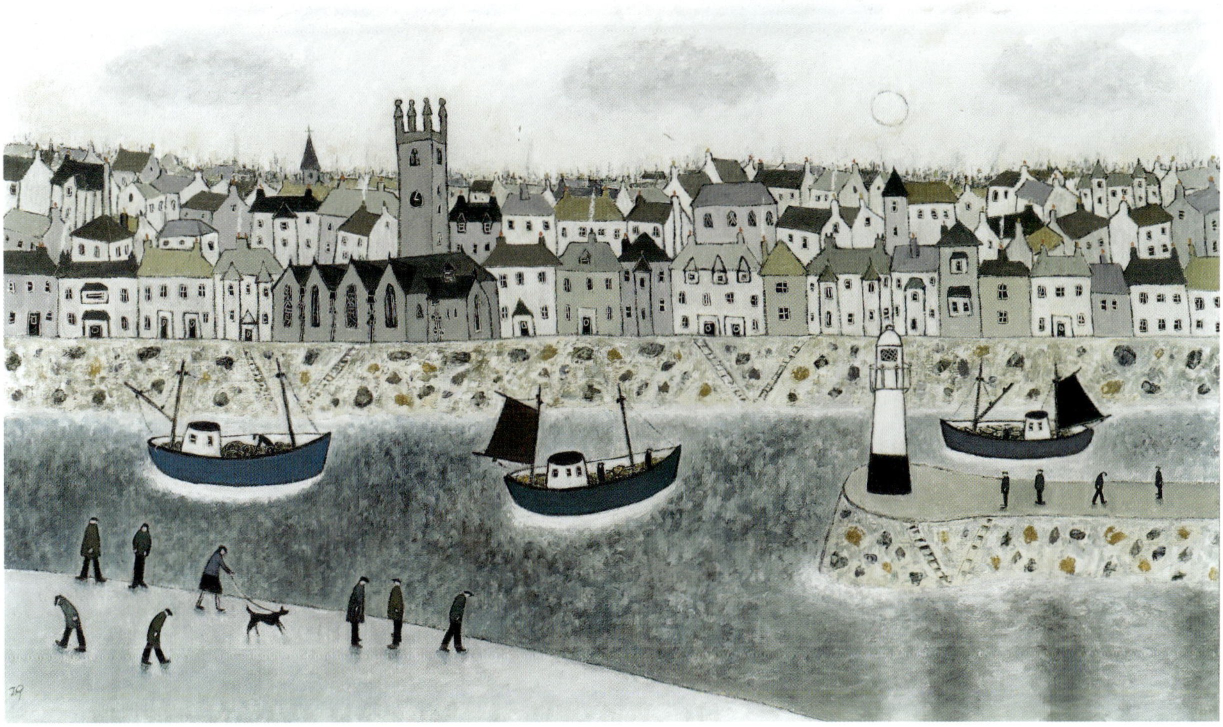
St. Ives Fishing Fleet

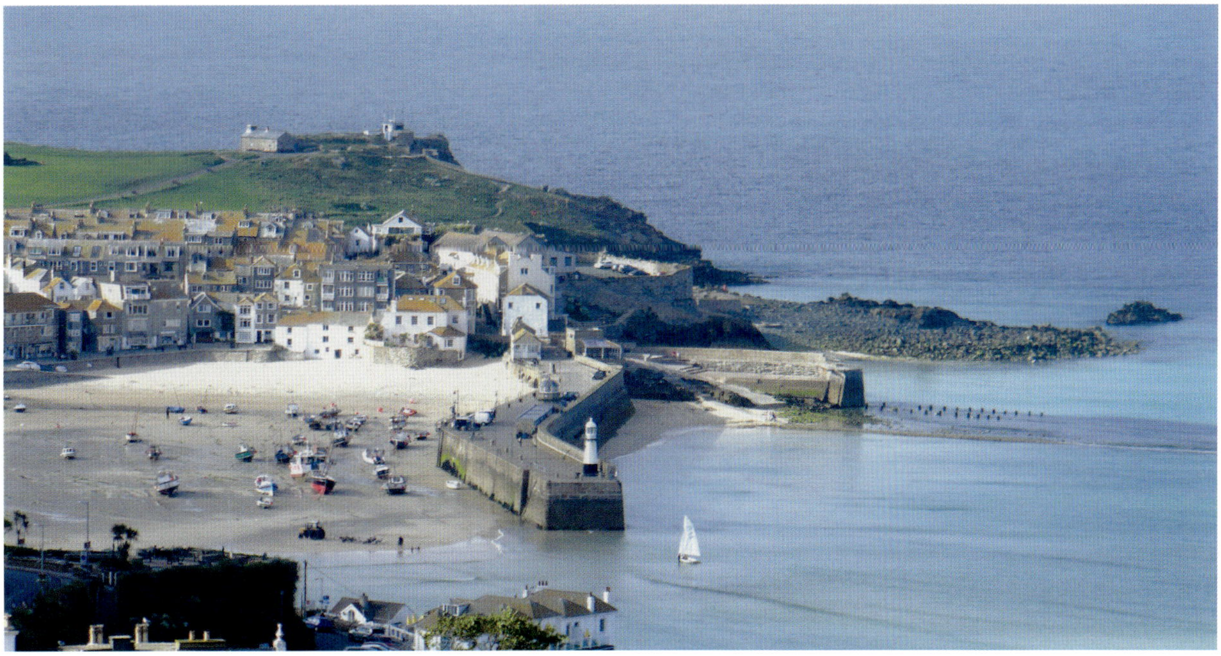
St. Ives Harbour, Low Tide, 2008

Other Artists - Heroes, Friends and Contemporaries

Alfred Wallis (1855-1942)

Joan never knew Alfred Wallis but she made no apologies for the influence Wallis and Christopher Wood (1901-1930) had on her work once she moved to Cornwall. After a spell in the workhouse at Madron Wallis died in poverty, aged 87. He was brought to St. Ives and is buried on the hill in Porthmeor cemetery and his grave is covered with tiles made by Bernard Leach. Mara, Joan's daughter, recounts that in later years when driving her mother to St. Ives they would always have to visit the grave and "say hello to Alfred..."

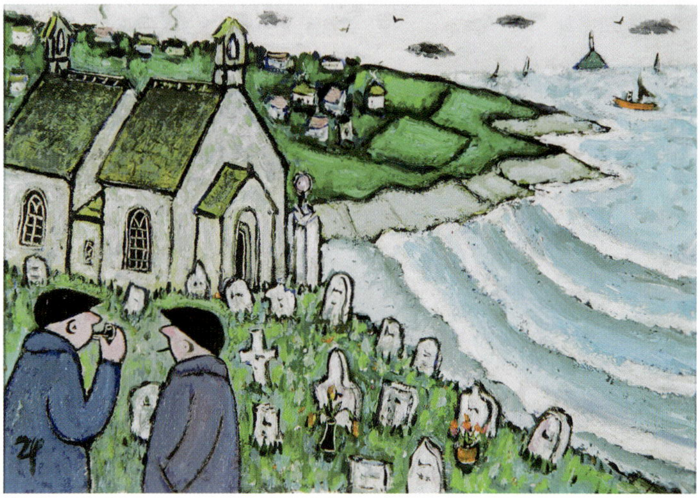

Porthmeor Cemetery

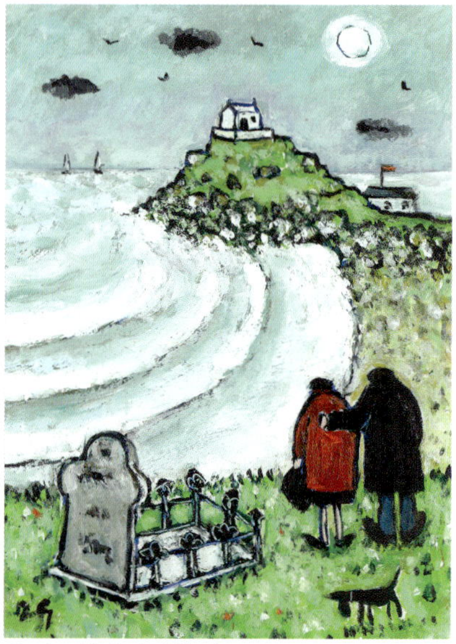

Saying Hello to Alfred

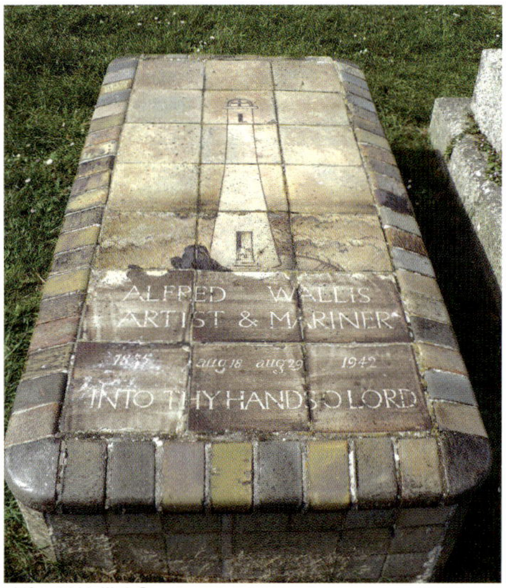

Alfred Wallis' Grave

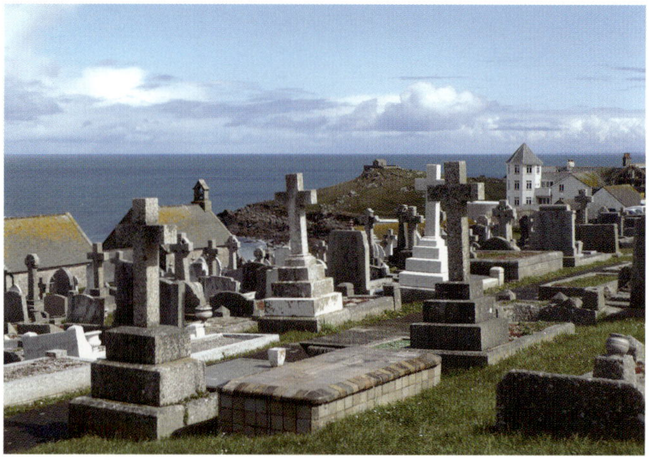

Porthmeor Cemetery 2008

Bryan Pearce (1929-2007)

He suffered as a child from Phenylketonuria, a rare cerebal disorder that prevents a child's normal development. He was encouraged to paint by his mother Mary, also a painter. Joan admired Bryan's work tremendously and was a a good friend to Mary. She admired the devoted care and encouragement that Mary gave to Bryan.

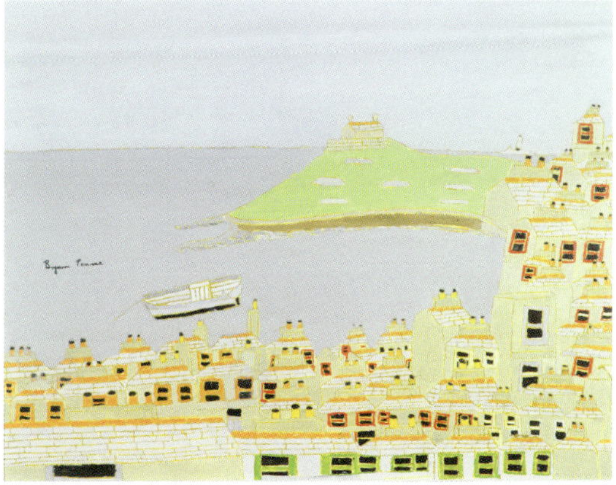

BRYAN PEARCE, View of the Island from Barnoon

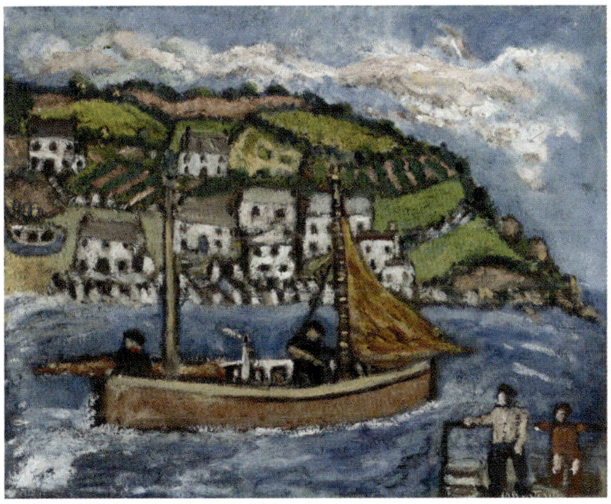

MARY JEWELS, Pilchard Boat

Mary Jewels (1886-1977)

A true Cornish painter who was born and lived in Newlyn. She was a member of the St. Ives Society and a founder member of the Penwith Society. She was quite an elderly lady by the time that Joan became friendly with her.

John Miller (1931-2002)

In 1961 he became a member of the Newlyn Society of Artists, serving as chairman for a number of years during the sixties and seventies and planned the first modernisation of the gallery in 1968. John encouraged Joan to exhibit at the Gallery and became a close friend.

JOHN MILLER, Penwith Sunrise

Barbara Hepworth (1903-1975)

Barbara Hepworth died tragically in 1975. Two years before Joan remembers going to Hepworth's 70th birthday party at her studio, Trewyn, in St. Ives. The room was full of the artists of the day, laughing and drinking whilst Barbara cut a very lonely figure who took no part in the proceedings.

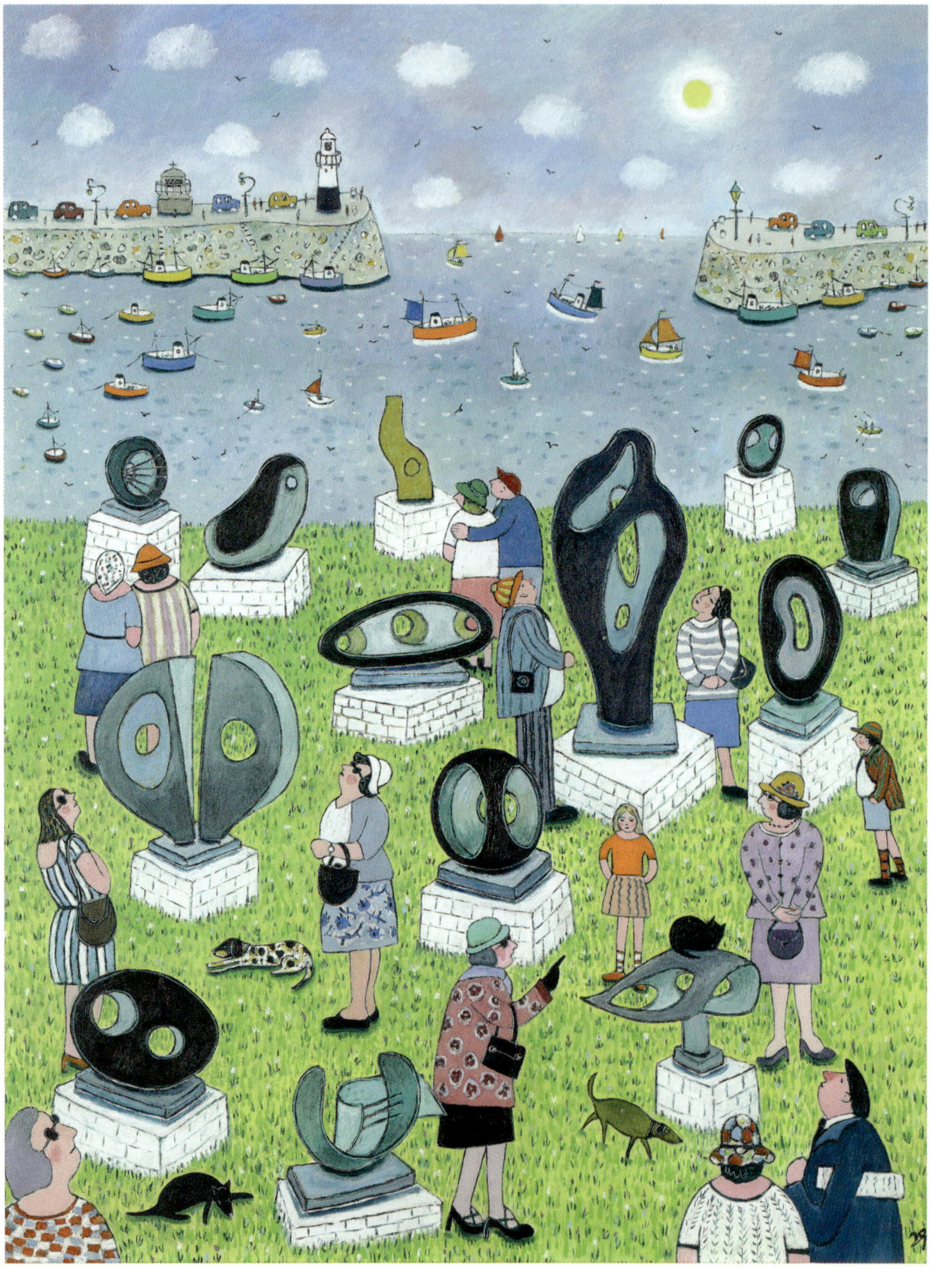

Barbara Hepworth's Garden

Beyond St. Ives

Lelant

Beyond St. Ives and Carbis Bay one reaches Lelant, the home of West Cornwall Golf Club. The lovely small church of St. Uny nestles right in the middle of the Golf Club with the sand dunes behind.

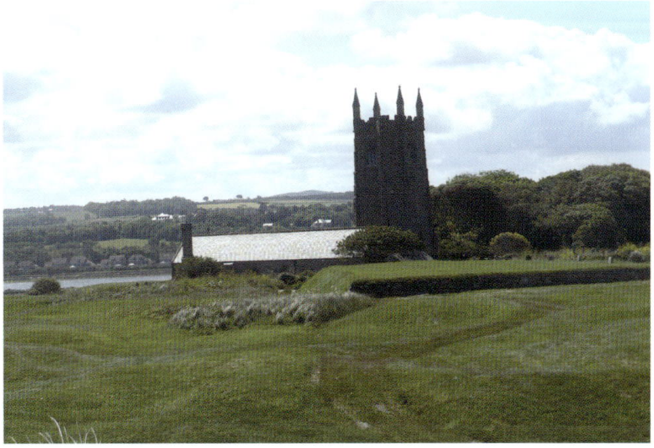

Lelant Church 2008

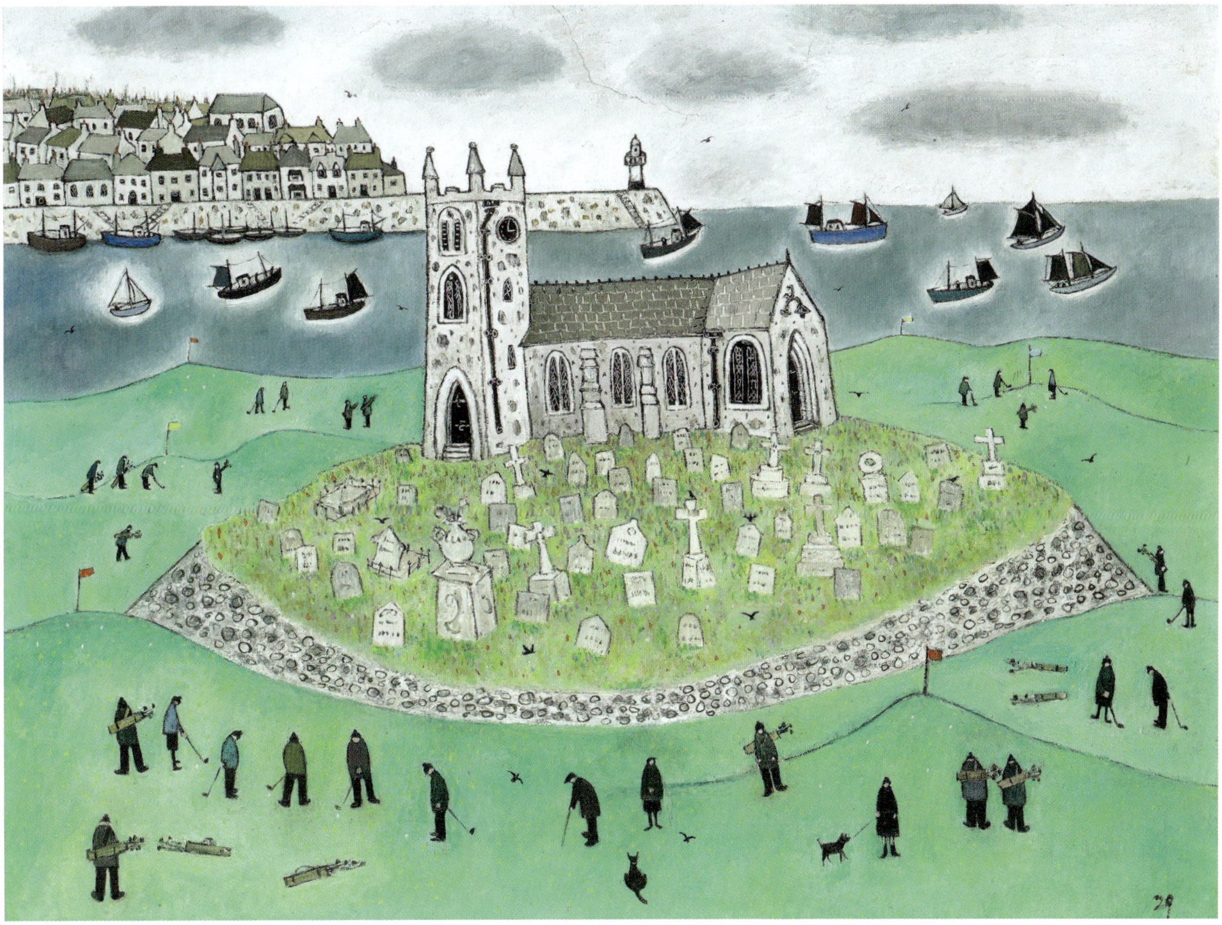

Golf in Cornwall

Hayle

Situated on the opposite side of St. Ives Bay, Hayle is famed for 3 miles of golden sand. It also has a tropical bird garden which was established in 1973. The flamingos in particular gave Joan very colourful subject material.

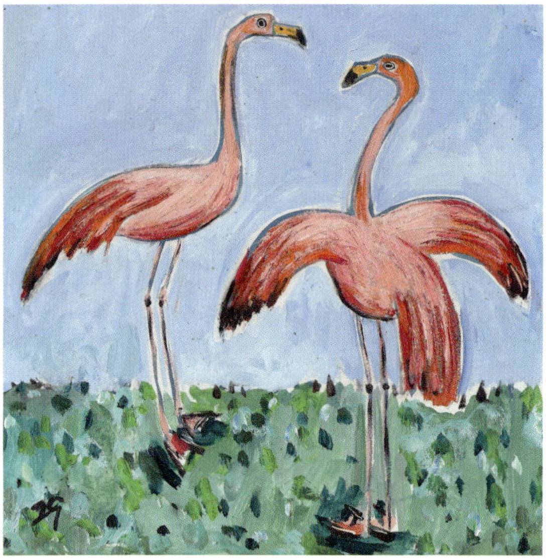

Flamingos at Hayle

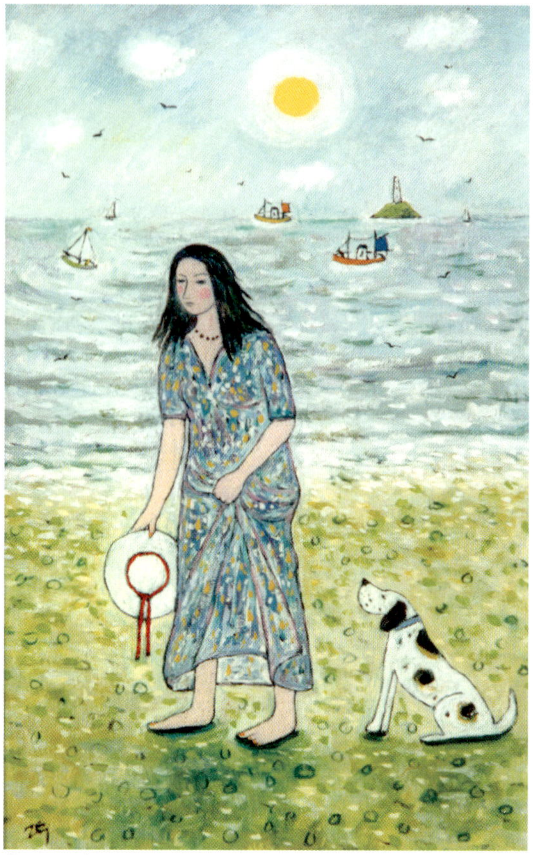

Summertime

Godrevy

A delightful spot to paint, read or just to soak up the sun.

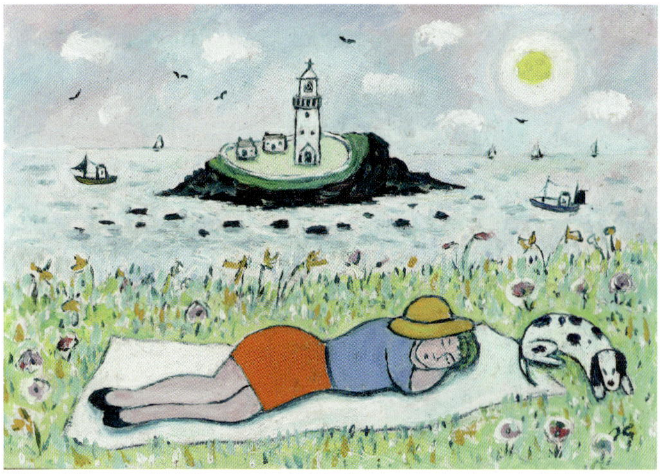

Perfect Happiness at Godrevy

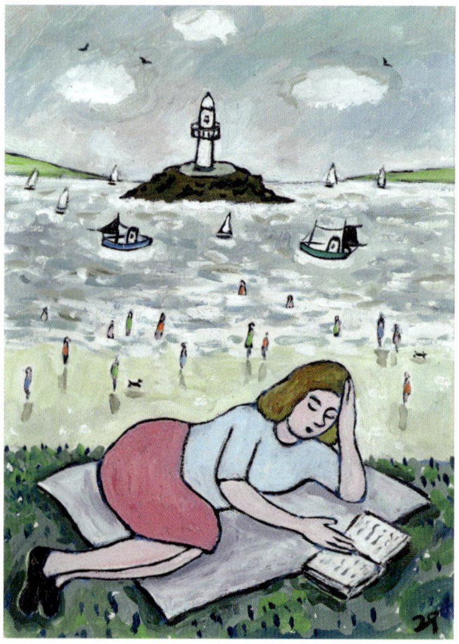

A Quiet Read at Godrevy

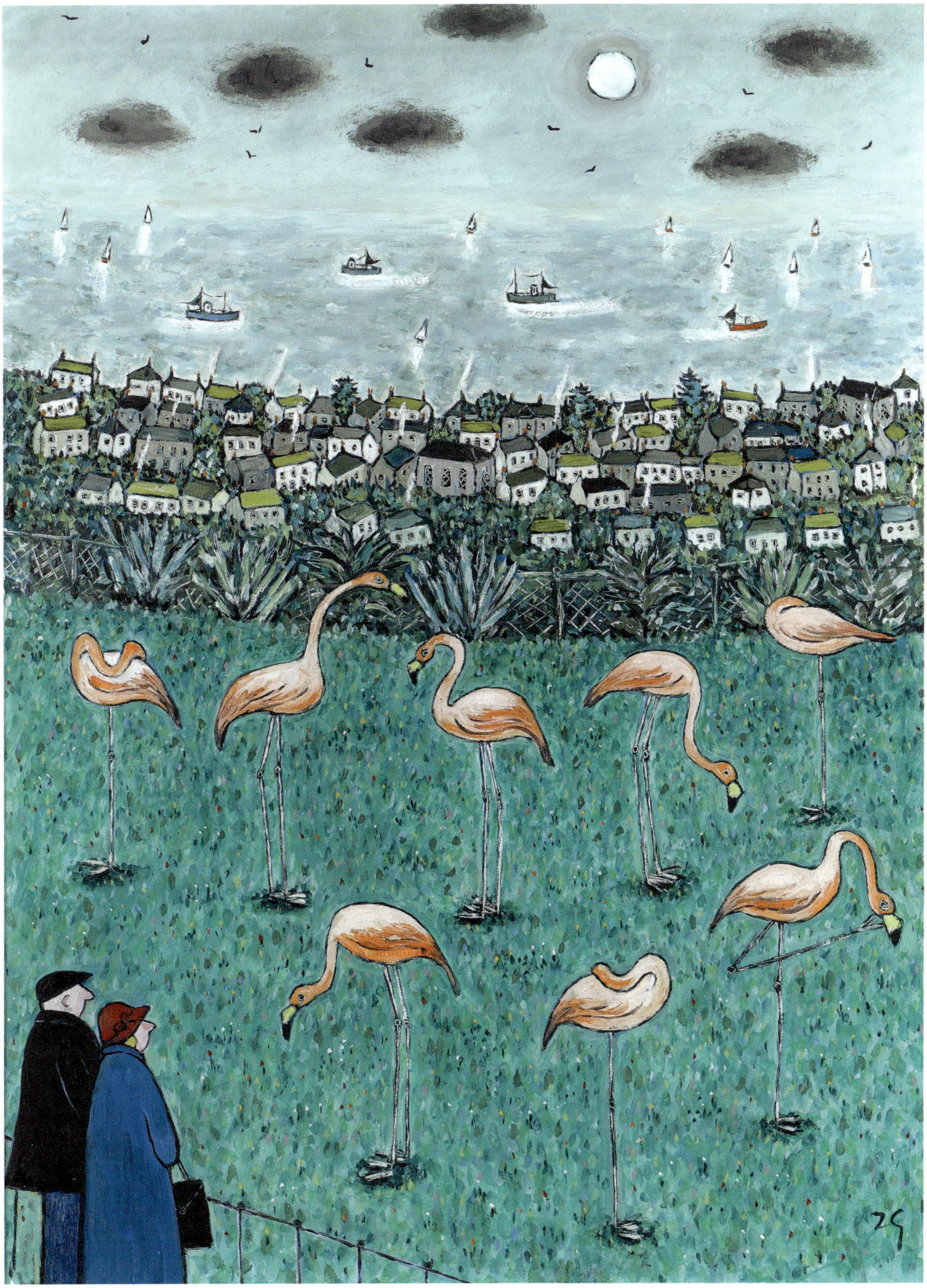

Paradise Park, Hayle

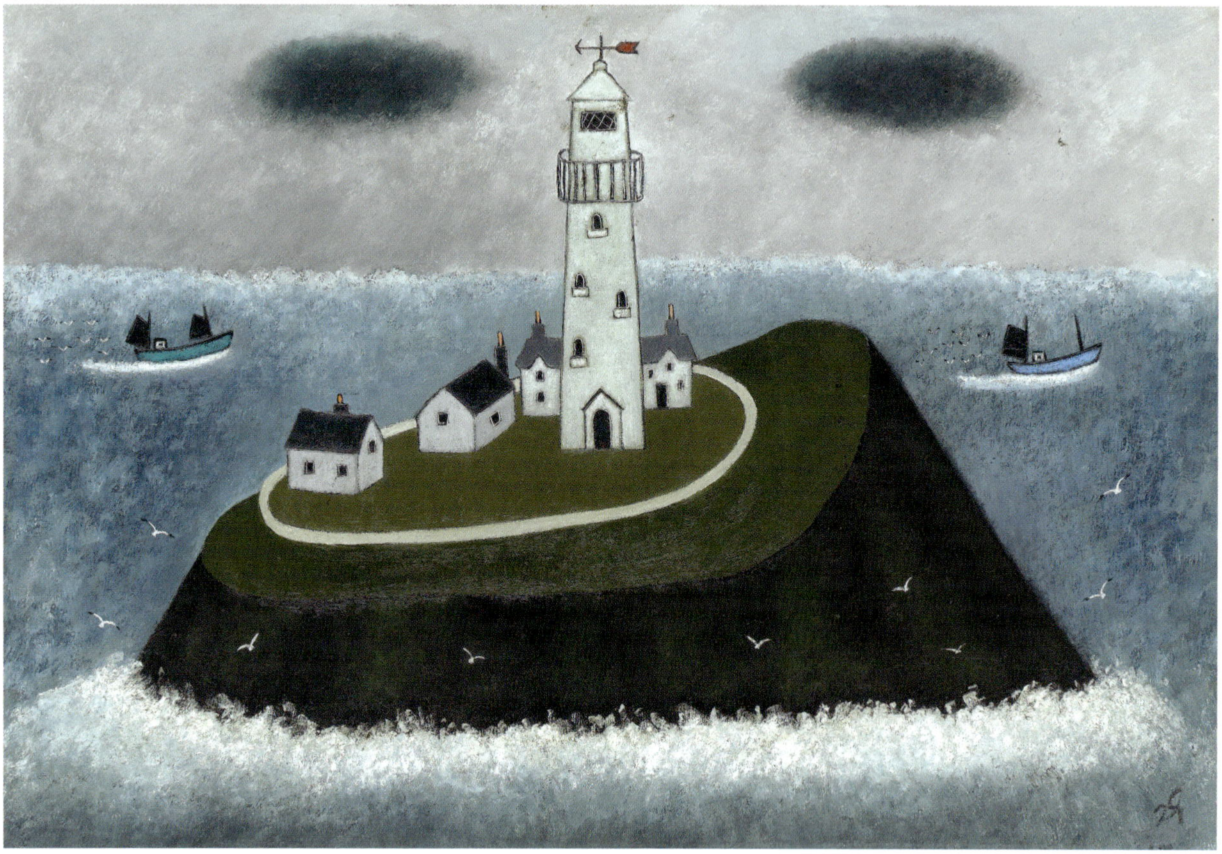

Godrevy Lighthouse

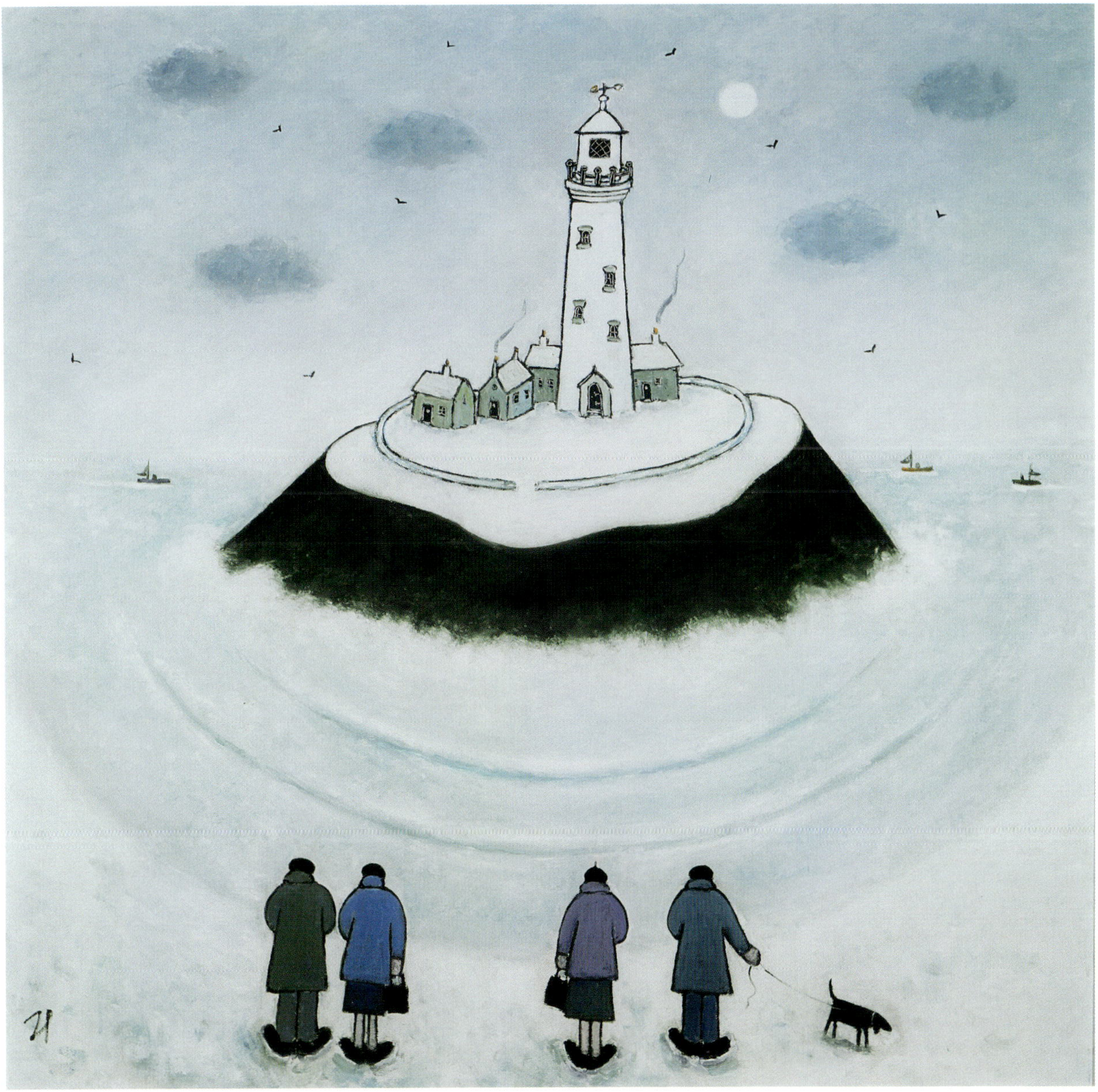

Visiting Godrevy Lighthouse, Wintertime

Chapter 8 Chapels and Churches

Coming from such a long line of eminent architects it is not surprising that Joan always loved the Cornish architecture that surrounded her. Churches and chapels feature prominently in her work.

"Buildings are in my Blood..."

The Methodist Tradition

The Methodist movement in Cornwall began in the eighteenth century. John Wesley visited Cornwall over 30 times between 1743 and 1787. Initially small meetings were held in people's houses, then larger open air gatherings before chapels were built and the Wesleyan Methodists were formed. Wesley's main preaching was aimed at the poor and uneducated miners and fishermen and their families. The established church was the church of the more prosperous. John Wesley had a profound effect on the religious life in Cornwall and today most towns, villages and hamlets have a Methodist chapel.

Joan's sketch books show that she must have spent many hours sketching these chapels for use in later paintings.

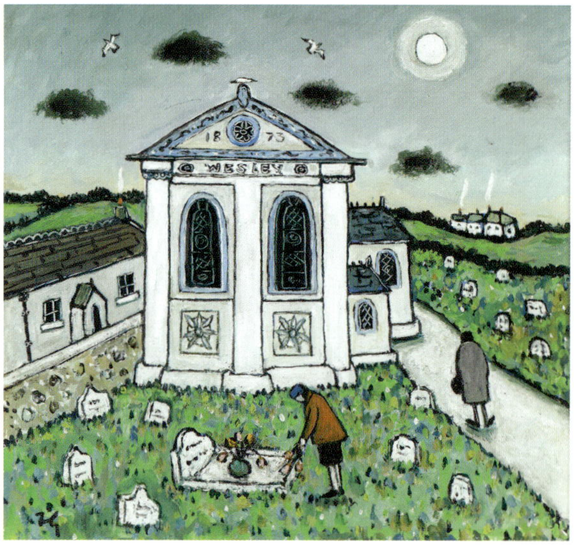

Sunday Morning

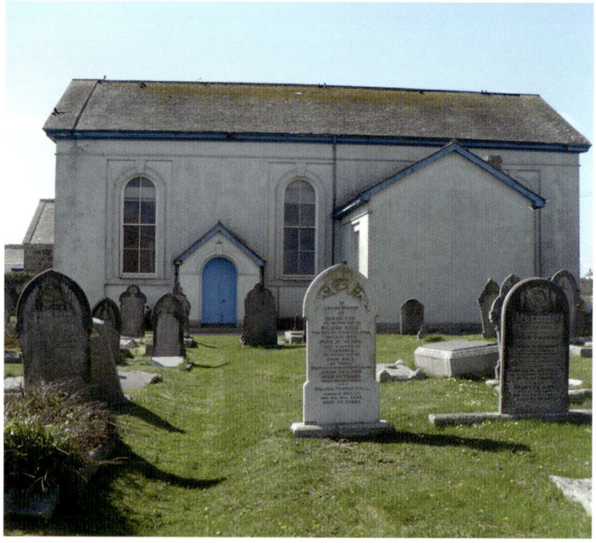

St. Levens Methodist Chapel 2008

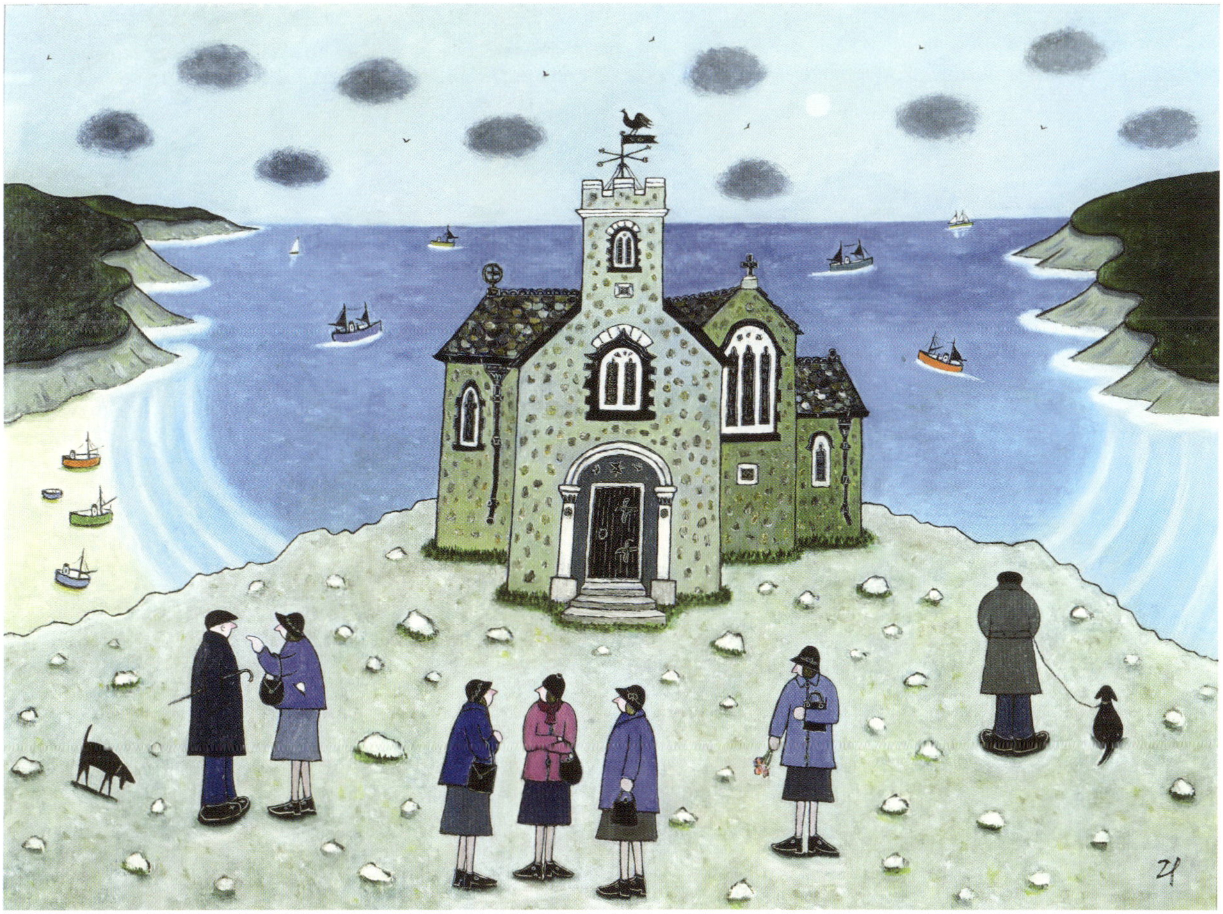

Visiting a Cornish Chapel

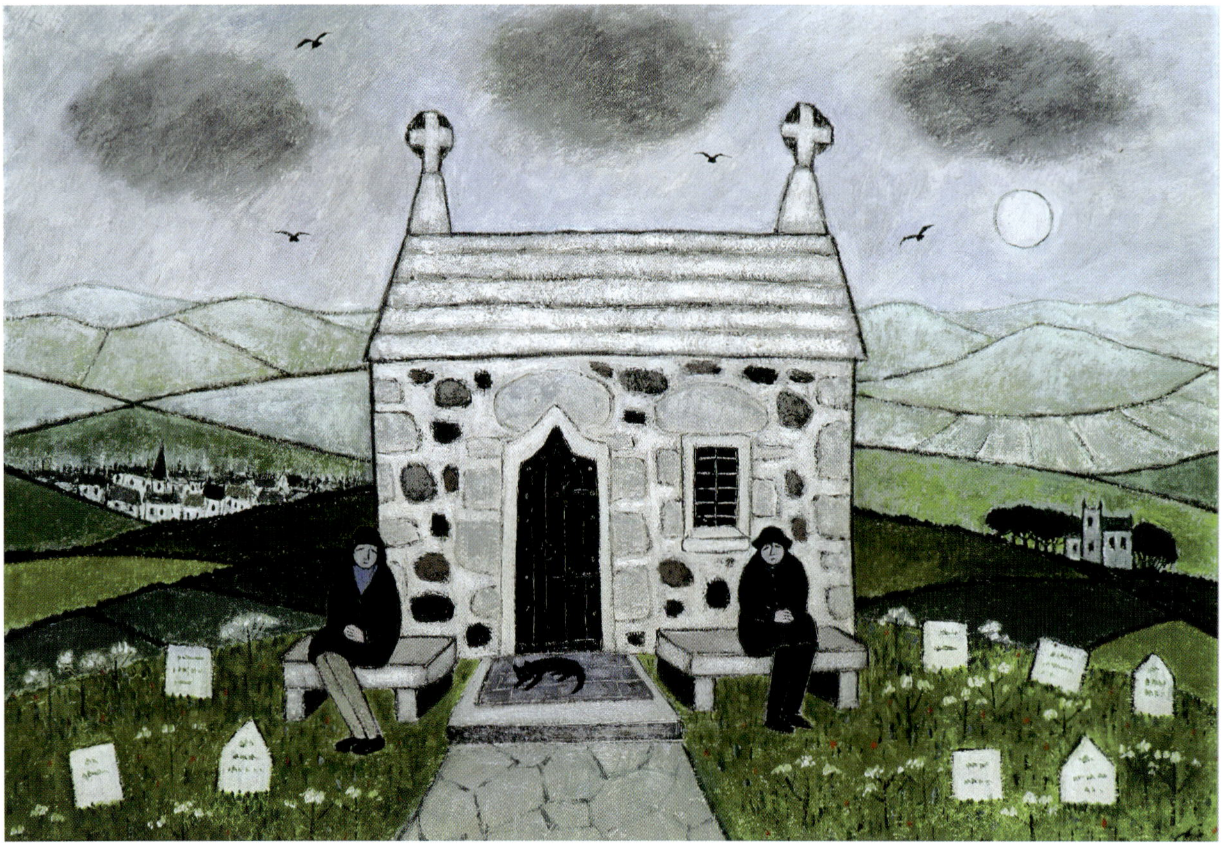

Cornish Chapel

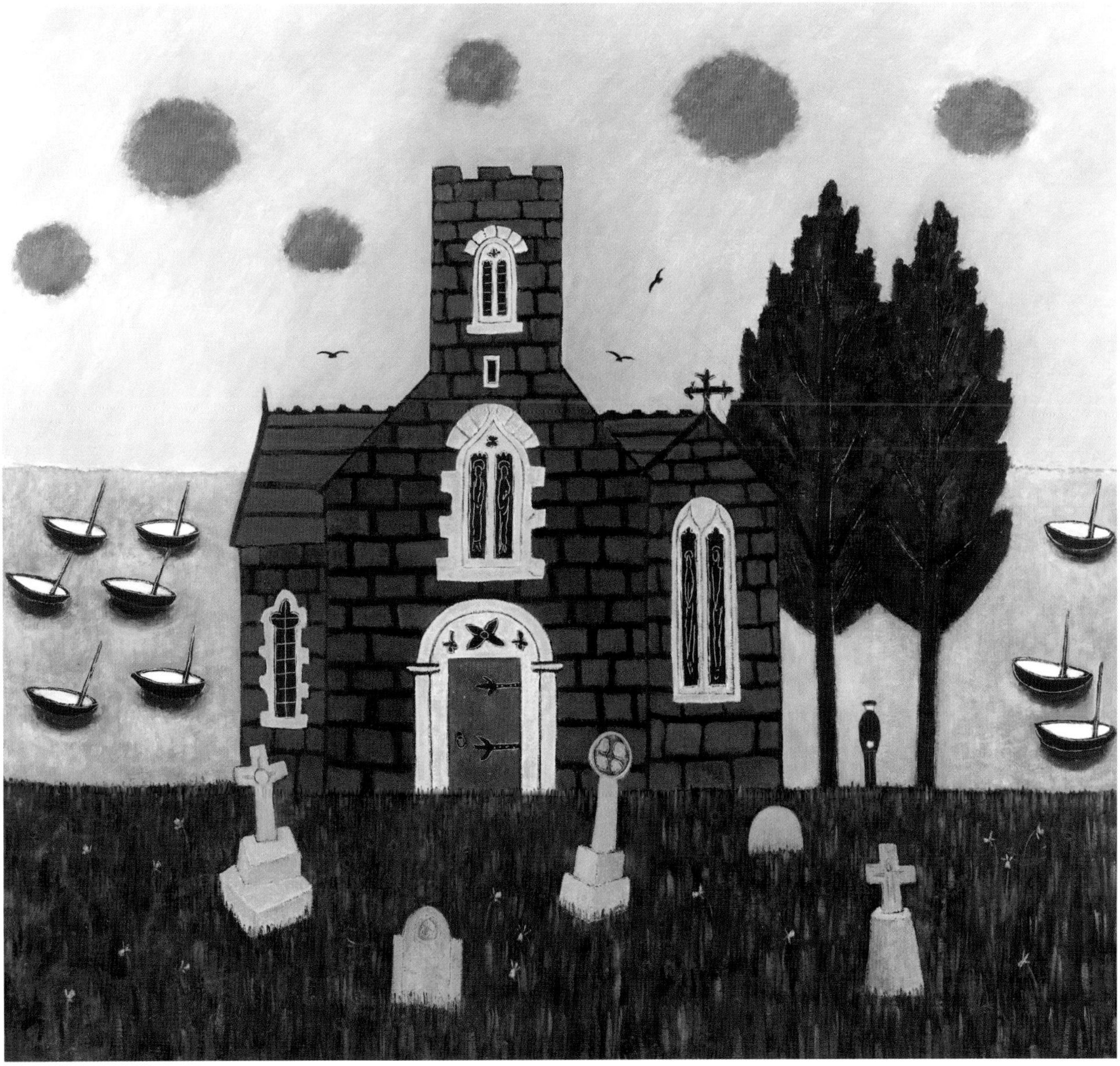

The Fishermen's Chapel

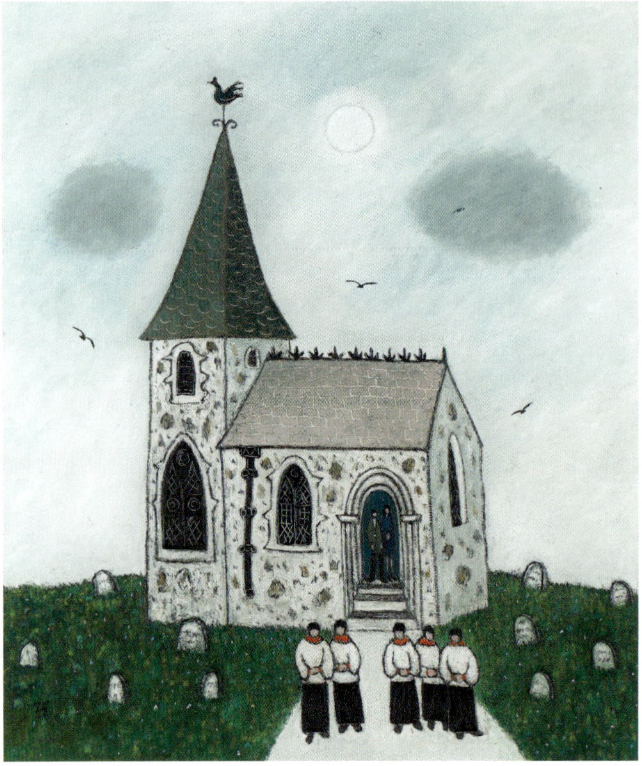

The Choir

Penwith Churches

Each town and village on the Peninsula has its own church. Mostly they are very beautiful and set in idyllic surroundings. Joan loved to capture some of the architectural features of these churches and use them as back drops to a number of her major works.

Festivals and Clergy

A recurring theme in Joan's work was the colour and texture associated with ecclesiastical life. Whether painting church furnishings, stained glass windows, bishops' robes or choristers' vestments, Joan's attention to detail was amazing. Frequently such works were full of mischievous humour.

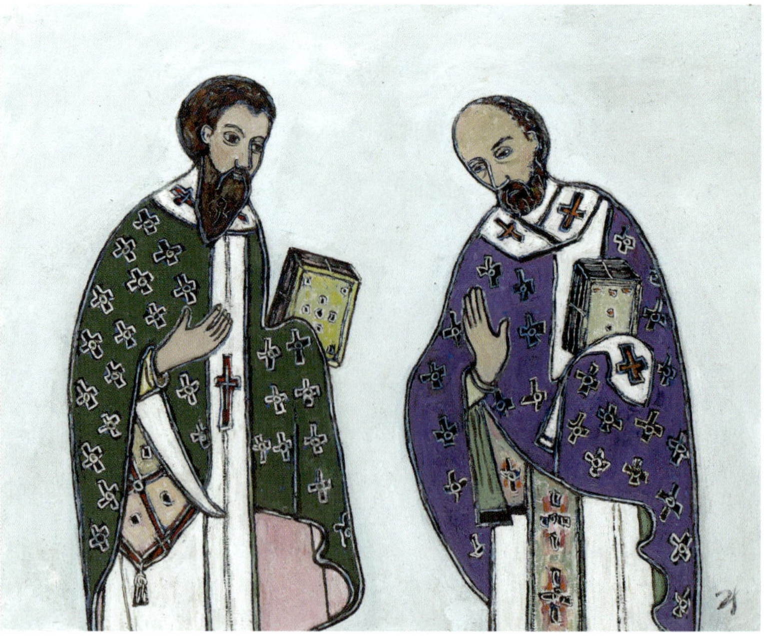

"You do look good in purple"

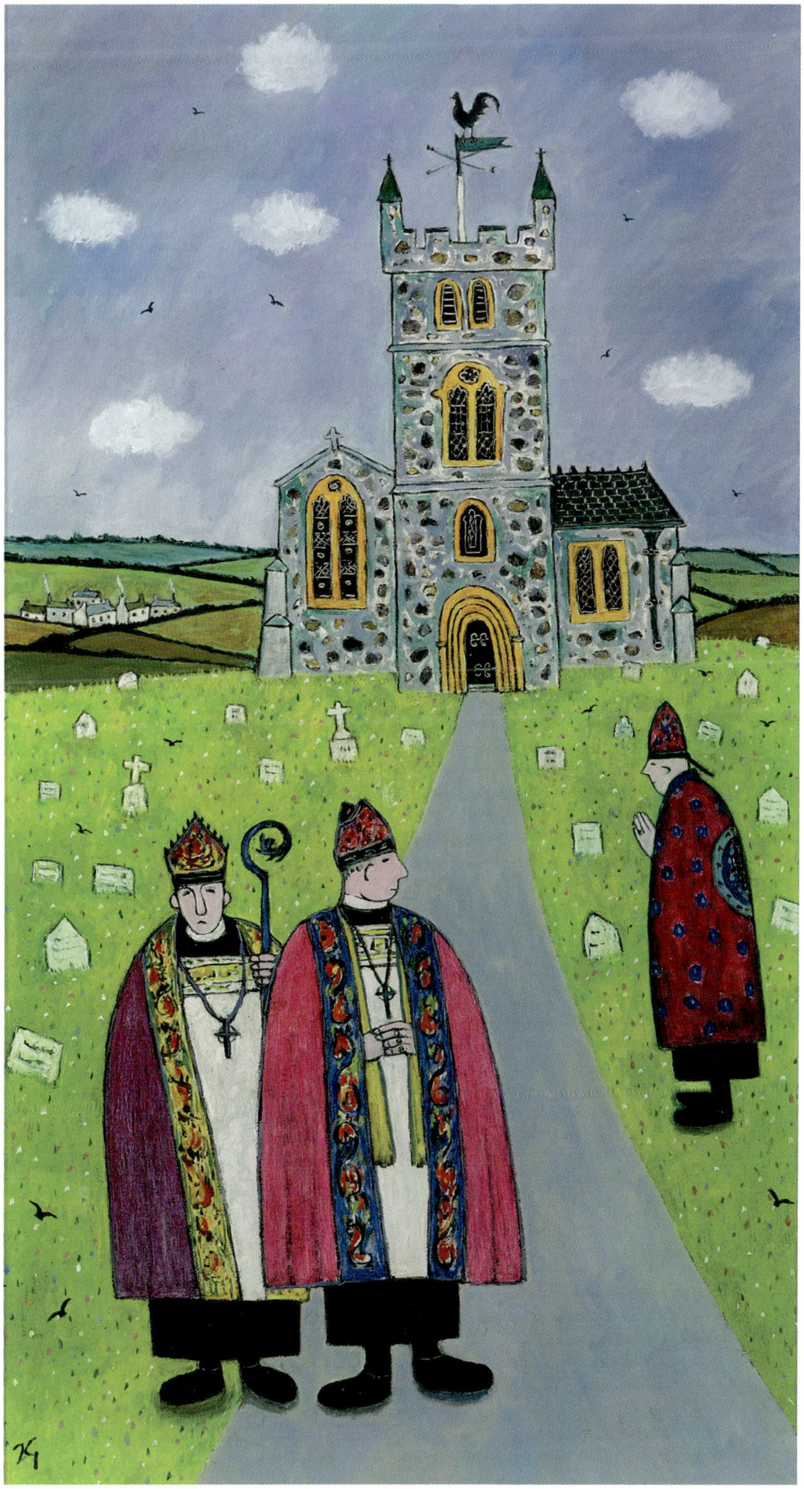

Easter Sunday

Weddings and Funerals

Such events gave Joan the opportunity to paint detailed scenes full of people and to capture the mood of the moment. Often her simple titles express a thousand "unspoken" thoughts.

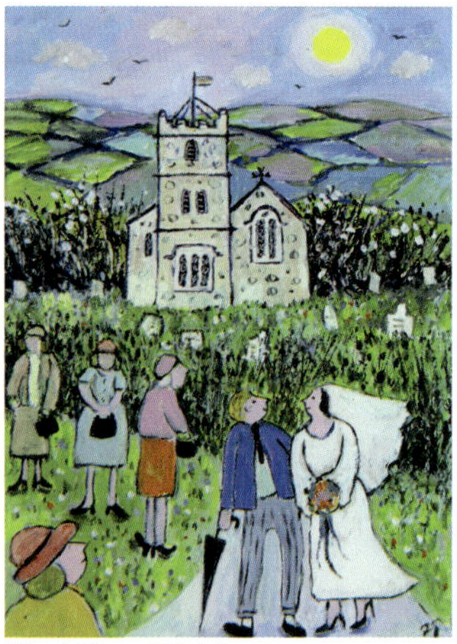

The Village Wedding

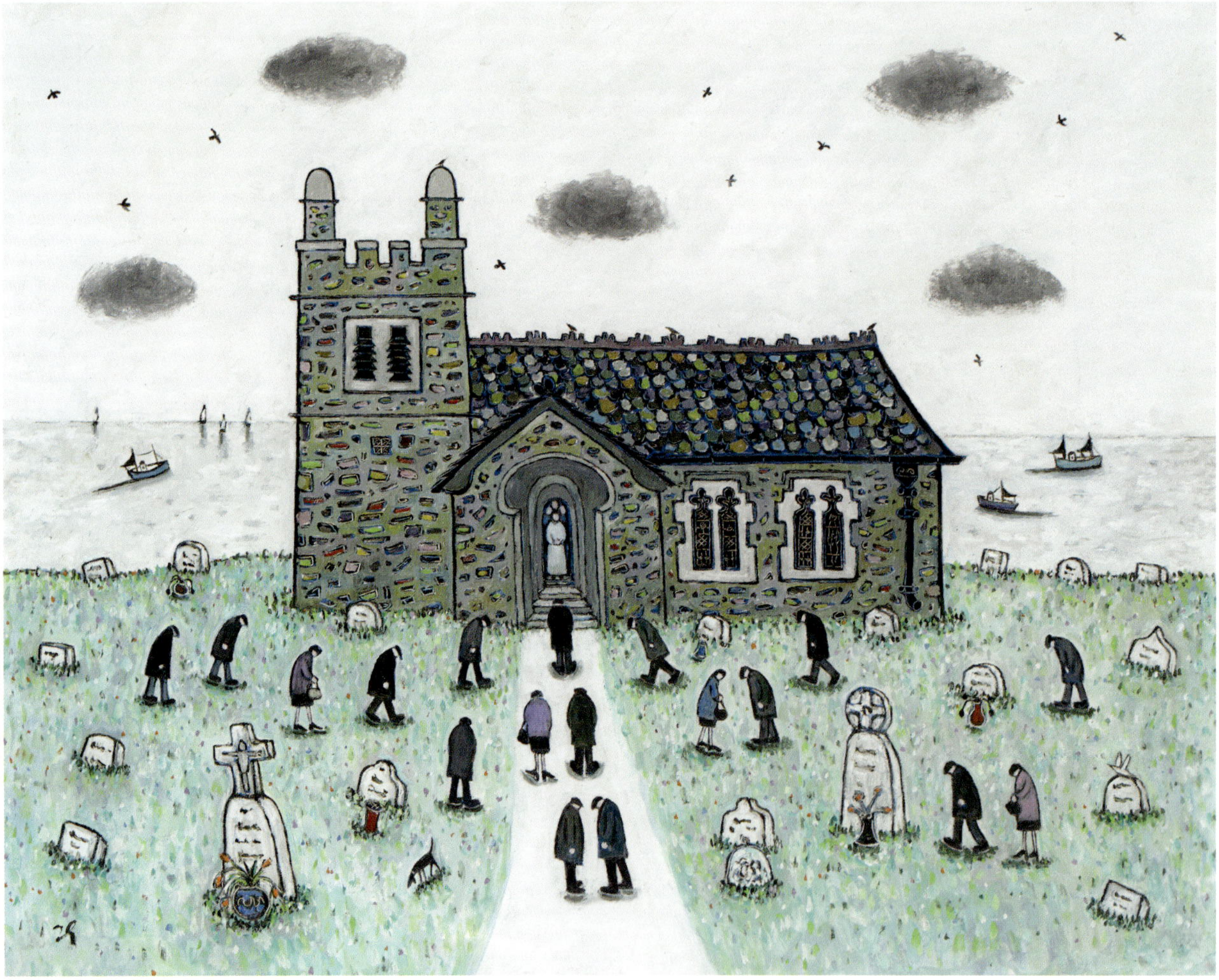

"Fancy Seeing You Here"

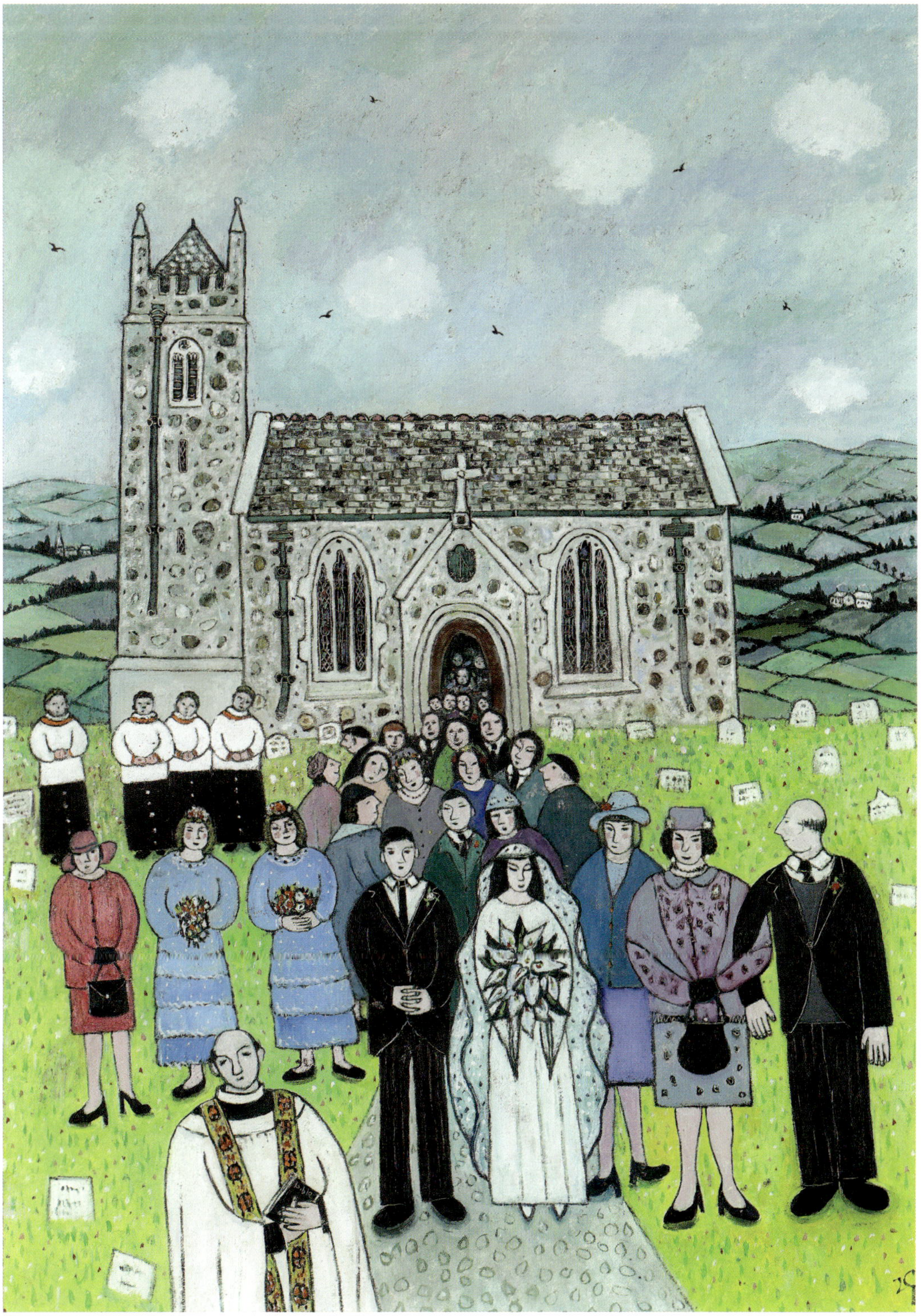
Her Big Day

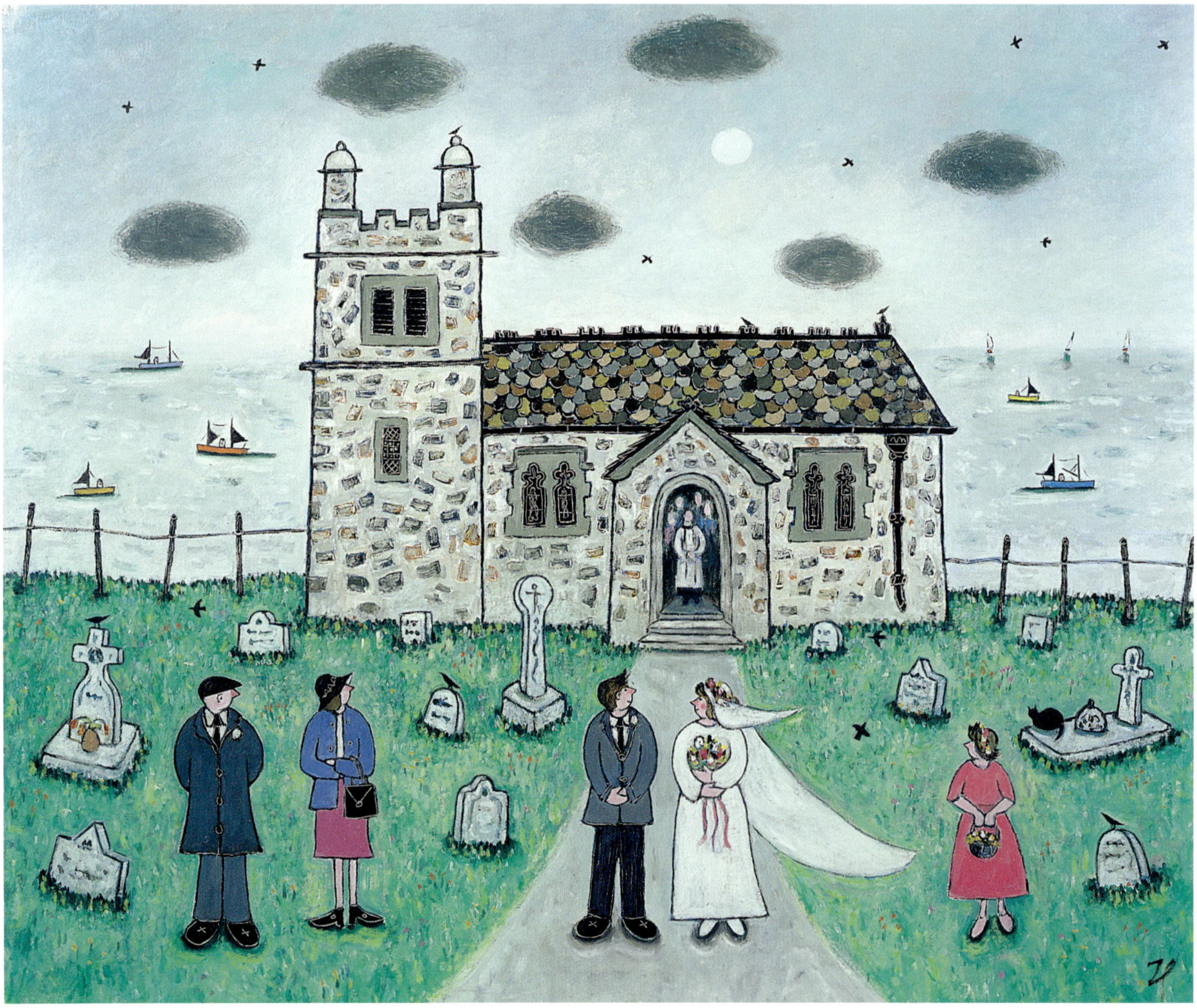
"What has she done?"

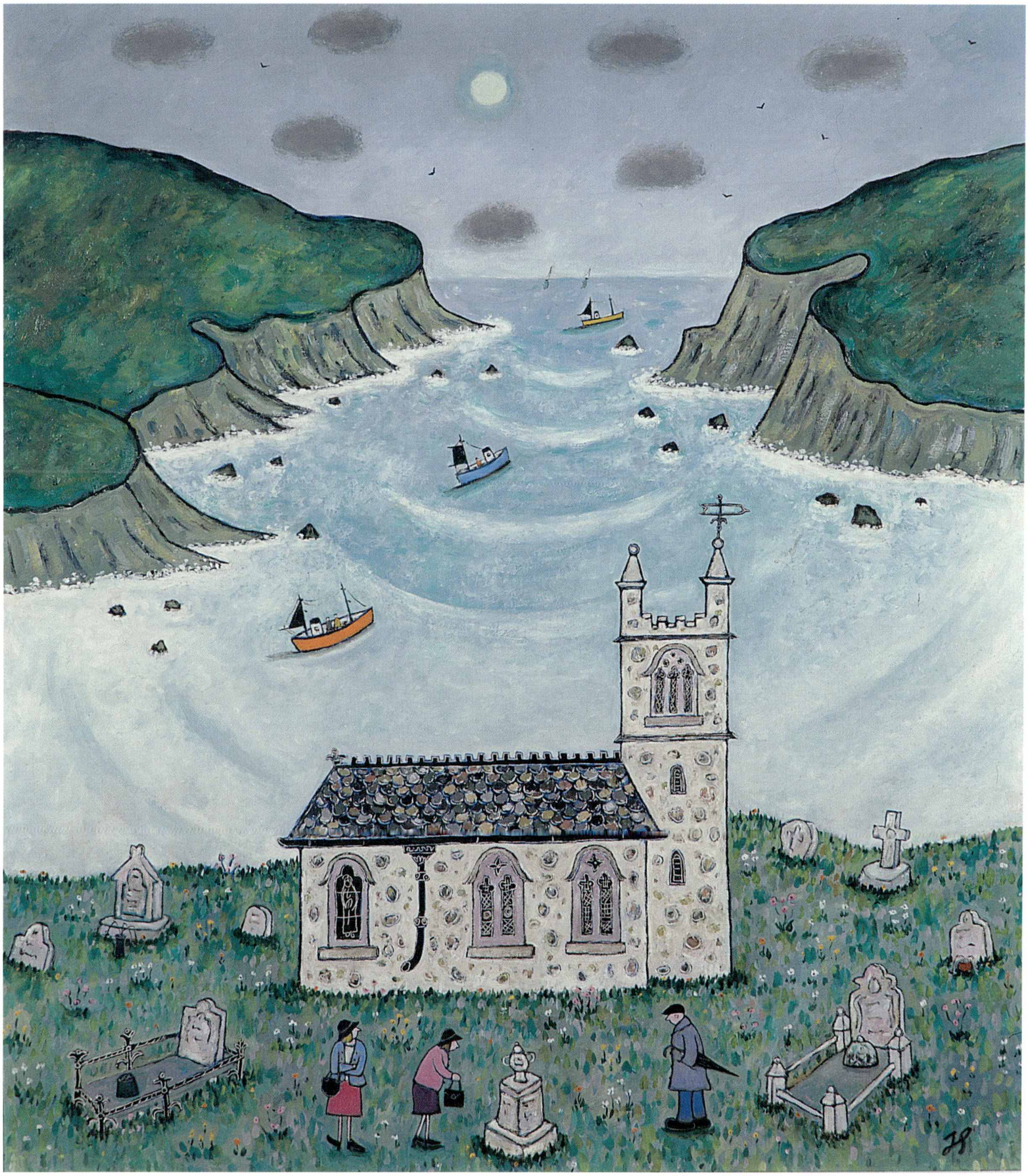

Discovering the Beauty of Cornwall

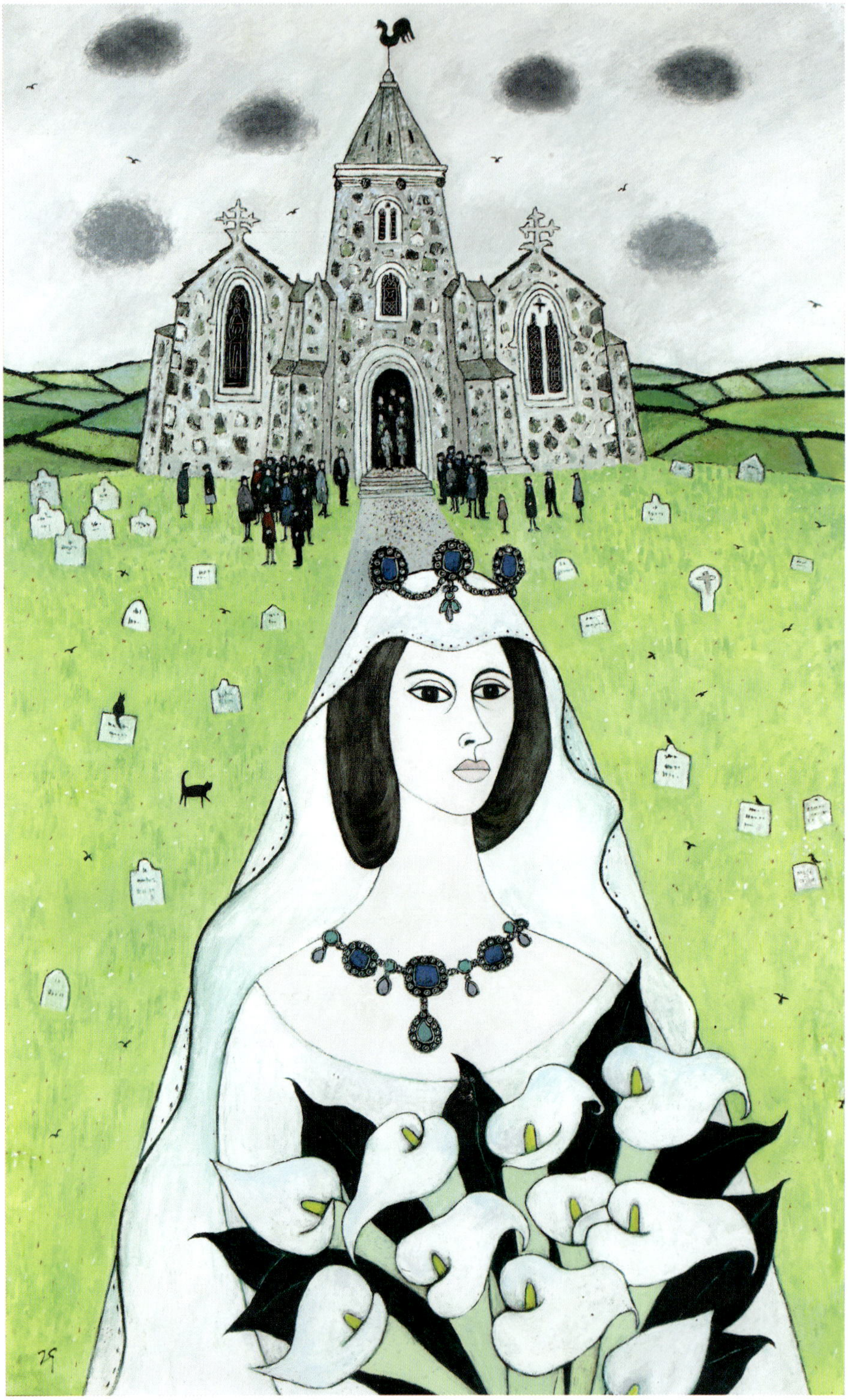

The Bride

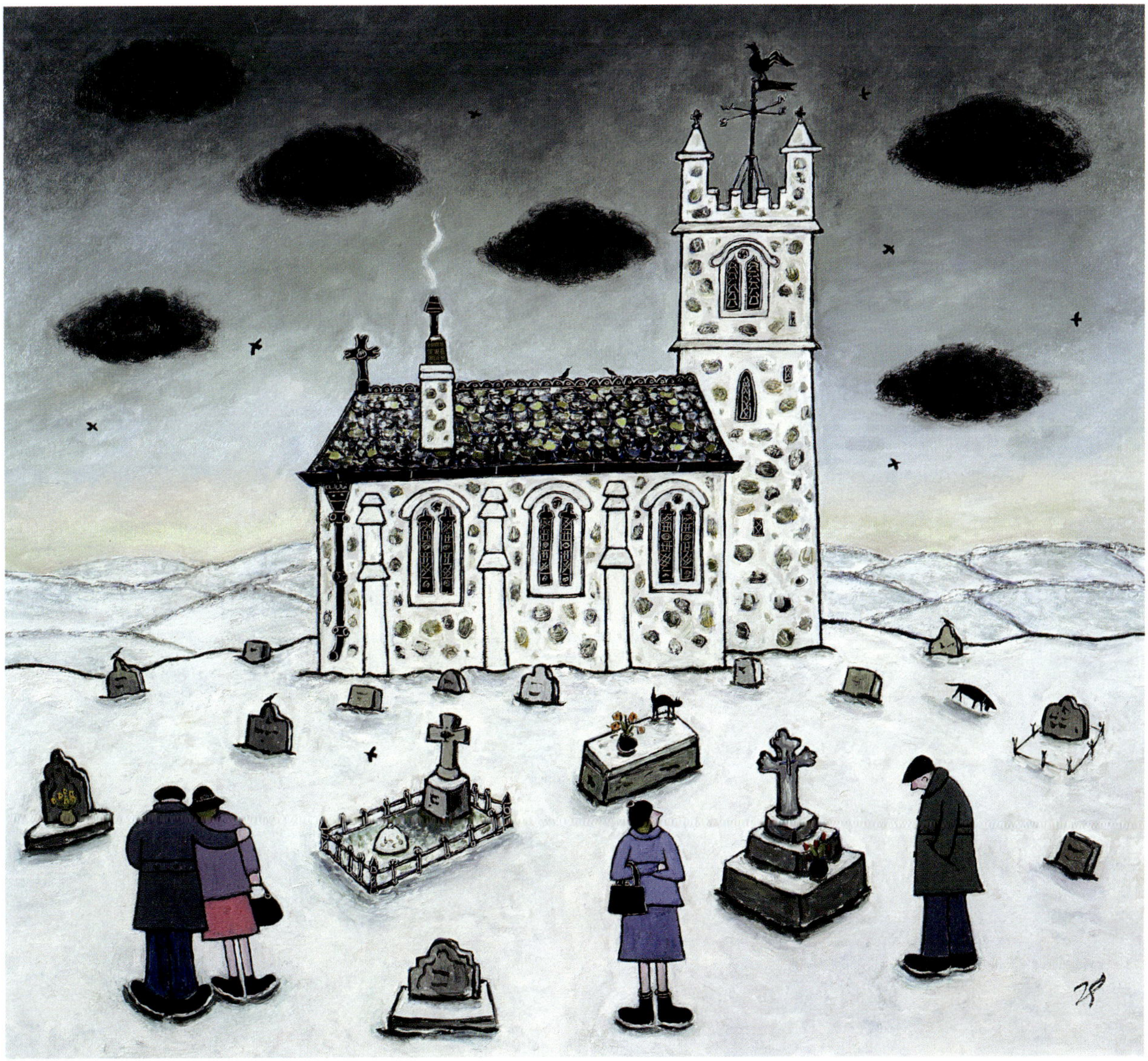

Paying their Respects

Chapter 9 The French Connection

Joan and France have come together many times over the years. In her mid teens she went to Paris and then with Adrian Ryan was a frequent visitor in the fifties and sixties.

There were also several memorable visits made in the company of her much loved brother Gil. He describes one such occasion, "A few years after qualifying I drove Joan and my wife Agnes through France to Spain. On the way back we stopped in Paris, where Joan knew a particular night club called Eve. For the cost of a bottle of champagne the three of us could stay all night. We had a hilarious time watching typical naughty French sketches."

Gil and his second wife Susan moved to France in the 1970's where he practised in Argentat-sur-Dordogne, Correze. It is a very picturesque area and Joan visited them twice in the 1980's staying at their idyllic home a short distance from Argentat.

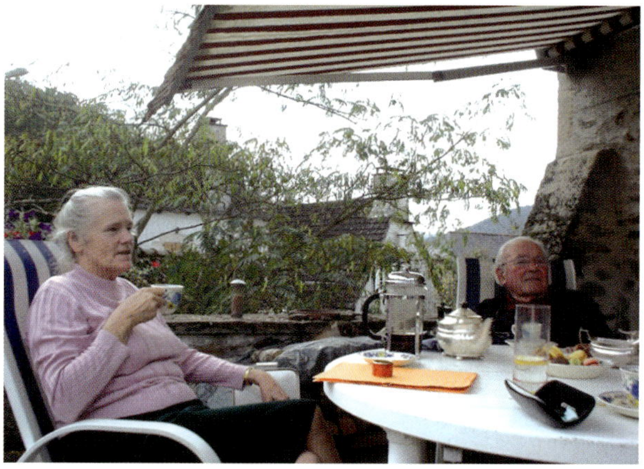

Gil and Susan at home 2007

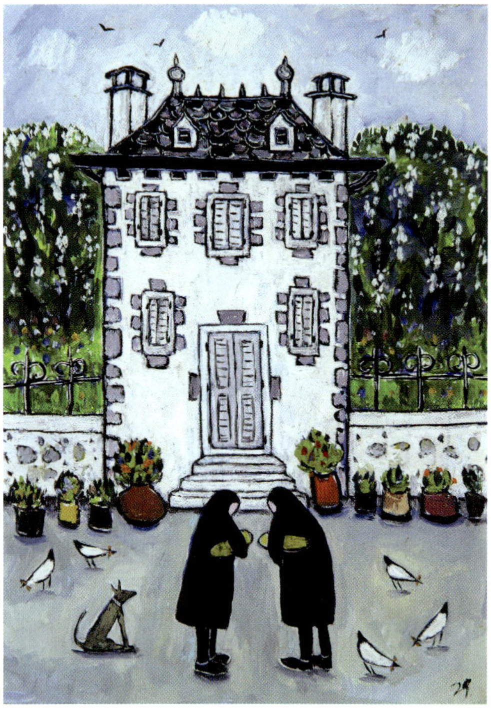

Maison Bourgeoise at Argentat

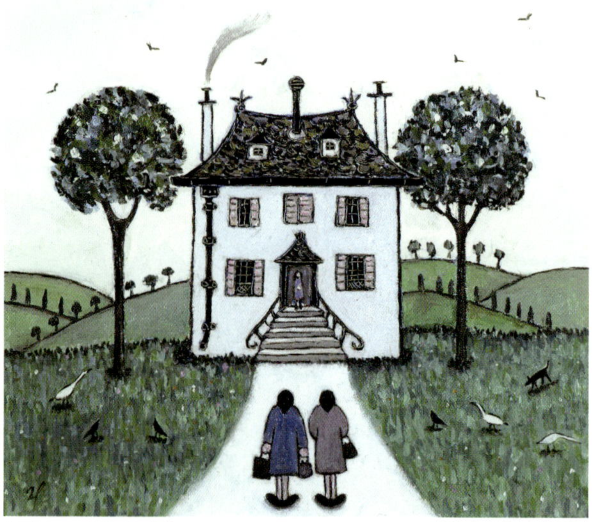

Cottage at Argentat

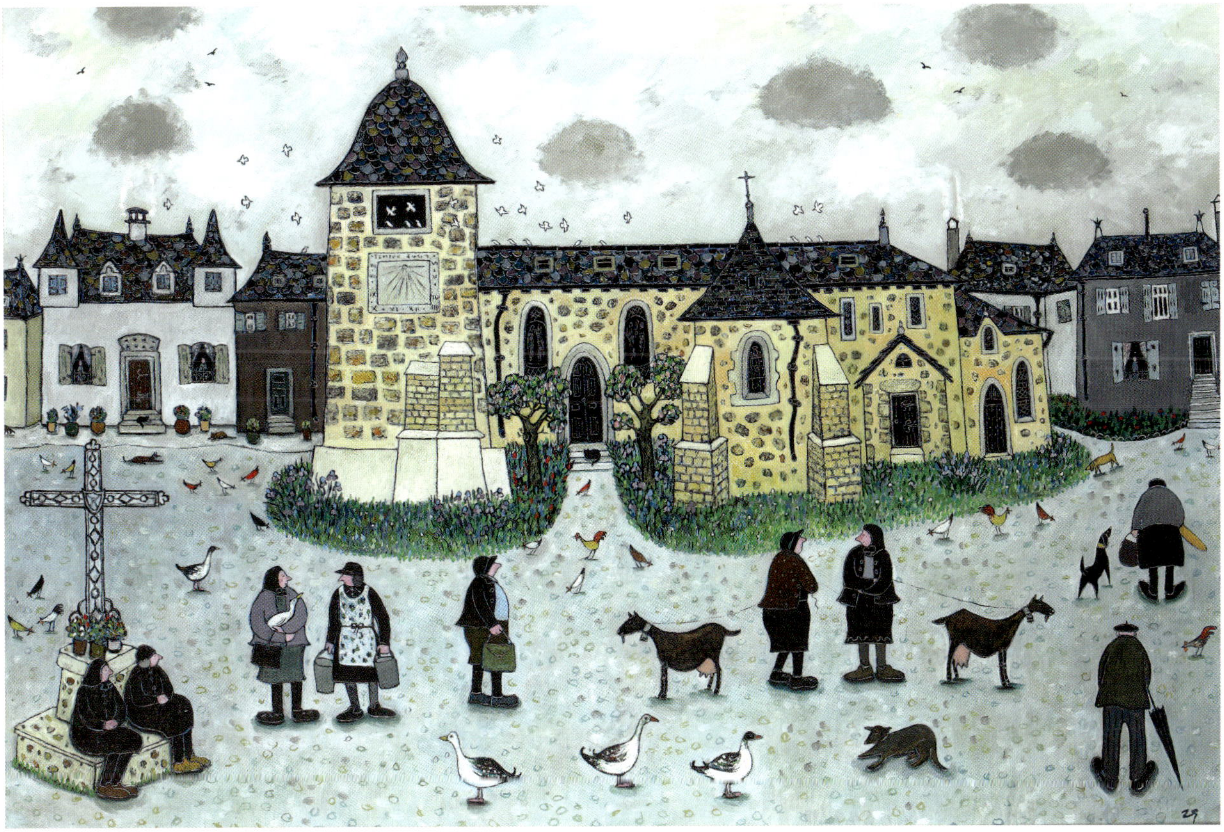

Market Day, Saint-Chamant

A splendid composition of French impressions. The main ingredient is the church at Saint Chamant. This village is the next village north of Argentat in the Correze district.

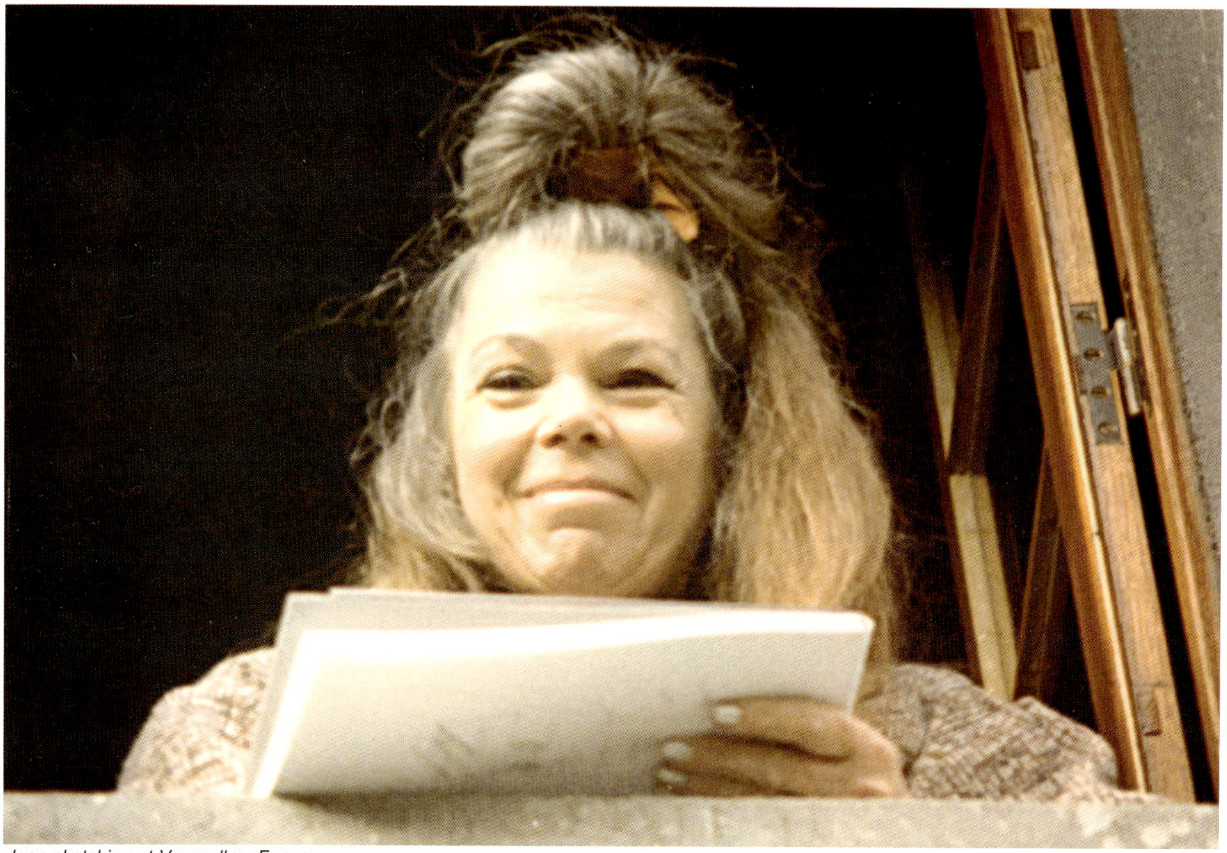

Joan sketching at Vergnolles, France

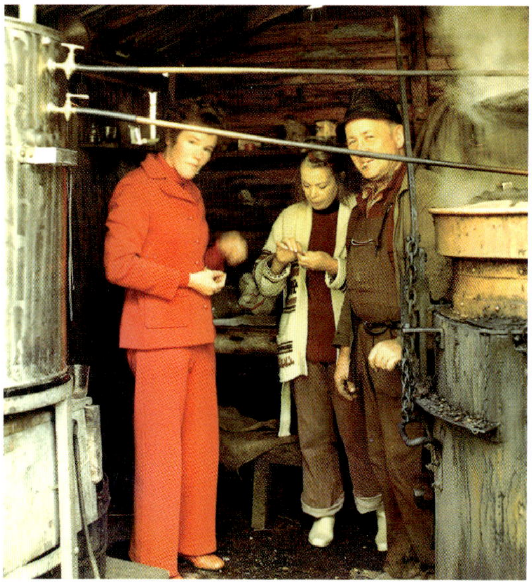

At Pont de Monceaux, eating walnuts

Gil and Susie drove her around the area where she sketched continuously, like somebody taking shorthand. Gil says "Often a few lines were enough for her to recall what she had seen and occasionally she would make a very detailed sketch of a feature that had caught her eye. She had an extraordinary visual memory, recalling subjects and people long after seeing them." These sketches were used to produce a series of marvellous pictures that captured the day to day lives of French people in their towns and villages, and the very distinctive architecture of the churches and houses in this region.

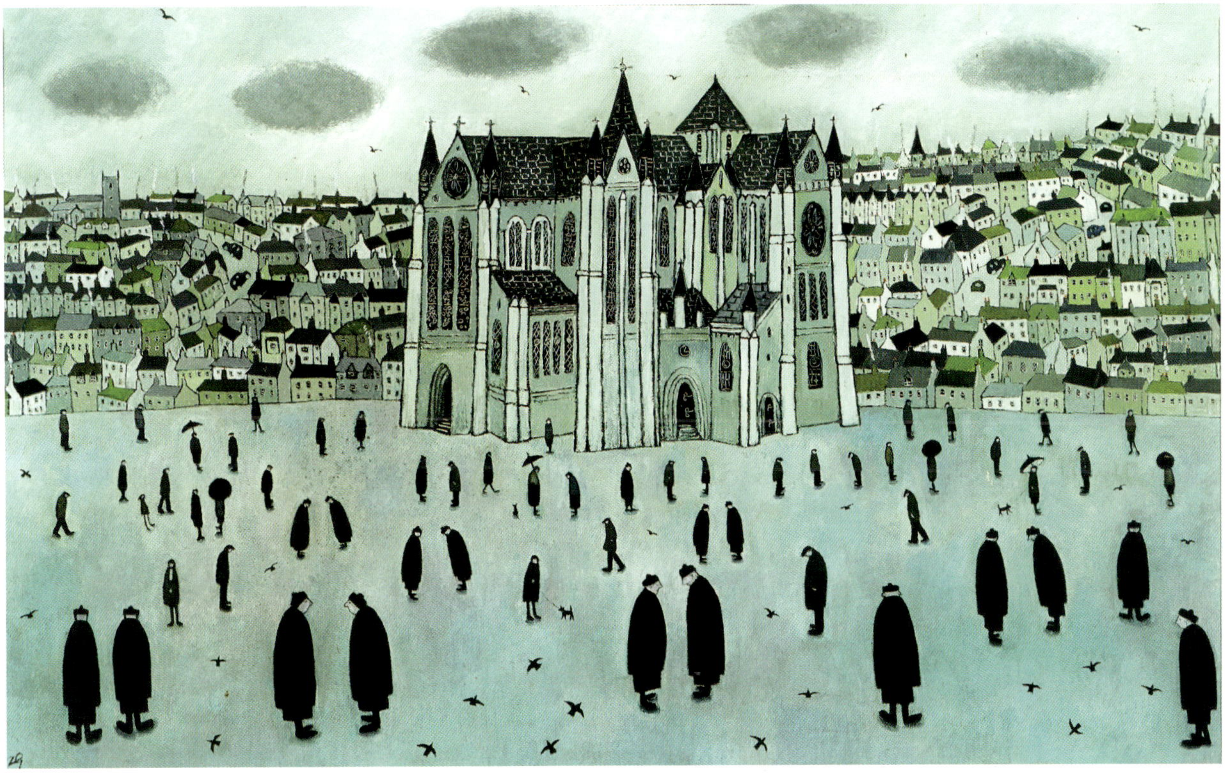
After Mass

This painting illustrates her fascination with ecclesiastical architecture and she found rich subject matter during her visits to France. The very detailed work is loosely based on l'Eglise St-Martin, Brive La Gaillarde.

French Characters

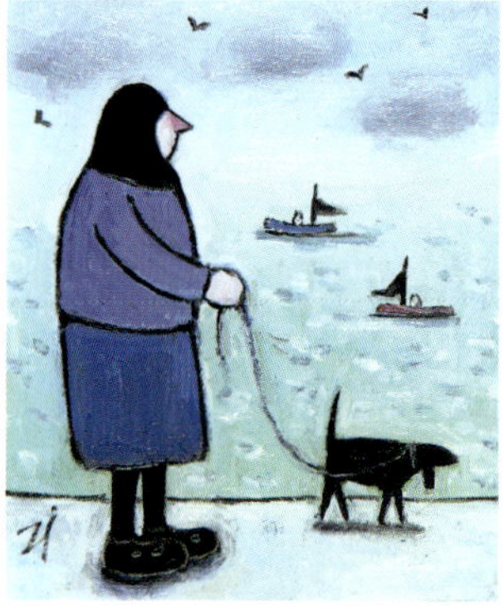

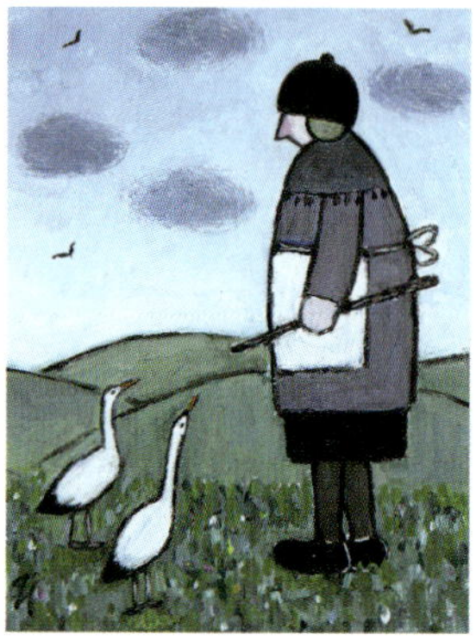

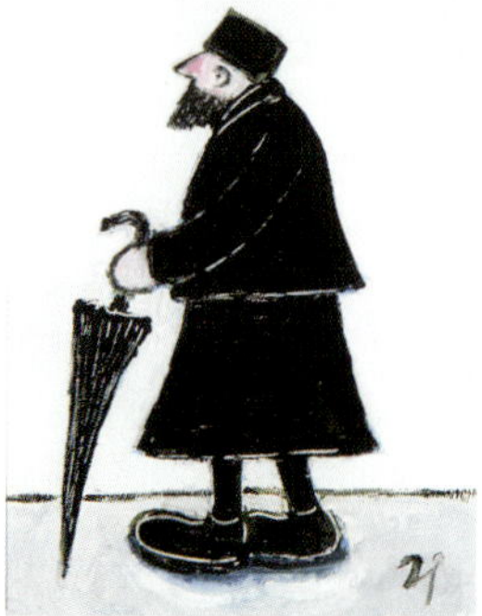

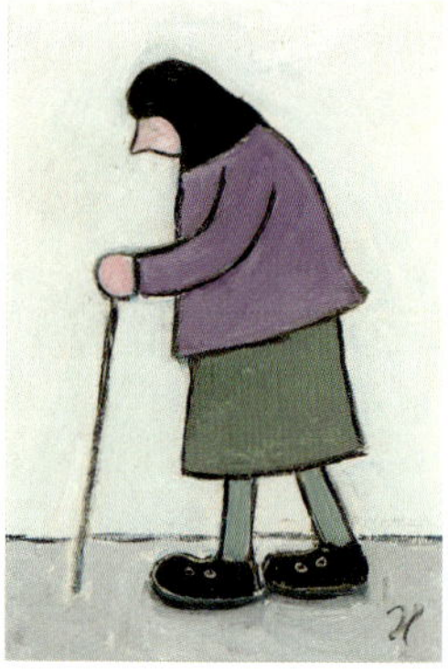

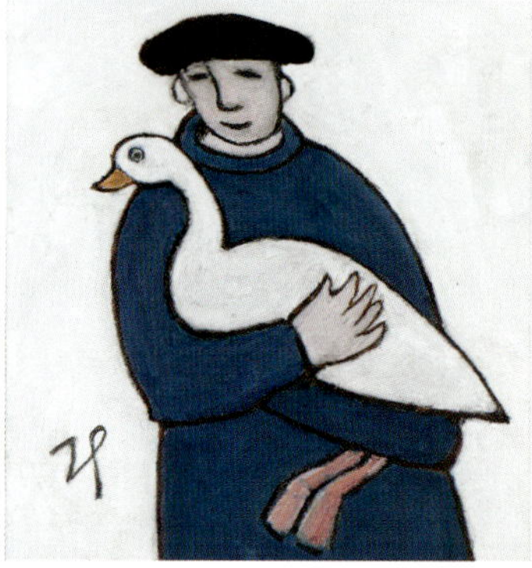

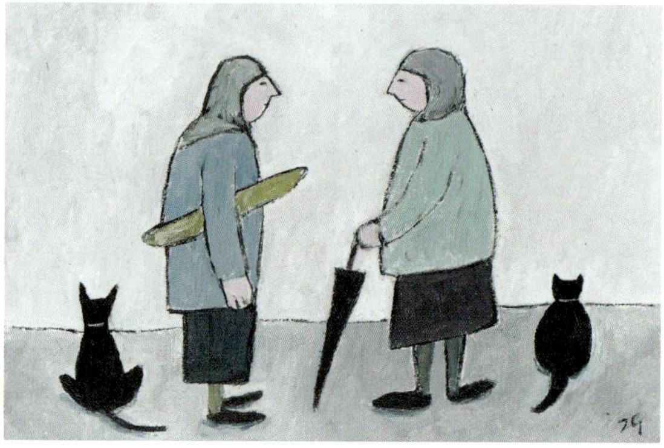

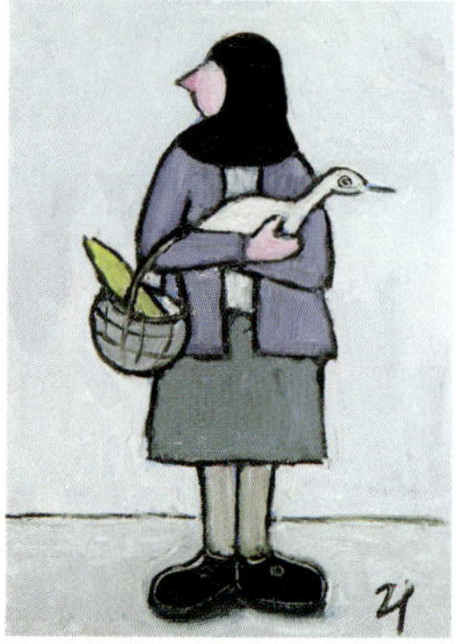

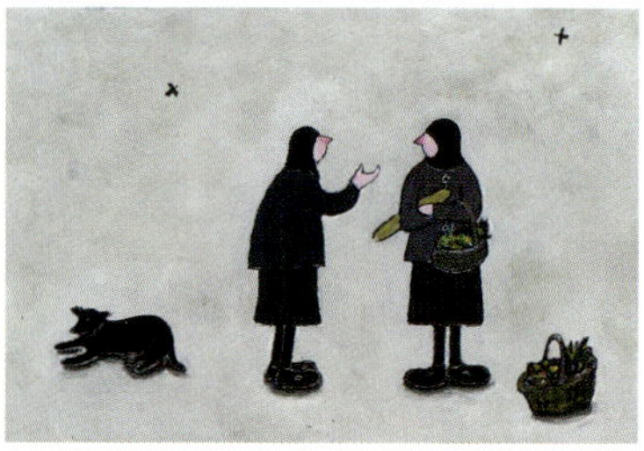

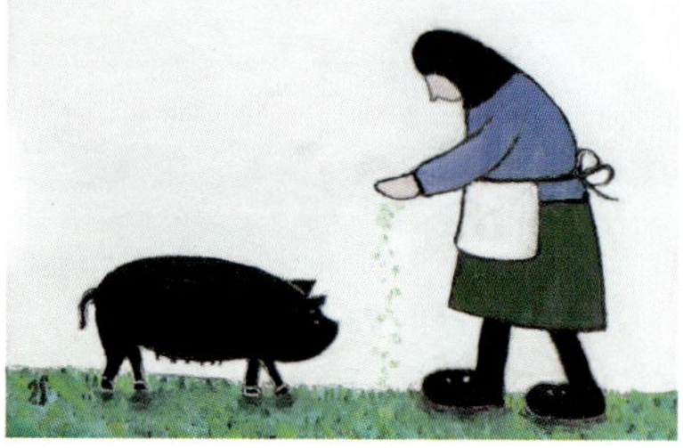

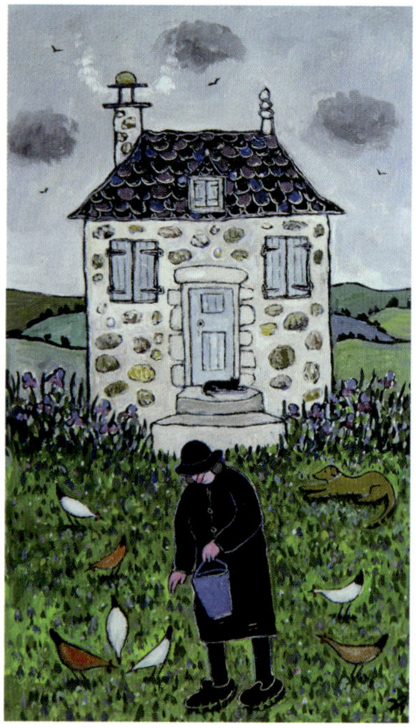

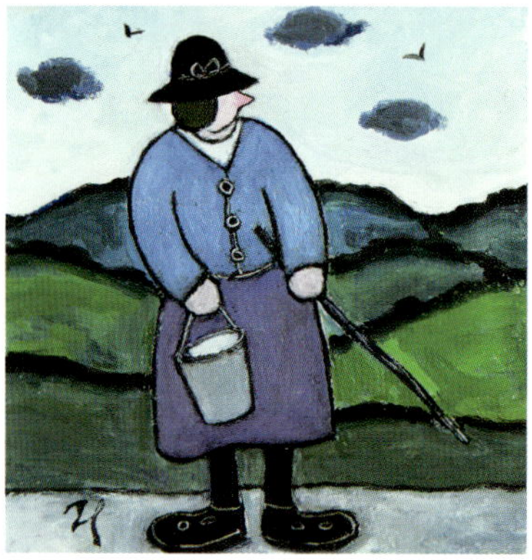

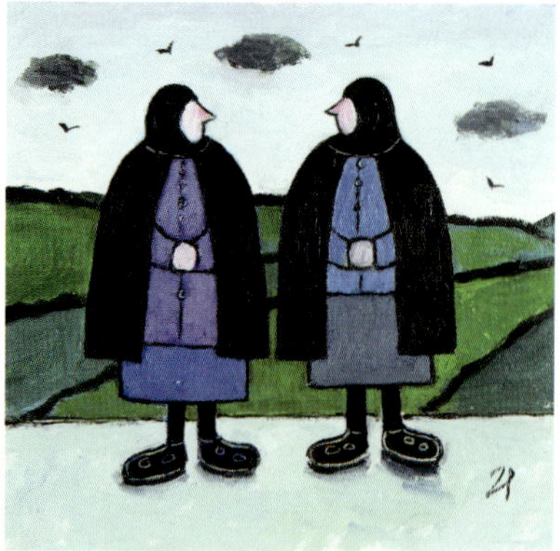

Chateau de Val

Chateau de Val on the Dordogne river near Bort-les-Orgues is one of the best conserved castles in the area. The imposing fortress is flanked by six machicolated towers with pepper-pot turrets.

Monceaux-sur-Dordogne

A charming village about four kilometres from Argentat.

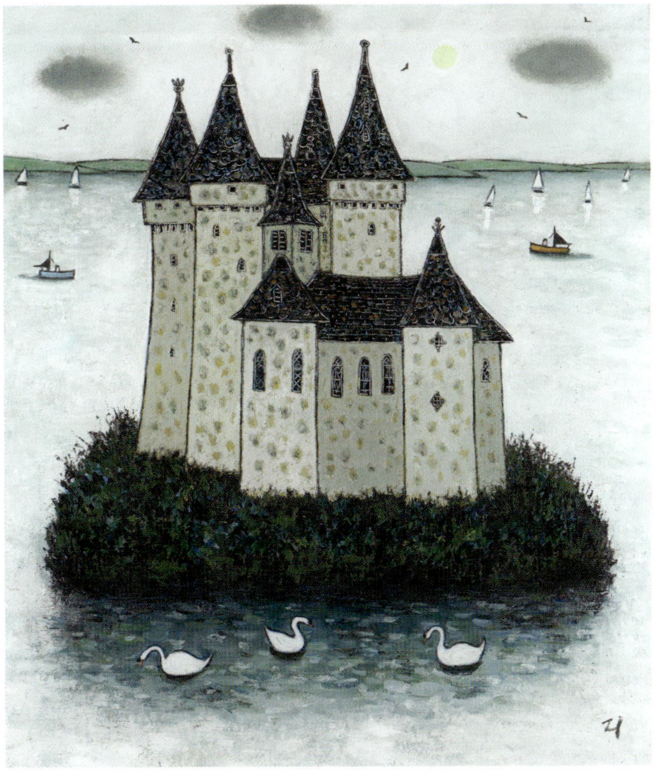

Chateau de Val

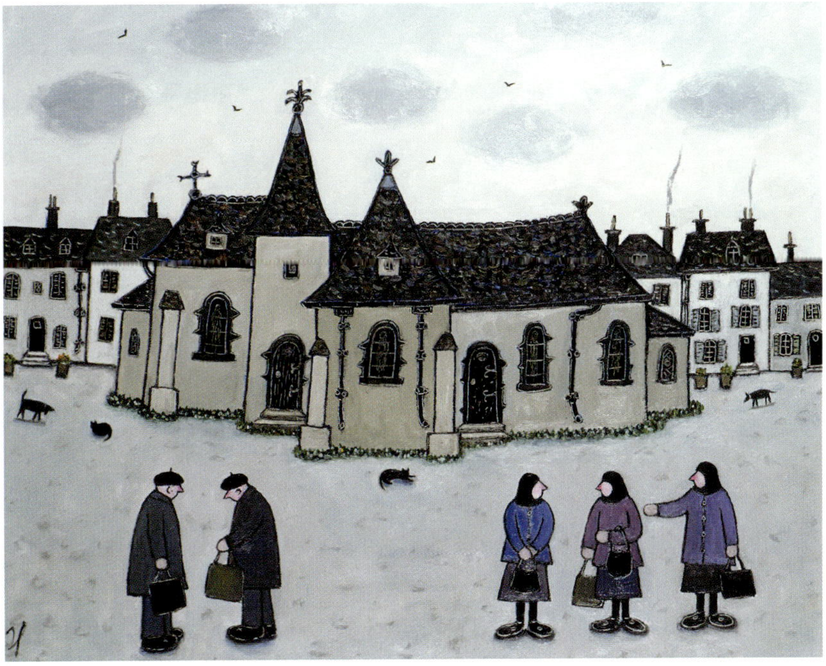

Village Square at Monceaux

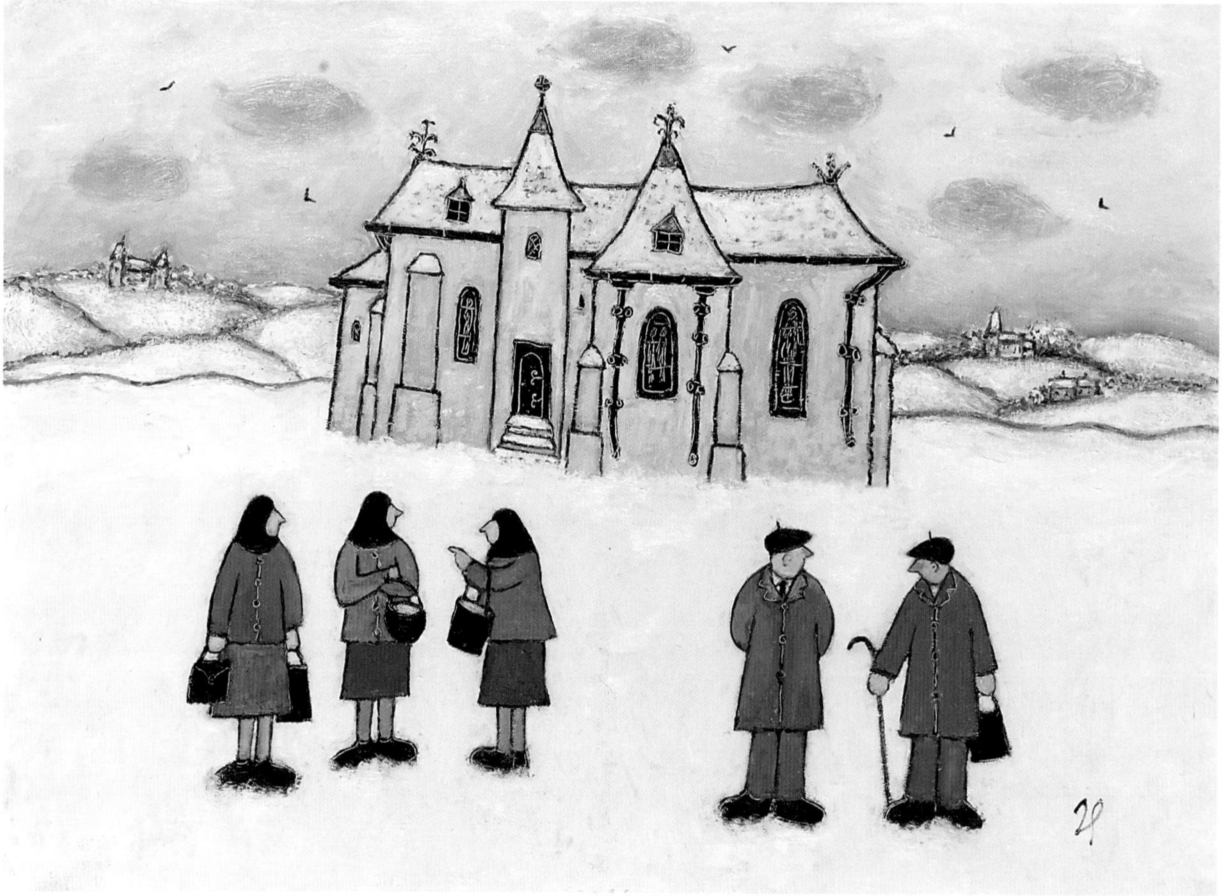

Chateau in the Snow

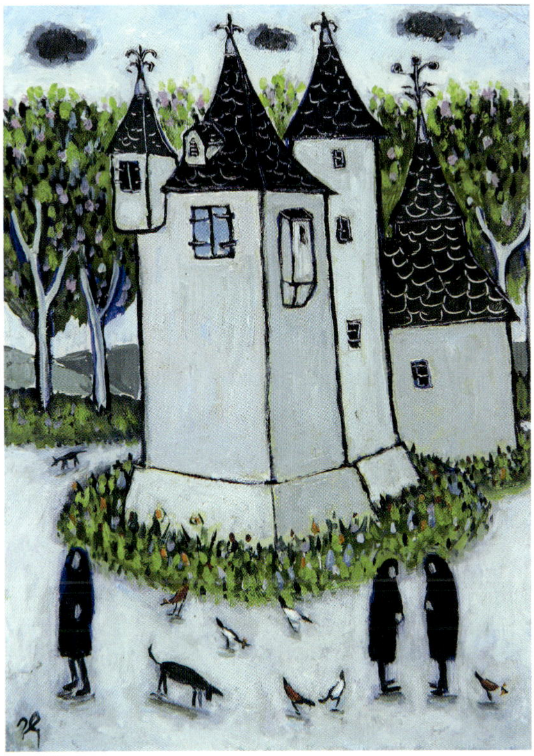
Bassignac le Bas

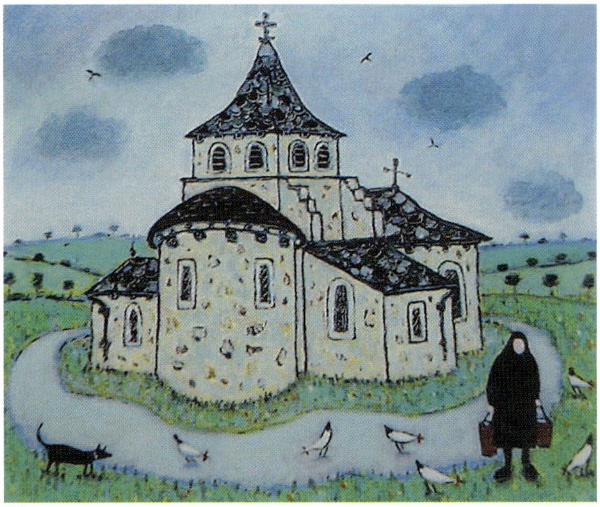
Mercoeur

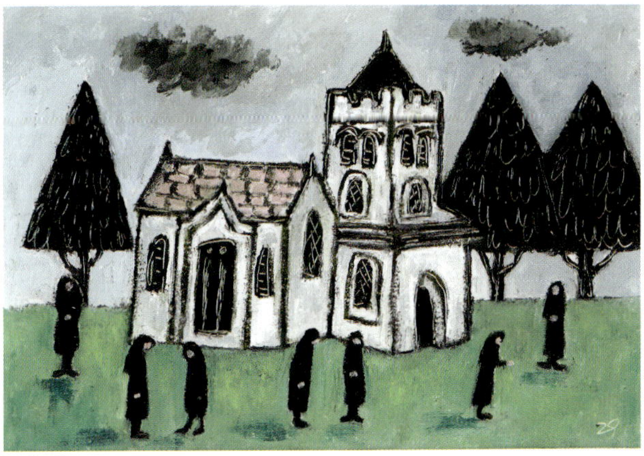
Small French Church

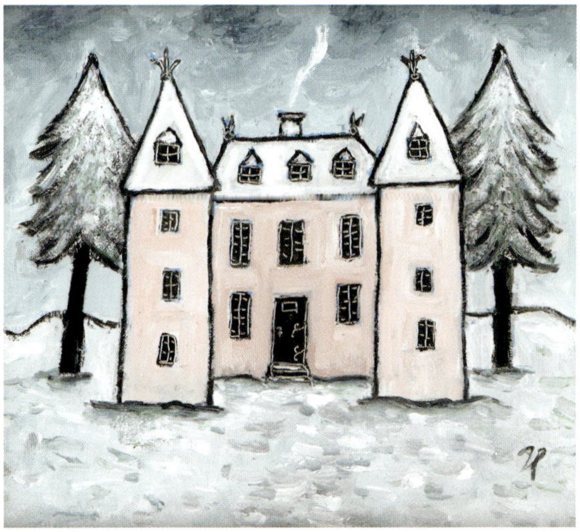
Pink Chateau

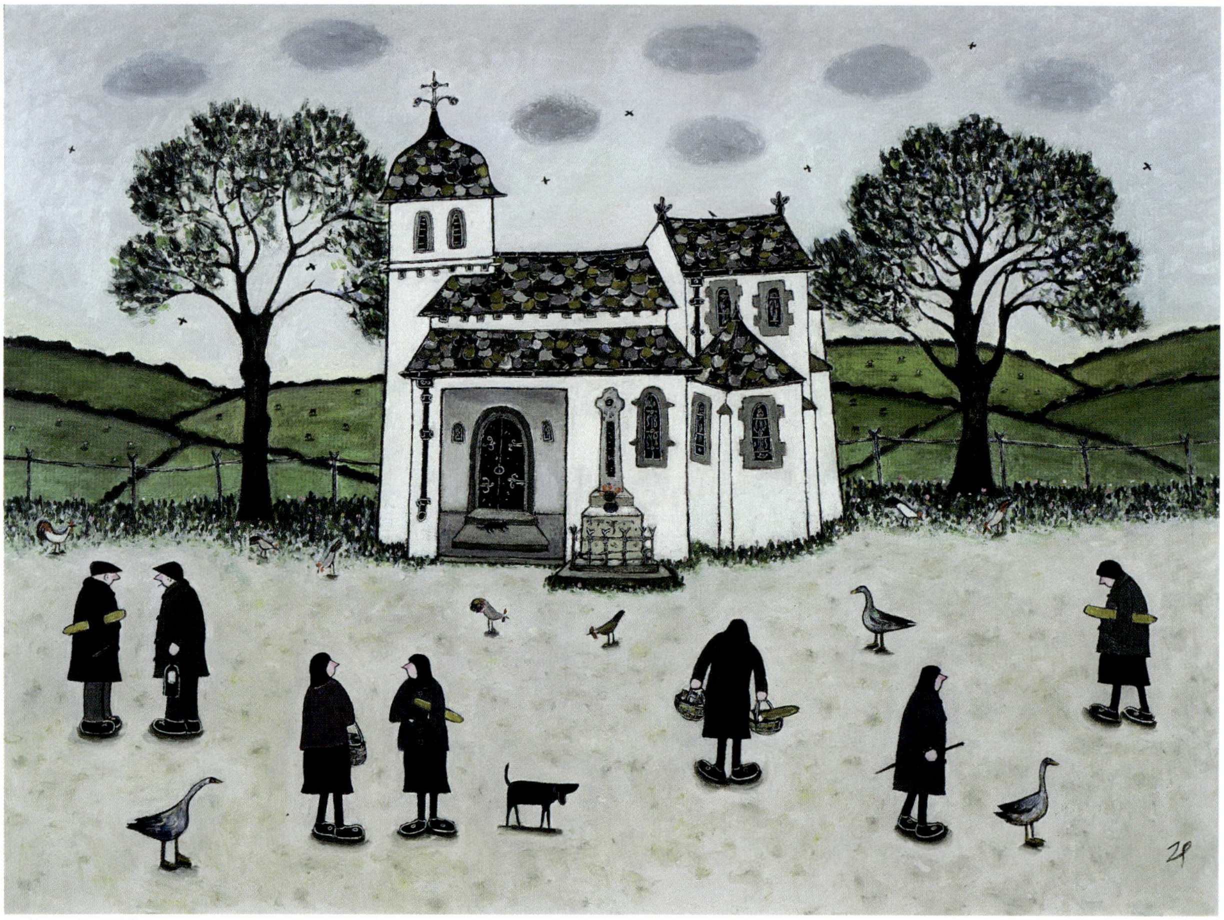

A Correzien Village

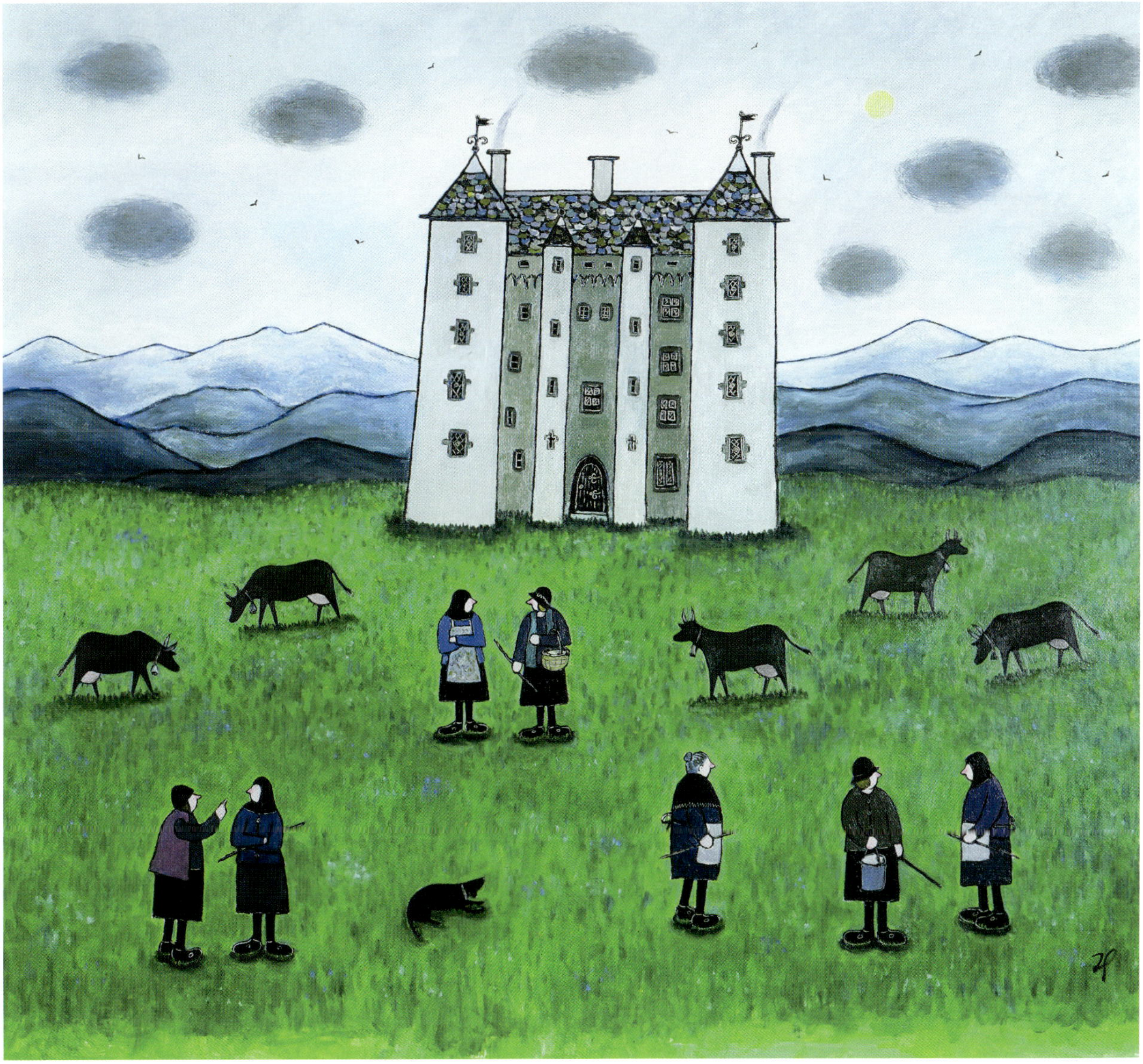
Chateau Chevenon

Chapter 10 Mousehole, Home for Fifty Years

From the moment Joan moved to Mousehole in 1958 her love affair with the village and its people began. A love affair which never diminished throughout the fifty years she lived in this idyllic spot.

Although in the early years she found it difficult to express herself through her art, once she broke free, painting became all consuming. Woe betide anyone who interrupted her in the studio! Mornings were for painting and nobody dared to call or telephone. Afternoons were spent driving her Morris Minor around the twisty lanes and tracks to find that perfect place to sketch and paint.

To put it kindly Joan's driving was somewhat erratic and her little car often ended up in places that no car should go. Paul, her son, reckoned that Joan's Morris was one of Cornwall's first "Off-Road" vehicles. A local man, Jack Way, remembers the time when her car was well and truly stuck in a muddy lane leading to a farmer's field where he was working. He helped to free her by jumping up and down on the bumper whilst she revved the engine furiously! He was rewarded for his trouble with a bottle of rum left behind the bar at the King's Arms.

Mousehole Harbour

This beautiful Cornish fishing village has barely changed in over a hundred years. Its tiny granite harbour is surrounded by a picturesque village of twisting lanes and alleys. Fishermen's cottages rise in tiers up the hillside from the harbour.

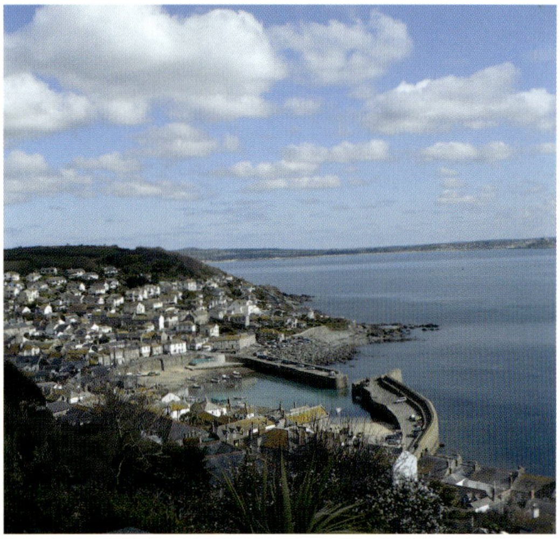

Mousehole Harbour from Raginnis Hill 2008

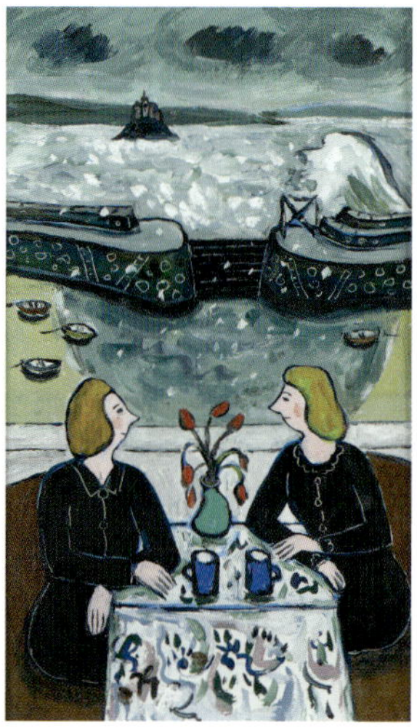

Stormy Day, Mousehole

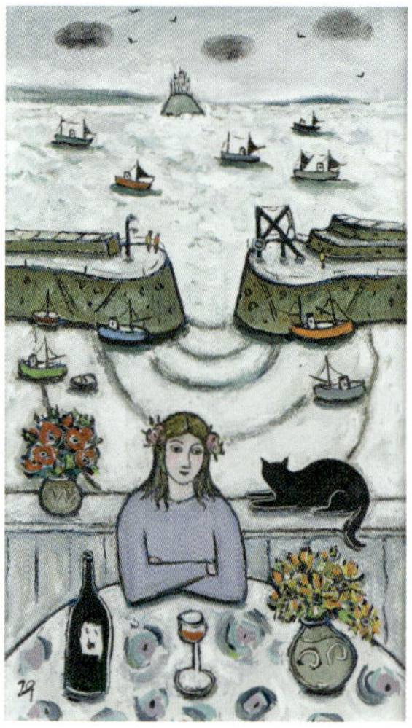

Flowers in her Hair

Mousehole, no longer the busy port, which was once crowded with pilchard boats, does however retain much of its old world charm, unspoilt by time. In winter timber baulks are laid across the narrow harbour entrance to protect the village from the worst of the winter seas.

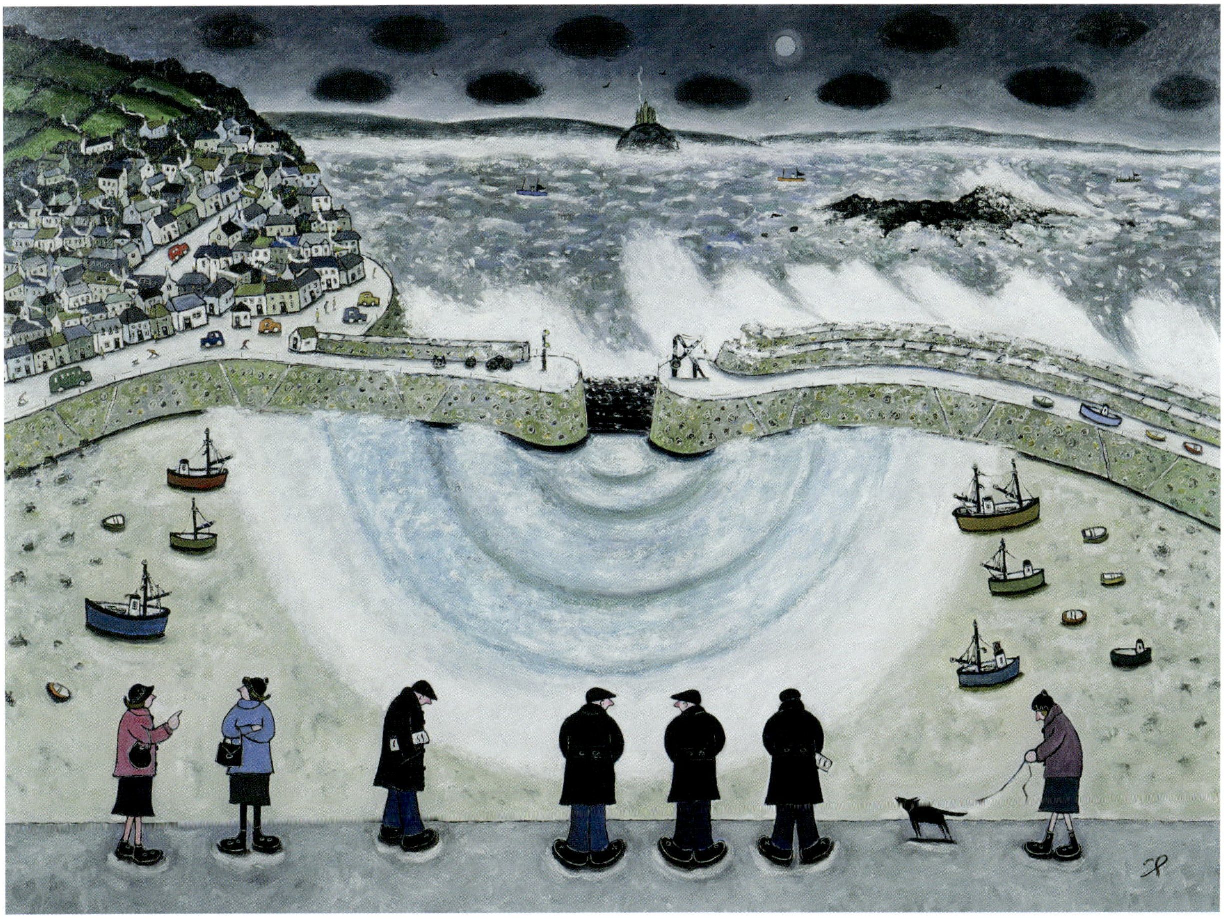

A Winter's Day, Mousehole

Joan had spectacular views of the harbour from her studio and greenhouse. There was always something different to paint. The sights and sounds of village life below were captured in so many wonderful works.

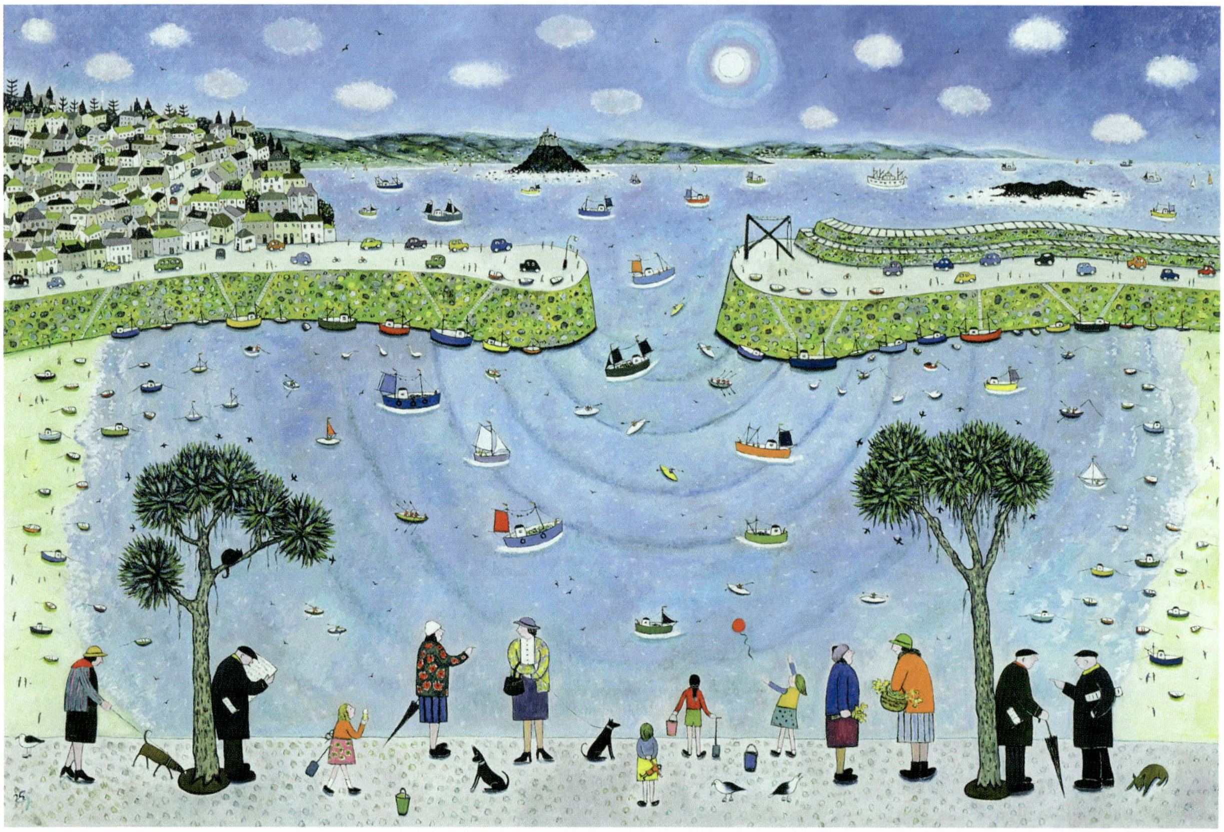

A Summer's Day, Mousehole

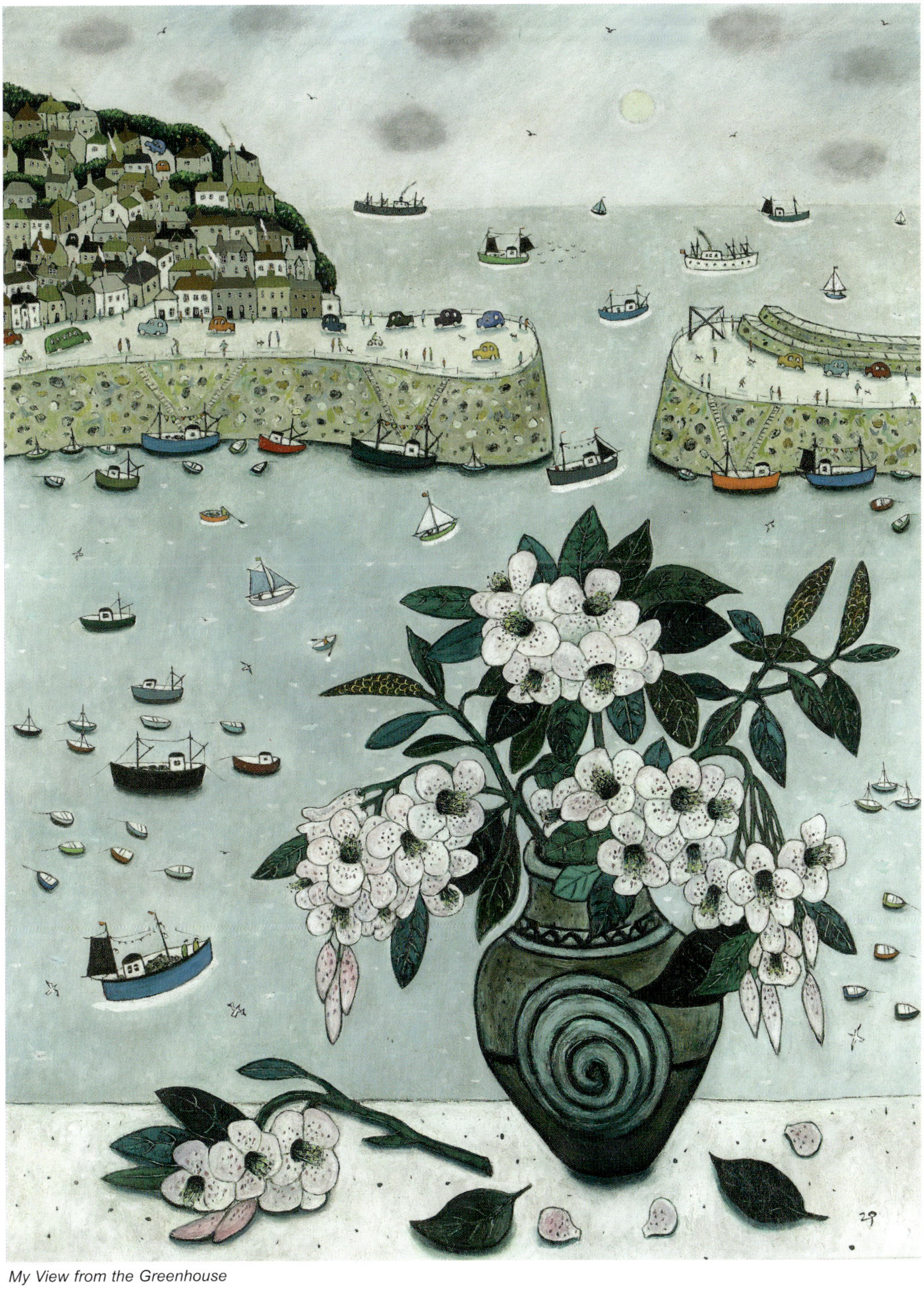

My View from the Greenhouse

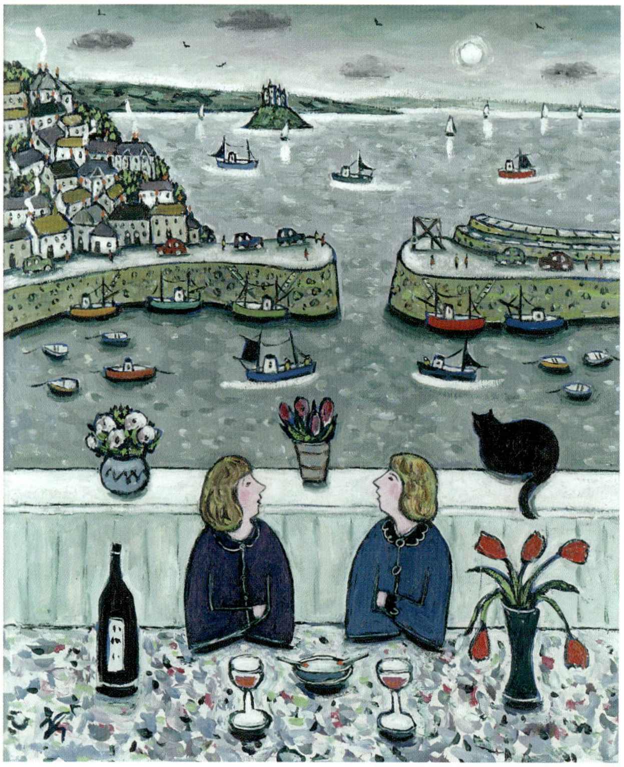

After Lunch at the Lobster Pot

The Lobster Pot

The "Lobster Pot" was world famous for its position overlooking Mousehole Harbour and for its delicious crab sandwiches. Much frequented by Joan and the setting for many of her humorous paintings. Regrettably it closed as a hotel a few years ago and has been redeveloped as apartments.

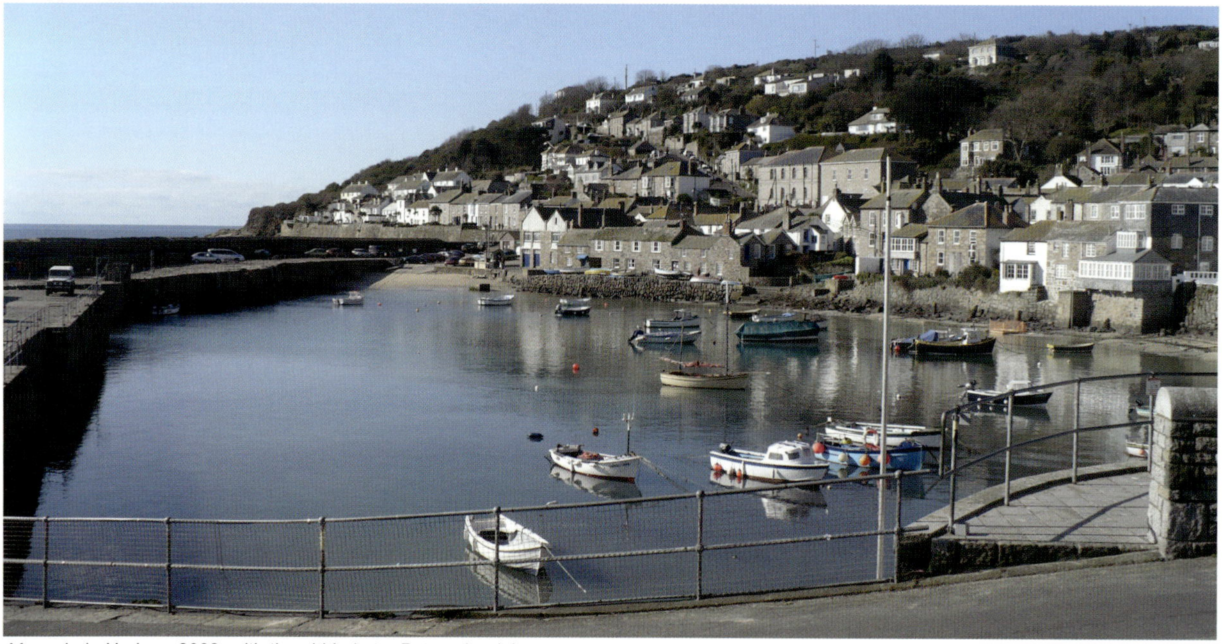

Mousehole Harbour 2008, with the old Lobster Pot on the right

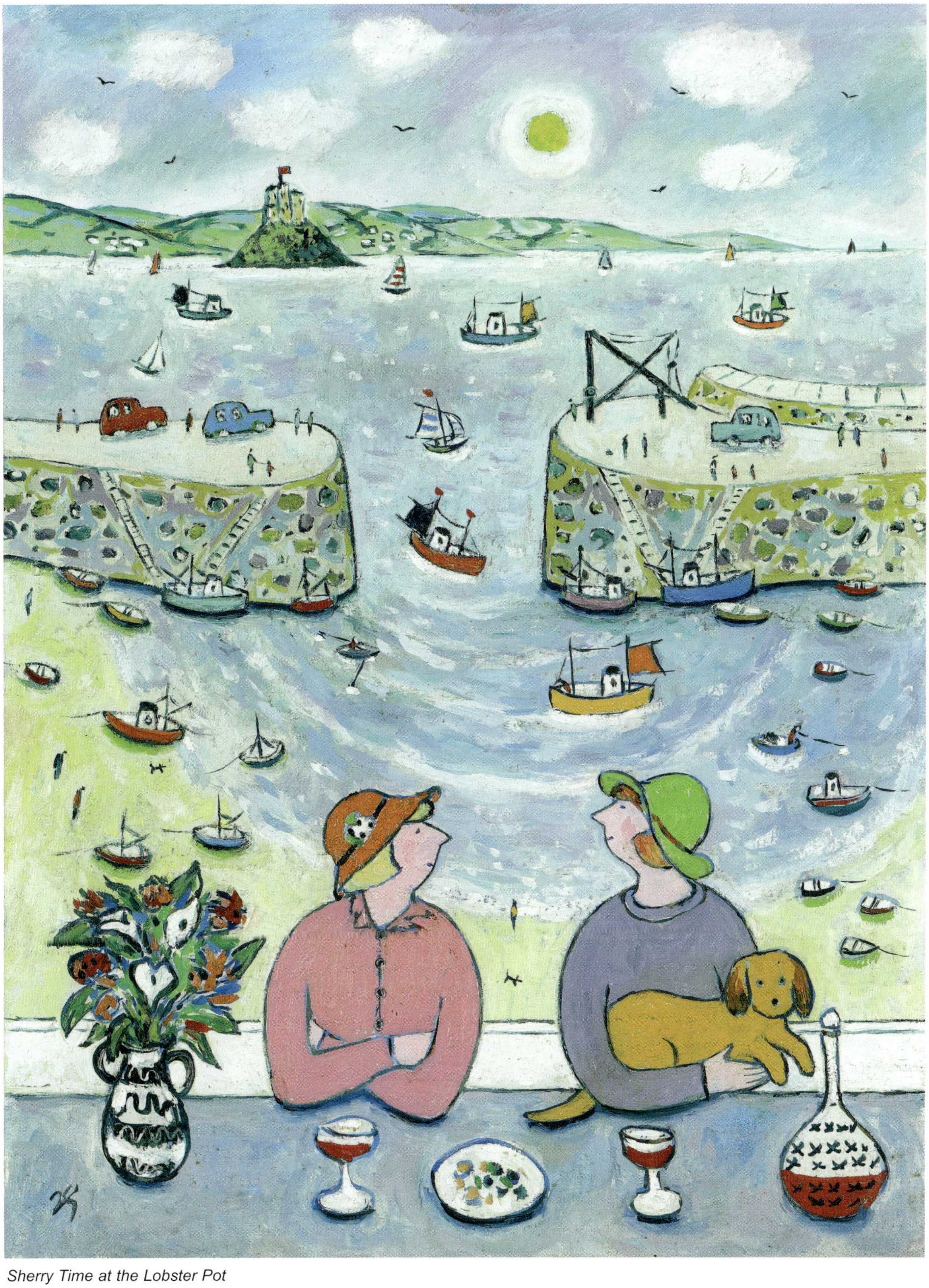

Sherry Time at the Lobster Pot

Mousehole Characters

Joan had many friends amongst the locals over the years. She had a special empathy with the fishermen who worked out of the harbour.

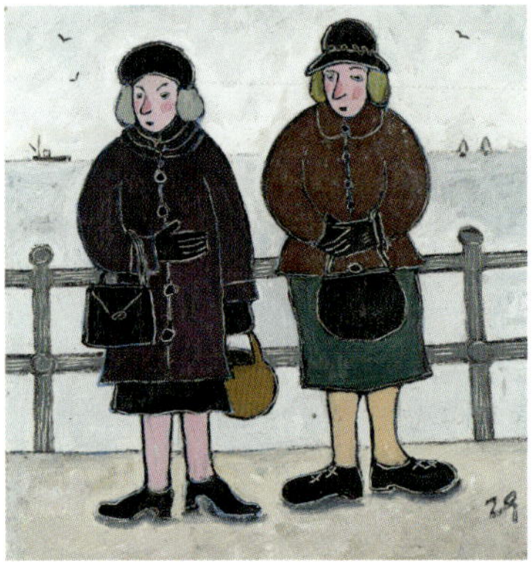
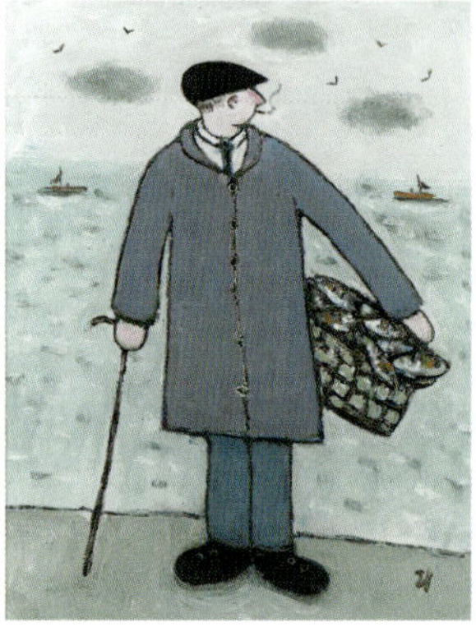
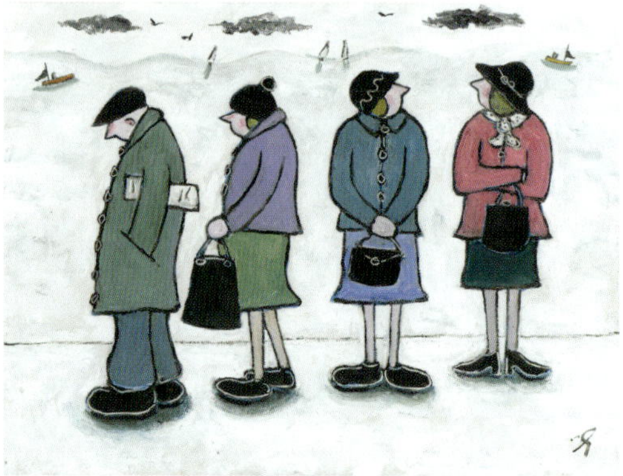
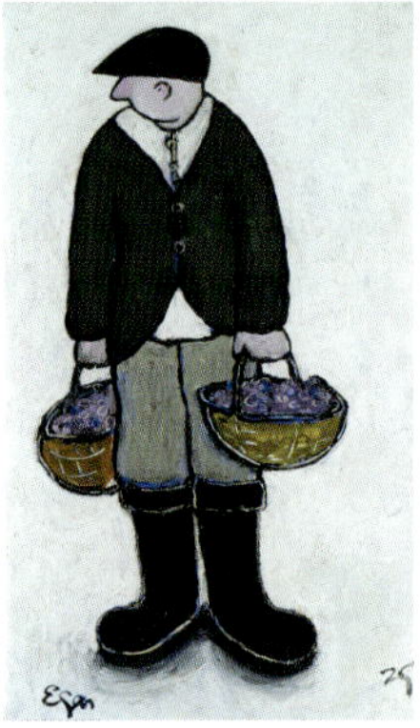
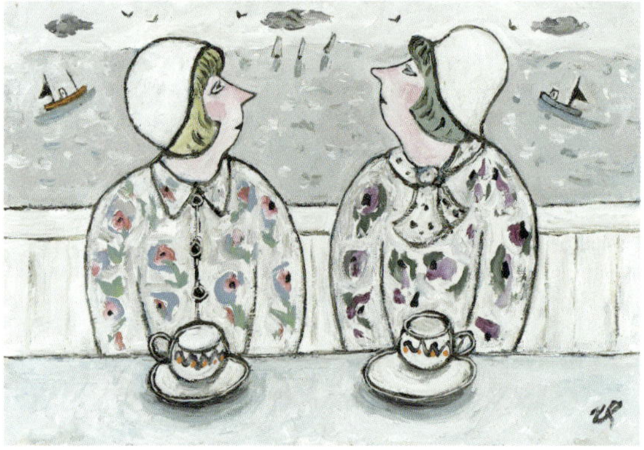
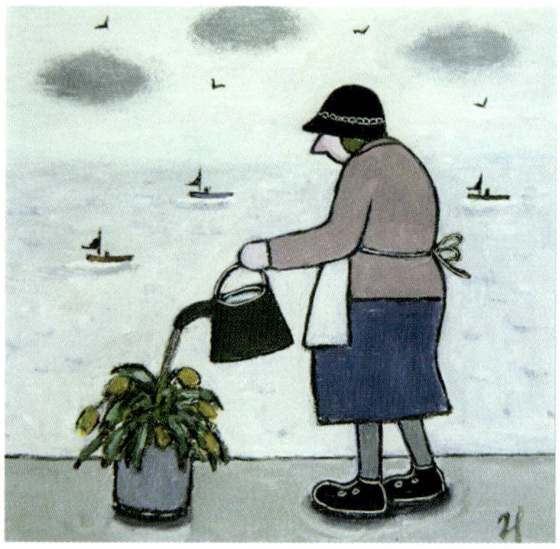
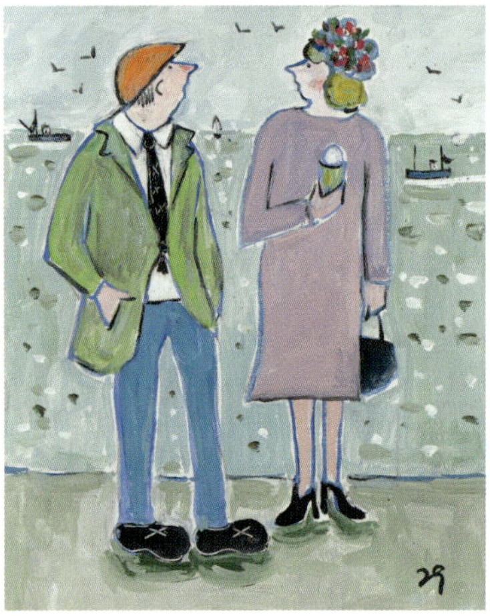
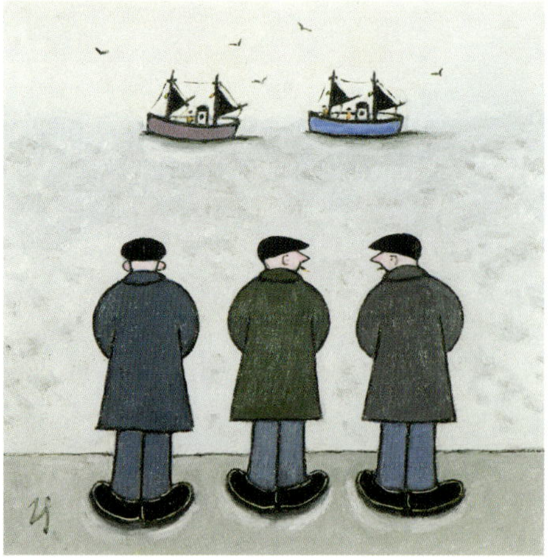
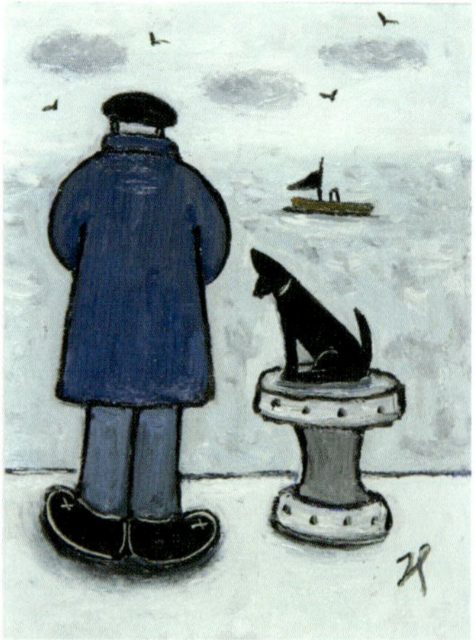

Jack Pender (1918-1998)

On the harbour there is a memorial seat to Jack Pender and it aptly states "A Man of Mousehole". Jack was born in the village, studied at Penzance School of Art, served with the Duke of Cornwall Light Infantry in the 1939-1945 war and returned to live in Mousehole. His cottage looks directly onto the harbour.

Joan knew him well and one can only imagine how many times these two amazing artists would have met and chatted together in the narrow streets where they both lived.

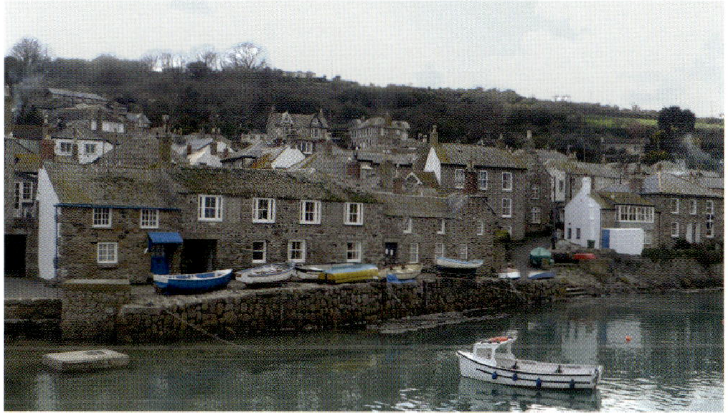

The Wharf with Jack's House far right 2008

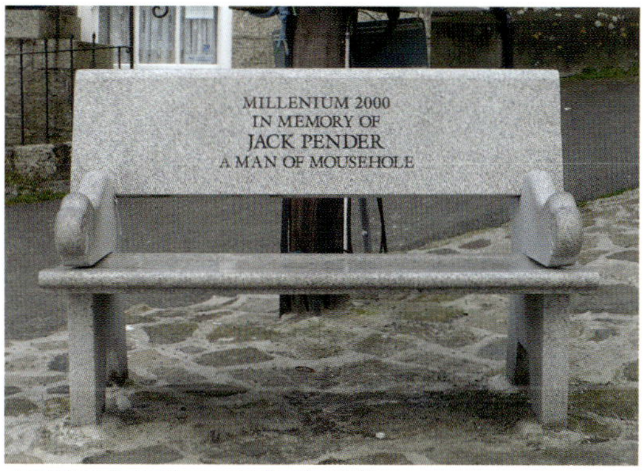

Jack Pender's Memorial Seat 2008

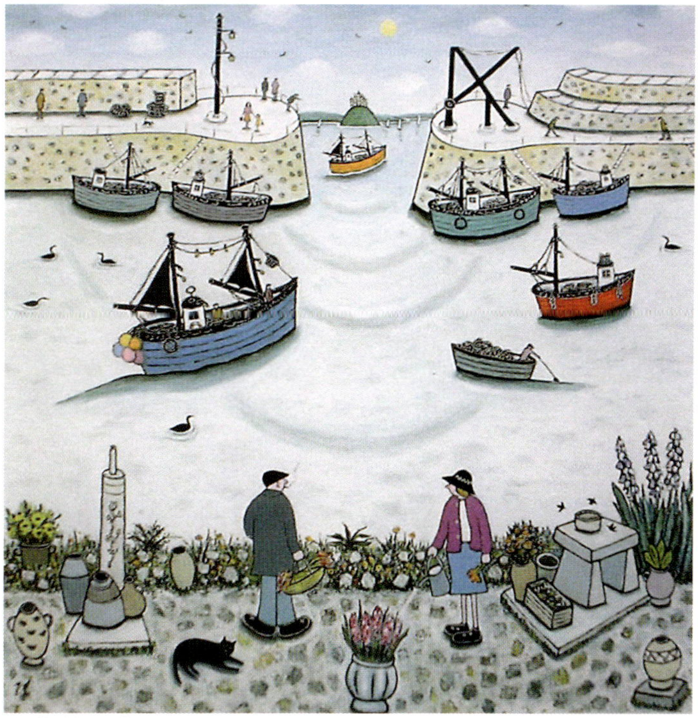

Jack's View of Mousehole

Joan’s Garden and Greenhouse

Another of Joan's great loves was her garden. The mild climate allowed her to grow many sub-tropical plants and trees. Her greenhouse was always full of the most exotic fruit and flowers grown from seeds or cuttings. Huge bunches of grapes would hang from the vines covering the glass roof. All this provided fantastic subject matter for Joan's still life paintings.

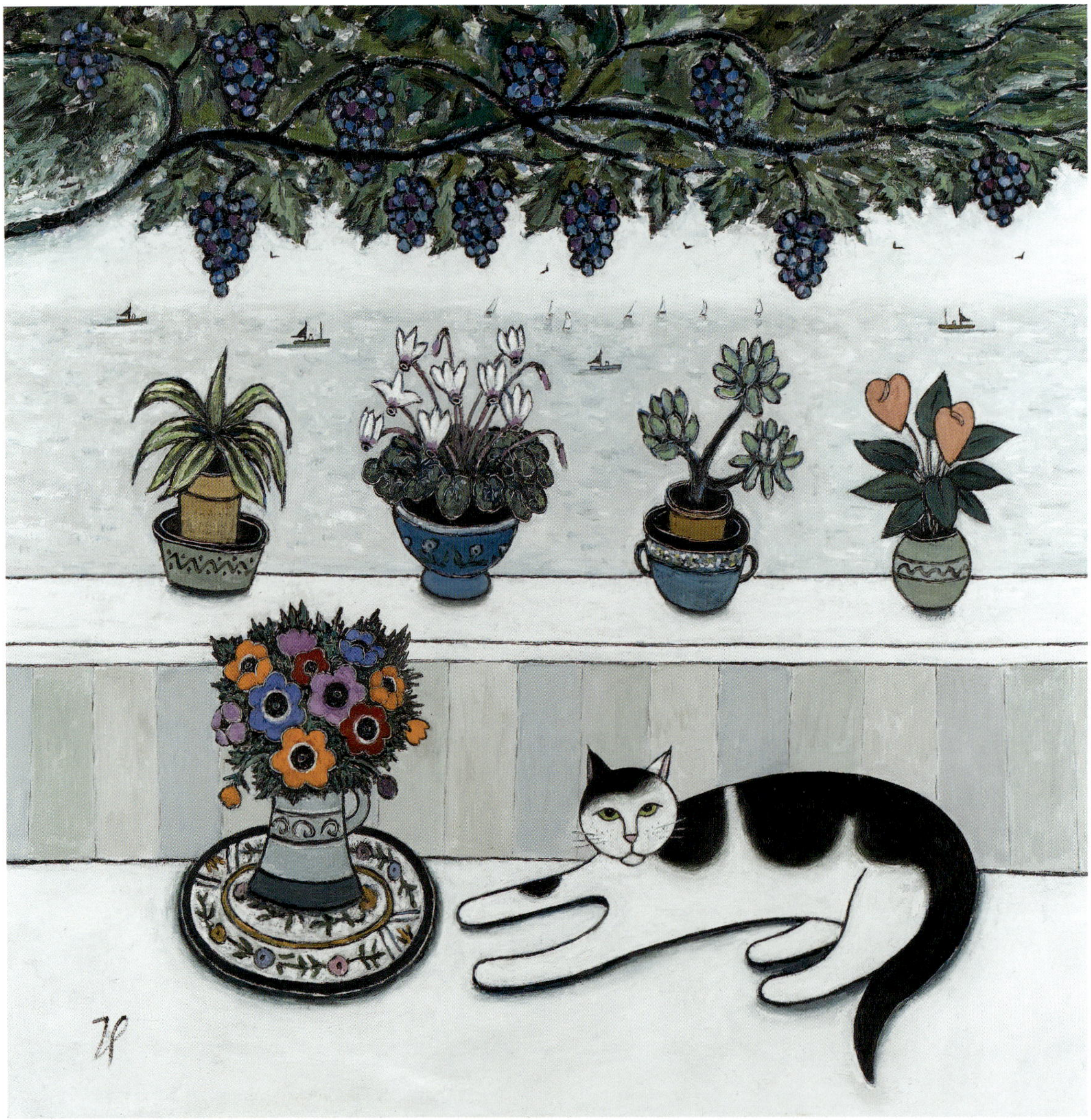

Titus in My Studio Greenhouse

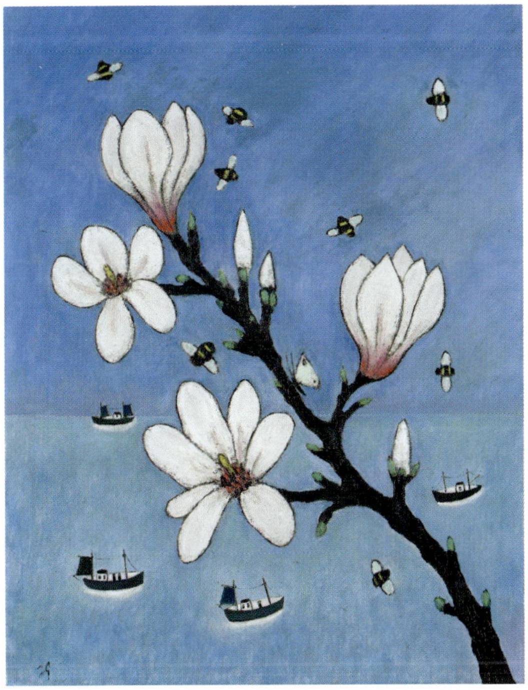

Tulip Tree in My Garden

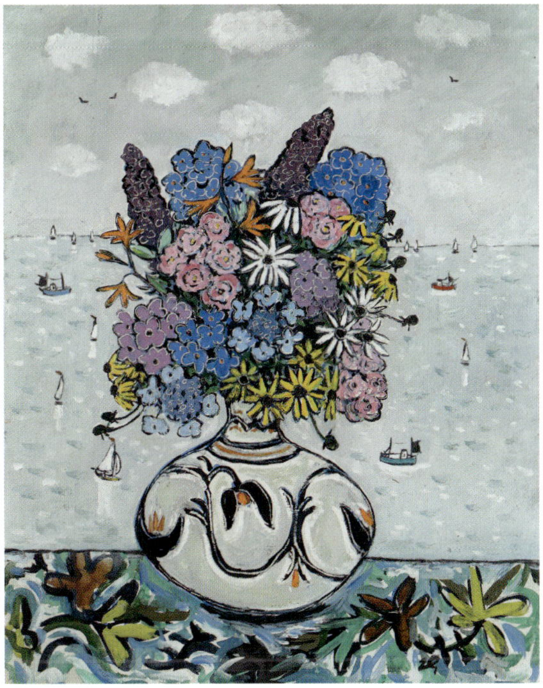

Flowers from My Garden

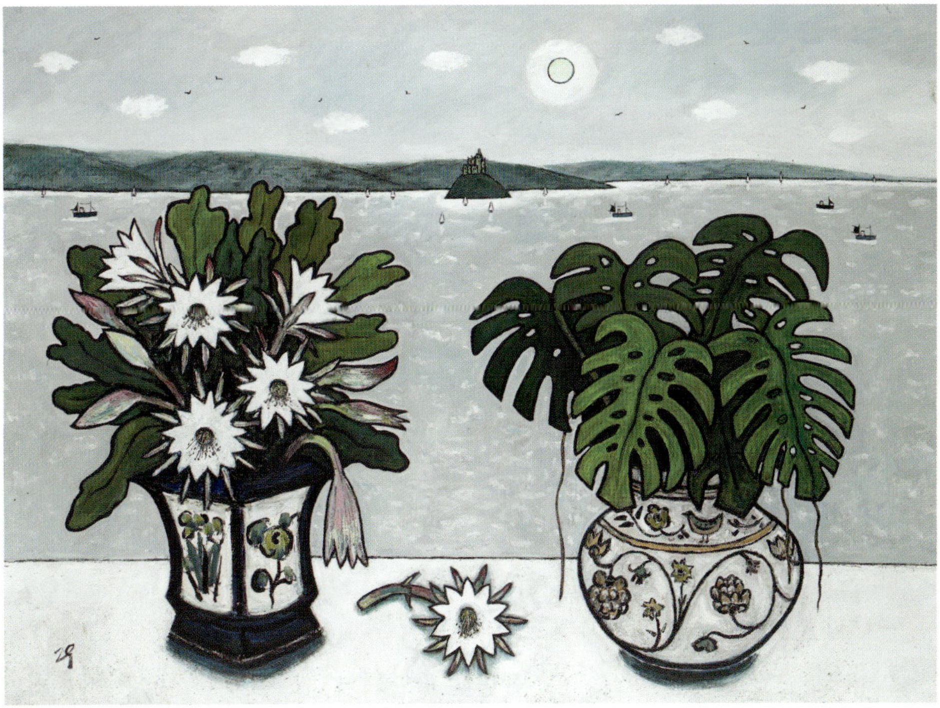

Cacti and Cheese Plant

Joan's Cats

Joan had a number of cats during her 50 years at Mousehole. Several were rescued or found abandoned and went on to live a life of luxury, being required only to pose frequently for their owner. Many shared the name Titus.

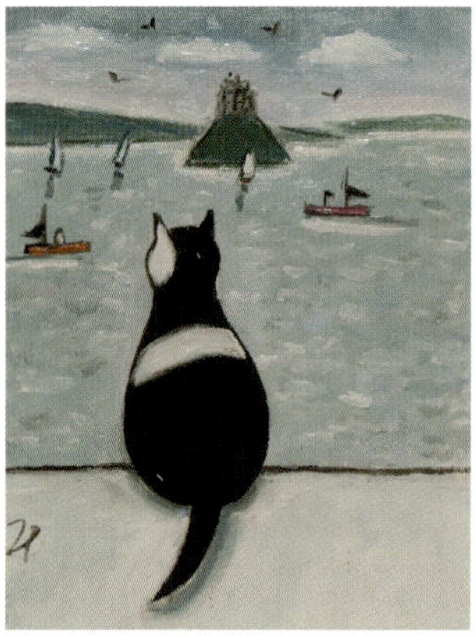

Titus Enjoying Life

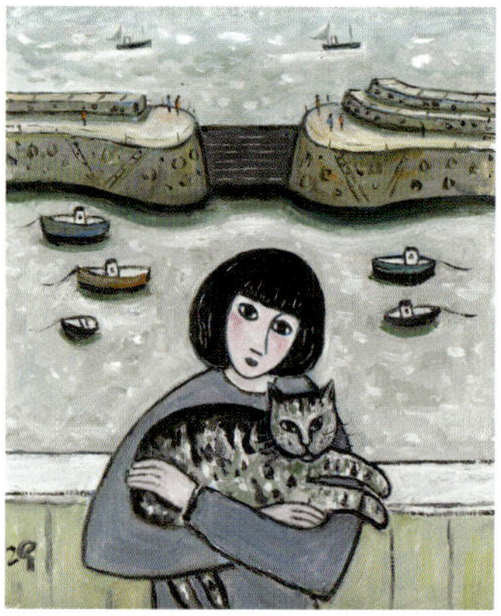

Simone with Titus III
(Simone is Joan's granddaughter)

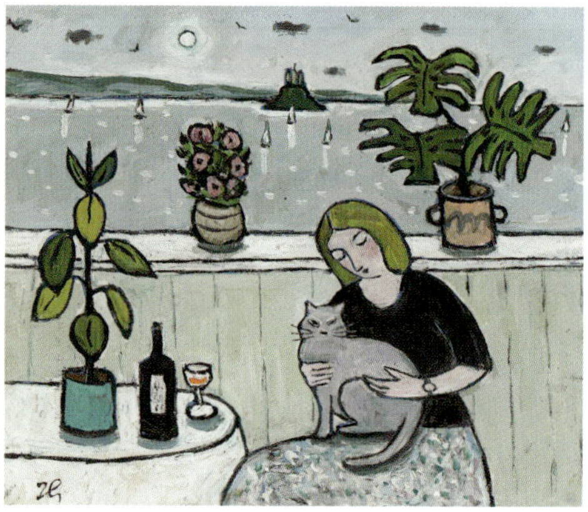

Titus I

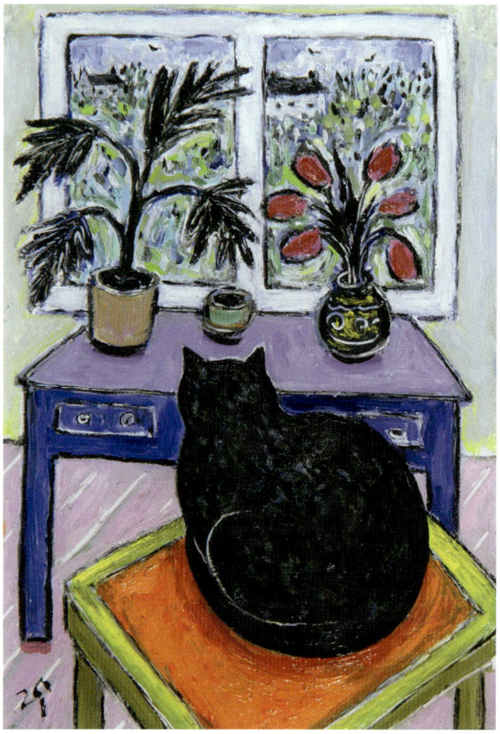

Black Cat on Orange Cushion

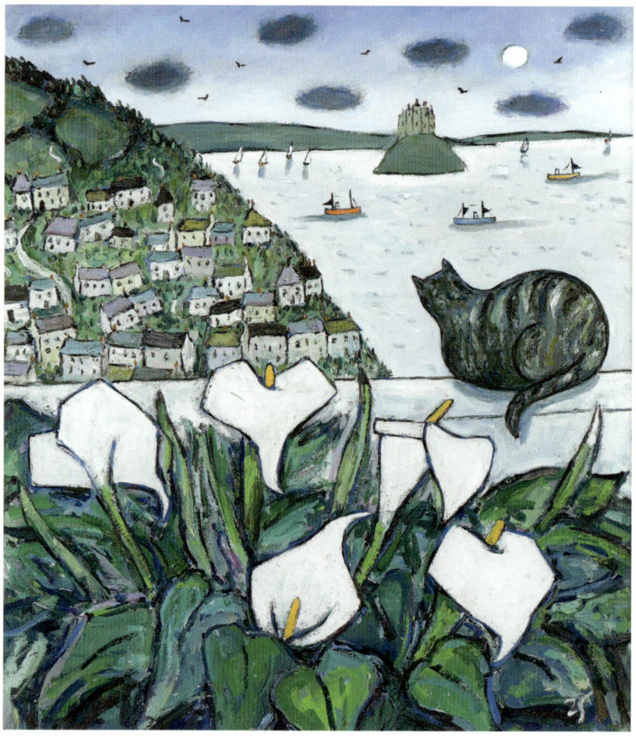

Titus III with Lillies

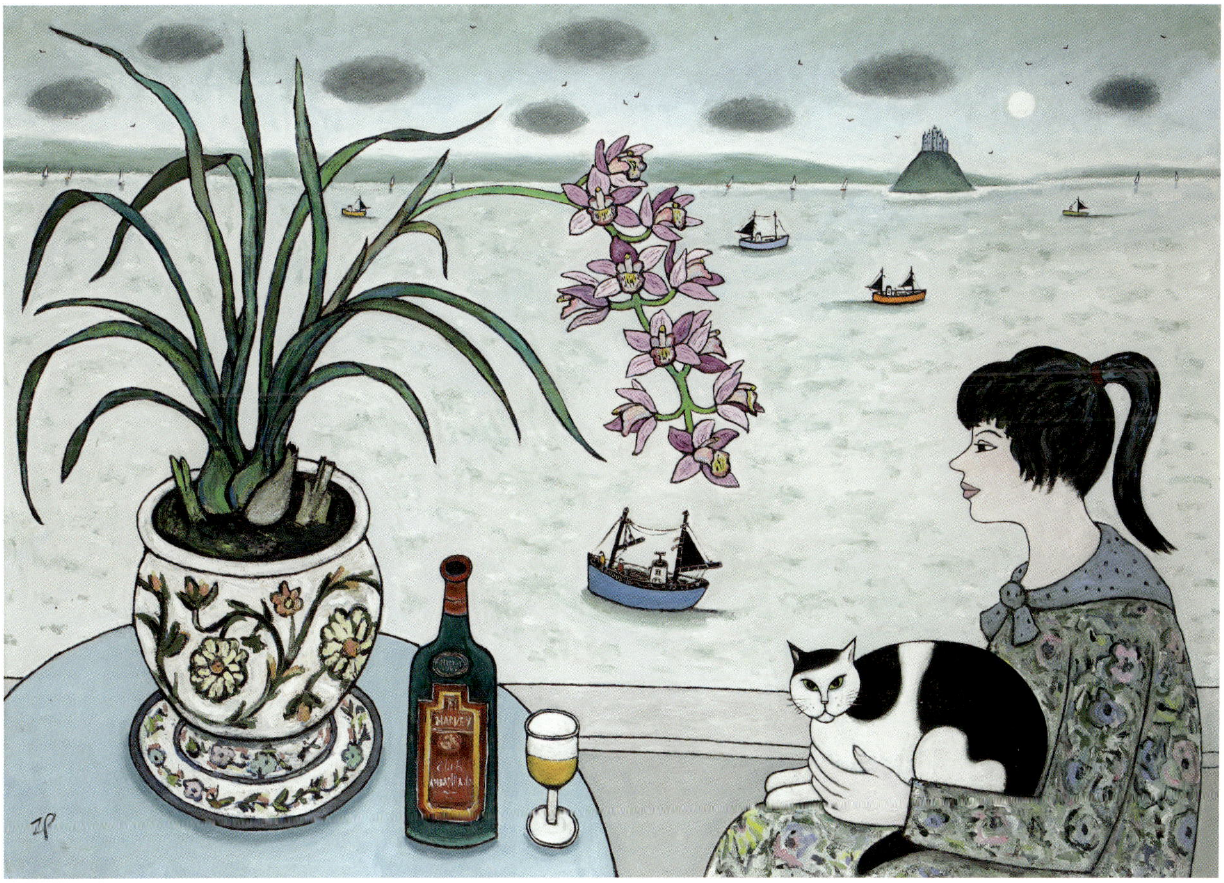

Sharing a Sherry with Titus IV

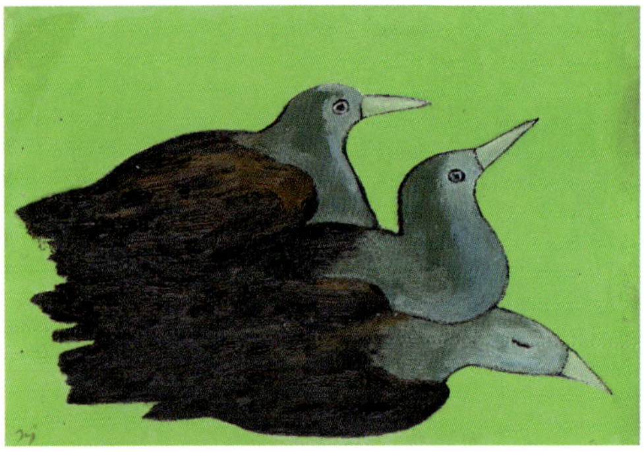

Oiled Birds after the Torrey Canyon Disaster

Joan's Birds

The Mousehole Wild Bird Sanctuary was founded in 1928. It became famous during the Torrey Canyon disaster in 1967 when 8,000 oiled birds were treated. Joan spent days helping with the cleaning and never forgot the distressed state of so many sea birds.

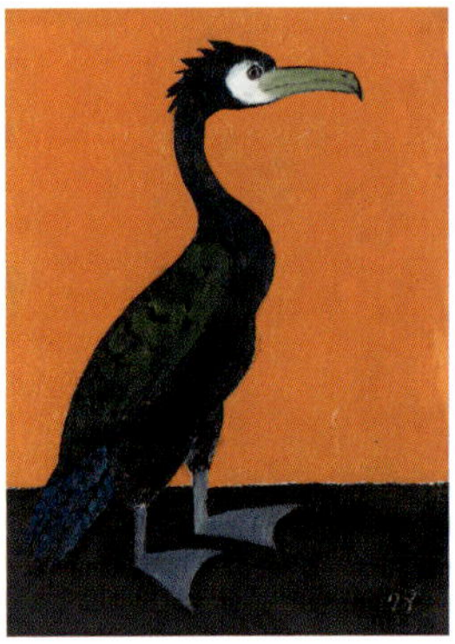

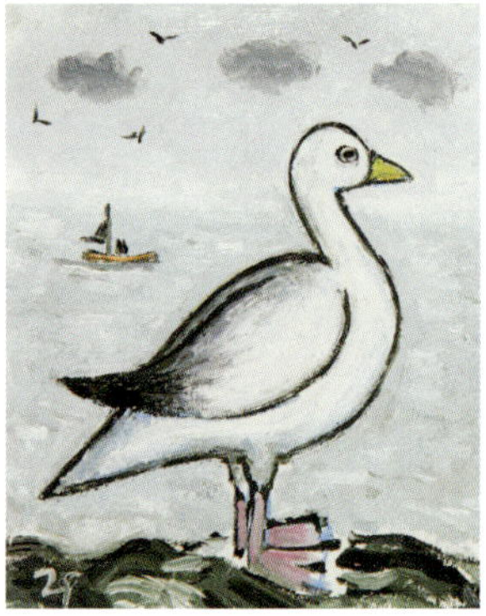

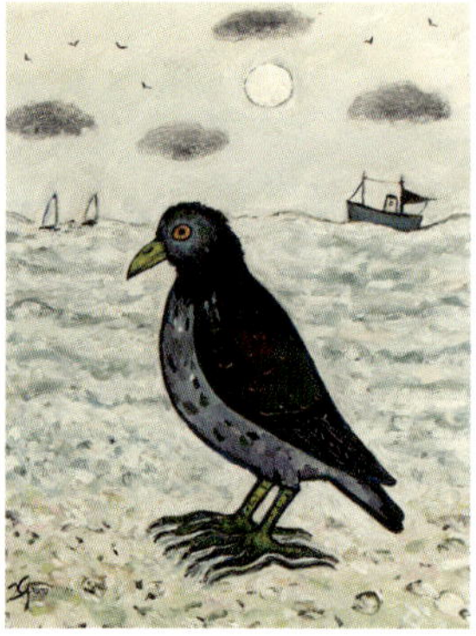

On a happier note Joan loved to watch all the sea birds and the great variety of small birds drawn by the plentiful food in her garden. She painted many in her own inimitable way.

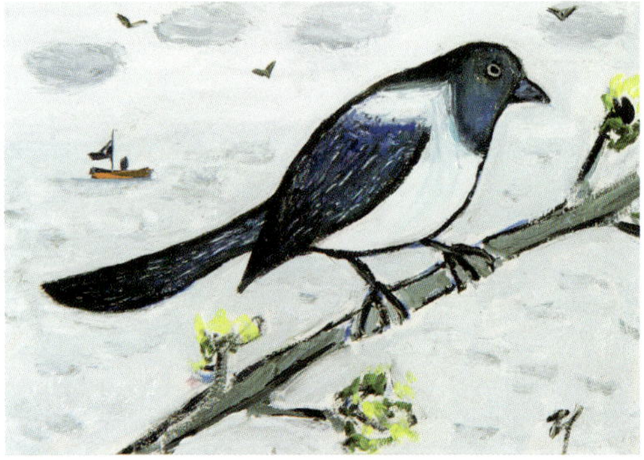

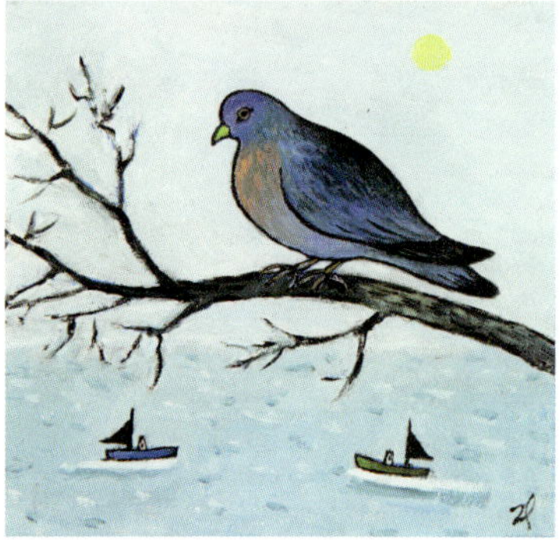

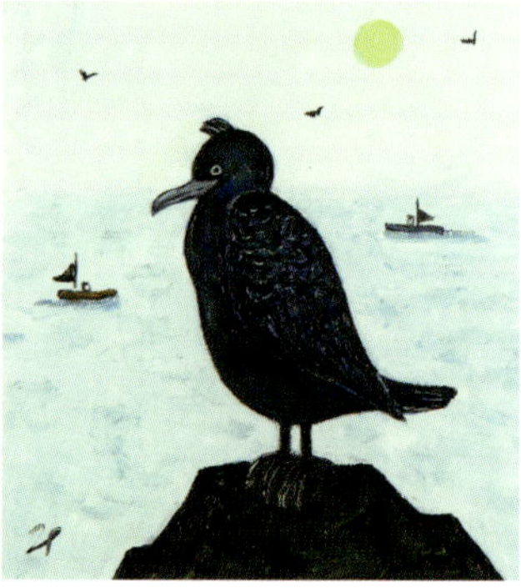

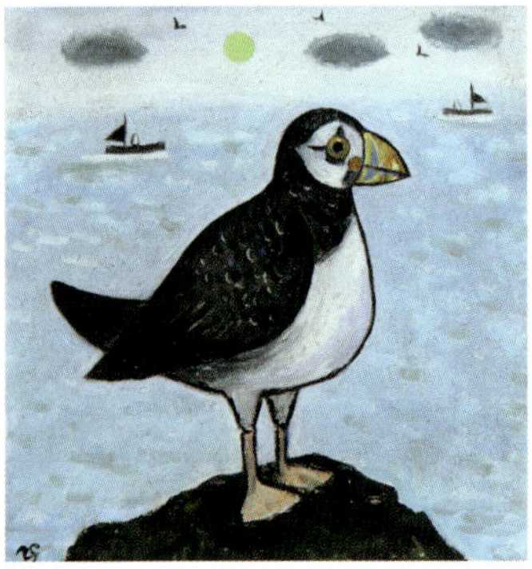

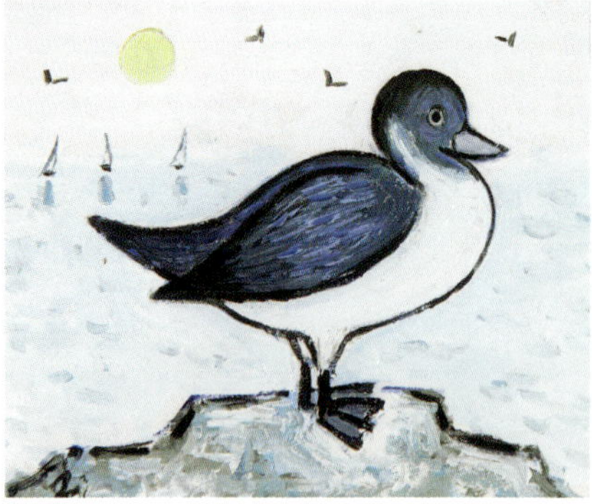

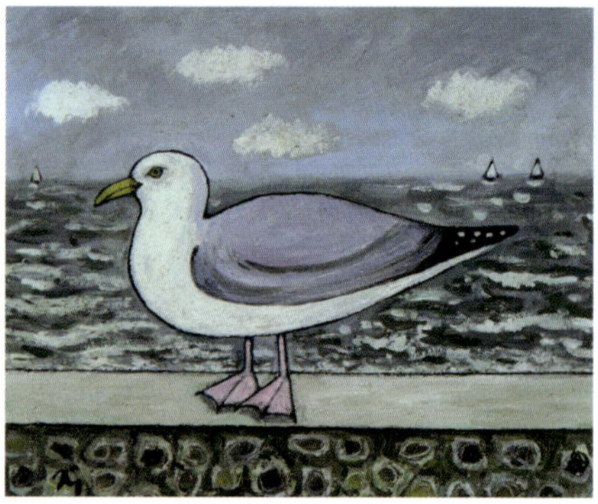

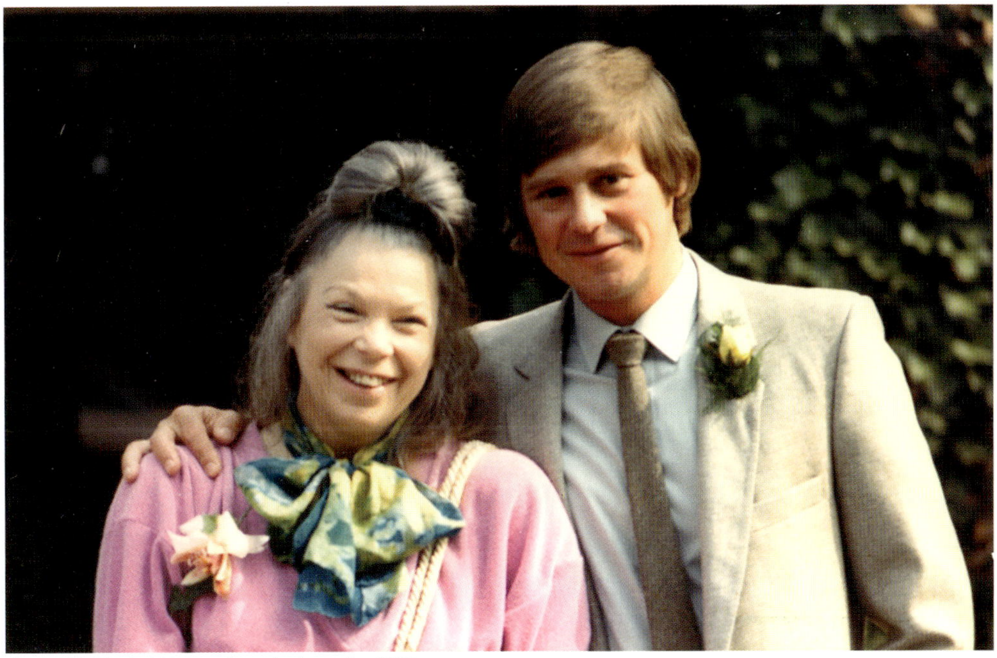

Joan with Paul at his marriage to Jeanette 1980

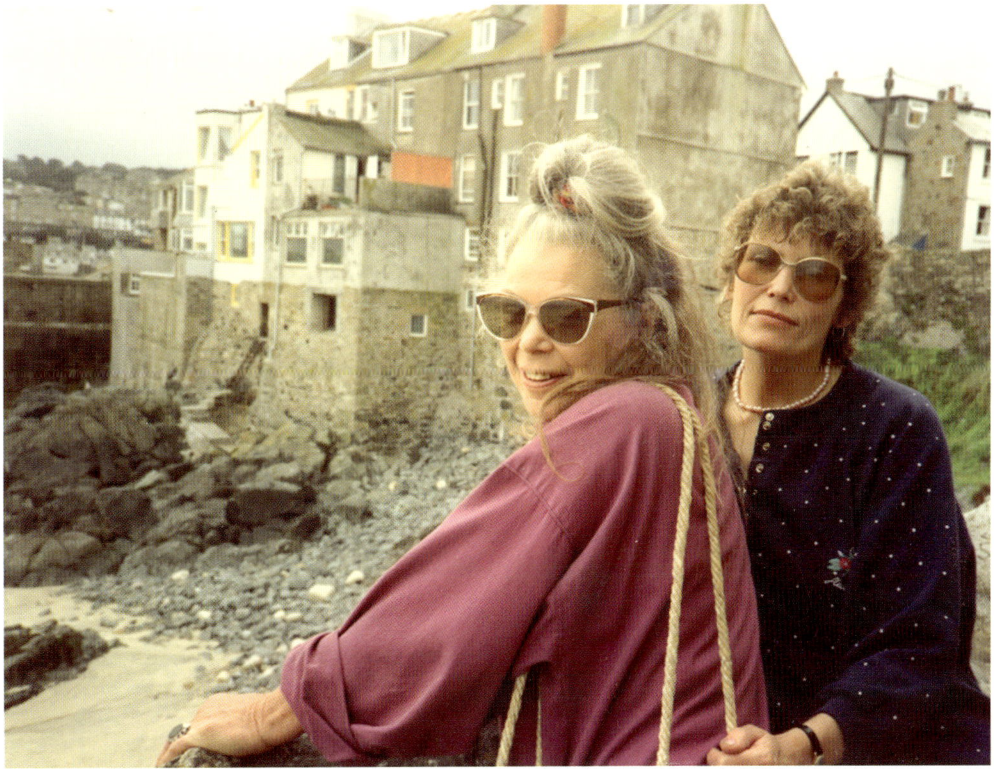

Joan with Mara at St. Ives 1985

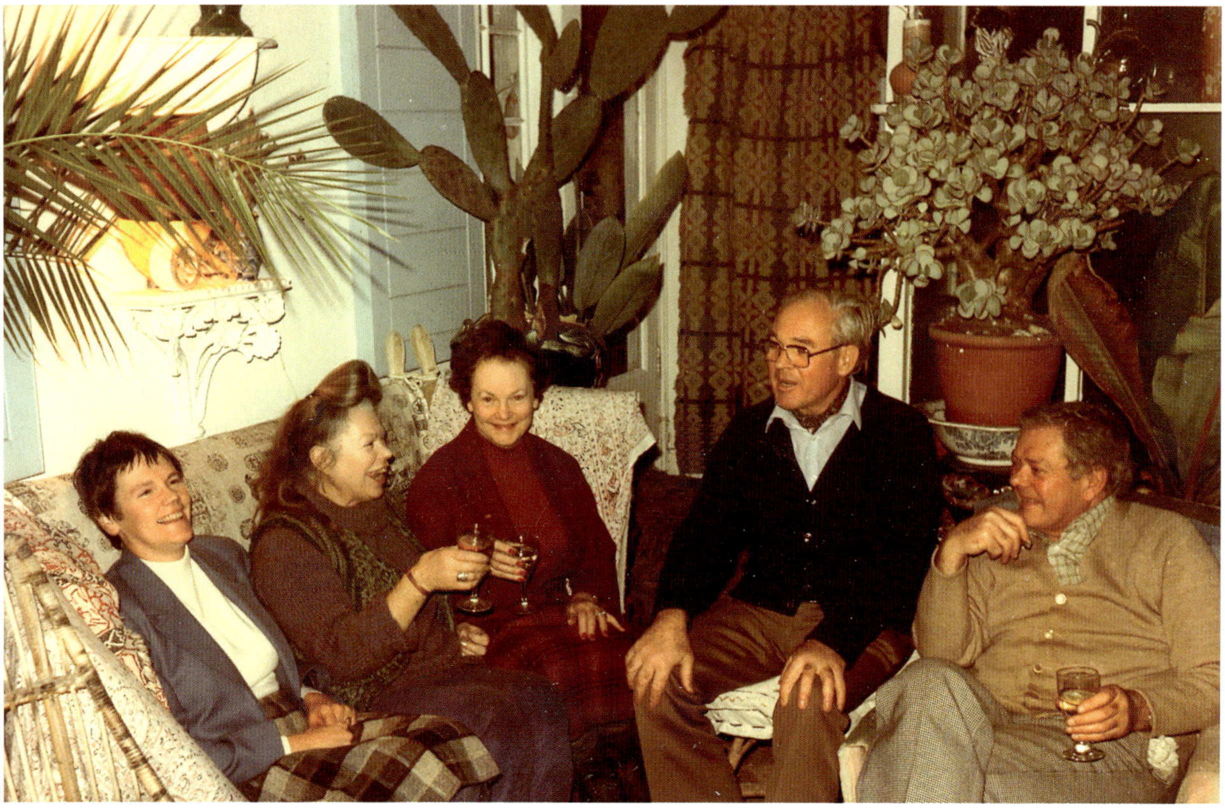

Susan, Joan, Betty, Gil and Michael in the Greenhouse

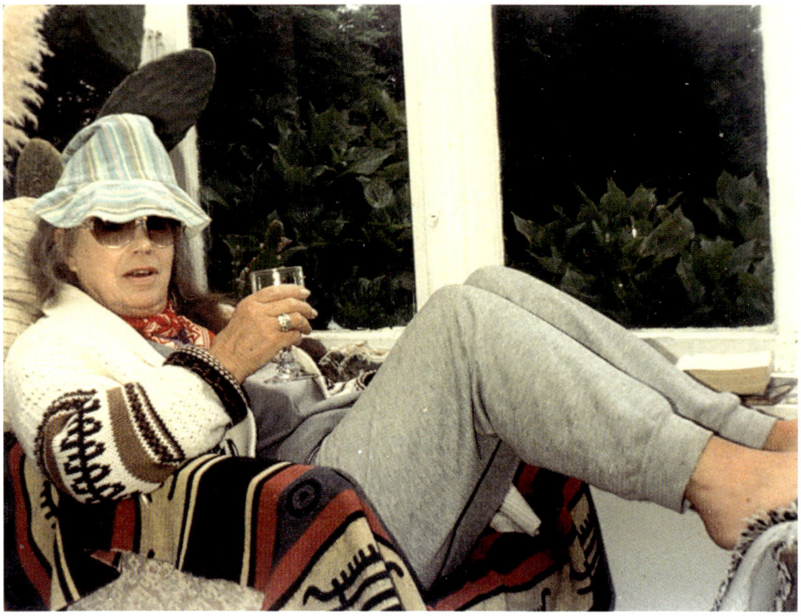

Sherry Time

Memories of Joan at Mousehole, from her brother, Gil.

"In the earlier years at Mousehole, after her children had married I would stay with her for a week in March each year, as we loved each other's company. (She had no telephone so I couldn't be contacted from the surgery!!) I was one of the very few allowed into her studio. Once I suggested that she should put figures into her paintings.

Joan was very happy at Mousehole and liked the locals, especially the fishermen. She lived on her own for a long time, except for a cat, but fortunately in later years her son and then her daughter came to live nearby. The house at Mousehole was very small, simple inside, with a coal fire in the living room, but home. She loved her lean-to greenhouse, where she grew large plants and her steeply sloping garden which was filled with azaleas, rhododendrons, camellias etc. She had a wooden shed built as a studio facing north.

She was very forthright, said what she thought, was sometimes quite rude but most of the time was a very friendly person. She was very generous, had a good sense of humour and a loud laugh.

Joan shunned publicity, having been approached many times by the media, including the BBC, but she always said that she didn't want people peering over the gate and saying "Oh that's where she lives..." For most of her working life she wouldn't go to other artists' exhibitions, saying she didn't want to be influenced in any way. She didn't like her work being called naïve - it was just HER.

Once "free from men" she sketched and travelled around Cornwall almost every day, driving in her much loved second hand Morris Minor.

I have always liked her pictures, naturally some more than others, but they are so pleasing in the home with their touch of humour, never ugly and should be looked at closely for their detail. "There is a real artist" said a very successful Dutch artist when he saw them"

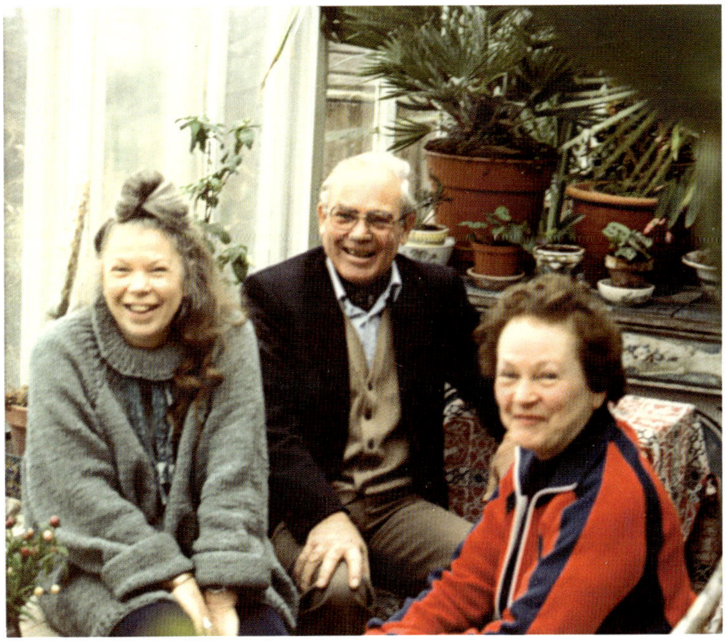

Joan in her Greenhouse with Gil and Betty, 1978

Mousehole Lights

One of Joan's legacies to the village of Mousehole is the world famous Mousehole Christmas Lights. Every year the village and its harbour are illuminated by an amazing display of lights and decorations. This spectacle has been growing ever since Joan put up the first string of lights outside her house in 1963. The event now draws huge crowds between mid-December and early January. The future of this tradition is safely in the hands of a group of volunteers, which includes Joan's grandson Sam Gillchrest.

Sam's Tribute

"Joan and I were very close. We would spend most Saturday and Sunday afternoons together in her conservatory overlooking the village of Mousehole. We would spend the time discussing anything and everything, from her views on the performance of the Labour Government, to the peculiarities of a new plant that she had added to her collection.

Joan had a great love of Mousehole and the characters of the village; she would often talk of friends and past events. Close to her heart was the carnival and she played a role as judge of the children's competitions. Generous as ever, she would award every child a prize who had made the effort to enter events such as the sandcastle and fancy dress competitions. One of Joan's favourite events was the 'tosher race'. This is effectively Mousehole's boat race, whereby all the fishermen take to the water in their brightly coloured boats and race around the bay, the first to finish winning a financial prize, often to be shared amongst friends in the Ship Inn. Joan also enjoyed the spectacle of the annual Lifeboat Blessing, an event where the lifeboats tie up in Mousehole harbour, and the Male Voice Choir sings hymns complimenting the readings of the local Methodist minister. Joan supported the RNLI throughout her time in Cornwall, her son Paul previously serving on the crew and today, her two grandsons Micky and I carry on the tradition. Although Joan was not one for baking cakes or rattling a collection tin on a street corner, she supported the charity in other ways. Last year she supplied the funds to buy a lifeboat barbecue, so that the crew could sell hot dogs and burgers to visitors on Lifeboat days, thereby raising more money for the charity.

When I was younger, I would earn pocket money by helping Joan to look after her garden. Her first love was her painting and her garden followed close after. Using the word 'garden' may be misleading, as Joan did not care for meticulous weeding, rather she preferred her plants to grow as they wished. The result was a collection of brightly coloured rhododendrons of massive proportions. Joan's policy towards her plants was often questioned by both my father and me. We were frequently called upon to repair fencing, or trim plants when they grew so wild, that they obscured the view of the sea from her conservatory. These tasks would be awkward and Joan would watch us carefully to see if we were damaging her plants. Woe betide he who cut more than she had specified. As I grew older, Mara took more responsibility for the garden. Once having spent a day meticulously weeding an area, Joan 'ticked' her off for making the garden look like 'suburbia.' One of my favourite stories revolved around the activities of a family of squirrels. These moved into the tree outside the conservatory and the individual members of said family feasted on the bird feeders. Joan thought this was a wonderful sight, however, the novelty soon wore off when Titus V (her large black and white cat, the fifth of the Titus dynasty) refused to go outside as the squirrels, in Joan's opinion terrified the cat. In my opinion the squirrels were an excuse, the cat being too lazy to move as going outside was far too much effort anyway. Dad and I were instructed to evict the squirrel family, without causing any harm to the animals. We purchased a humane trap, and subsequently became experts in capturing them. A trail of peanuts leading them into a subtly camouflaged trap proved to be most effective. Having captured the animals, they were released elsewhere. As I was learning to drive at the time, this proved to be an excellent excuse to have an opportunistic driving lesson. From these anecdotes, I hope that you can begin to understand Joan as being a caring, generous, yet wonderfully eccentric individual.

We all miss Joan, and it continues to be difficult to come to terms with her passing, however, we are all fortunate to have years of wonderful memories, and as was said at her funeral "she will live on in her paintings and in our hearts forever," and for all who knew and loved Joan, and for all who enjoy her work, this sentiment could not be more appropriate."

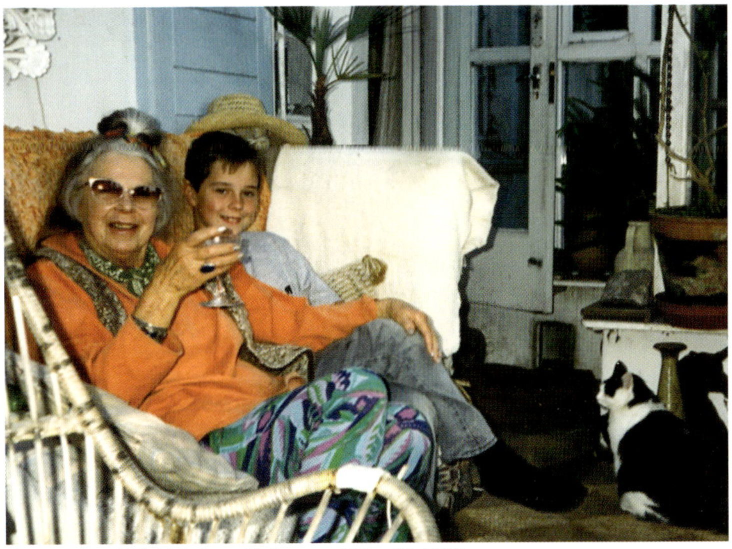

Joan on her 80th birthday with Sam and Titus IV, 1998

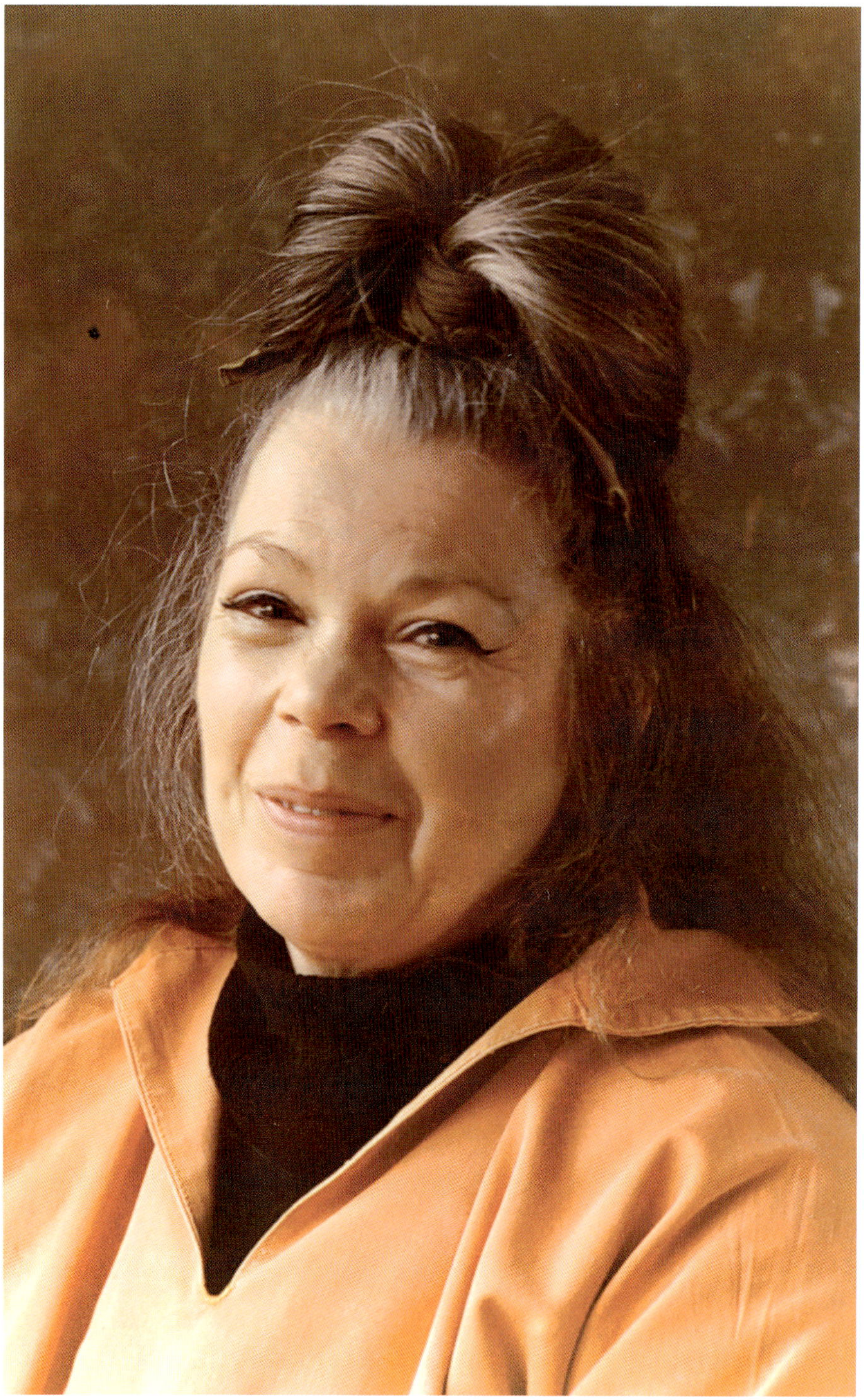
Joan Gillchrest

Up The Hill to Paul

The village of Paul sits high on the hill above Mousehole. The 15th century church, overlooking Mount's Bay is the main church for Paul and Mousehole. It was to feature in many of Joan's paintings.

Within the church is a memorial to the crew of the Penlee lifeboat lost in 1981. This tragic loss was felt deeply by Joan and her family as many of the crew that night were close friends.

For many years her son, Paul, was a member of the lifeboat crew and the tradition is being carried on by grandsons Mick and Sam.

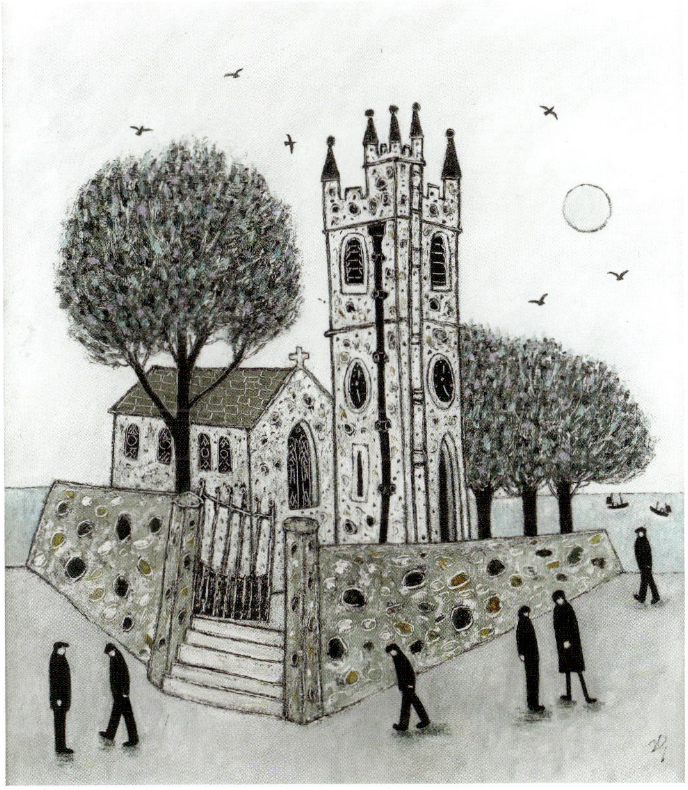

Paul Church

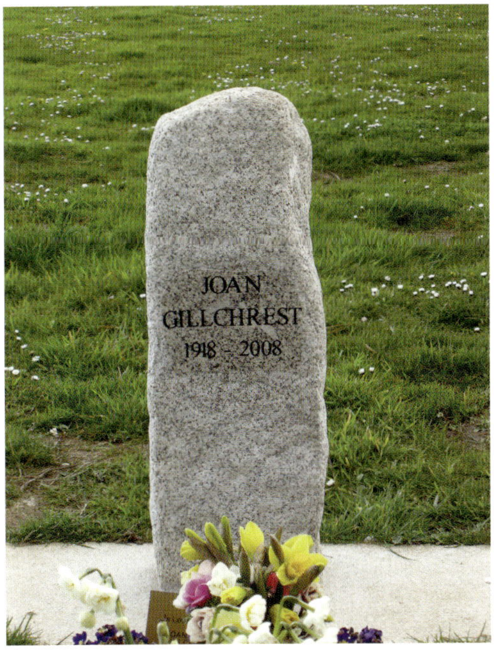

Joan's headstone

Joan Gillchrest (1918-2008)

In January 2008 a simple but dignified service was held for Joan in Paul Church and she was buried high on a hill above her beloved Mousehole.

Acknowledgements

This book would not have been possible without the help and encouragement of Joan's immediate family. Special thanks to Mara, Paul, Dennis, Jeanette and Sam. They treat me as one of the family and I will always be grateful for their warmth, hospitality and friendship over the years.

I have received so much information from Joan's brother, Gil and his wife Susan. I visited them at their home in deepest France coming away with lovely stories of Joan, family photographs and examples of her early paintings. Joan's French paintings are an important part of the story and the contribution from Gil and Susan in Chapter 9 has been invaluable. Many thanks to both of them.

Joan's cousin, Margaret Powell, provided me with details of the Gilbert Scott family tree when I visited her in Lamorna. I thank her for this information.

I wish to thank the family of the late Adrian Ryan for granting me permission to reproduce one of his works. I also thank the executors of the estate of the late Bryan Pearce for granting a similar permission.

For correcting all my split infinitives and other grammatical howlers I am grateful to Ron Sparrow.

Paul Rolls, from my printers, Manor Creative Ltd. has been a tremendous help in the design and production of this book. His technical knowledge plus his keen interest in the total concept have made all our timescales possible. As always Glynn Clarkson's photography of many of the paintings is of a very high standard. Many thanks go to Blair Todd, Exhibitions Manager at the Newlyn Art Gallery and The Exchange, and Steve Tanner for the photograph on page 70.

Last but by no means least I want to thank my colleagues at Wren Gallery. Thank you to my business partner Chris King for his encouragement and for doing the things I should have been doing whilst I have been researching the material. Thank you to our Gallery Manager Christine Cherry who has helped with the research in Cornwall and France and who took many of the recent photographs that appear in the chapters. We are fortunate that one of our colleagues, Alison Walmsley has extensive computer knowledge. She has spent hours working alongside me, designing the page layout, fitting in the text, scanning and sizing the images and preparing the book in the form you see it today, thank you Ali.

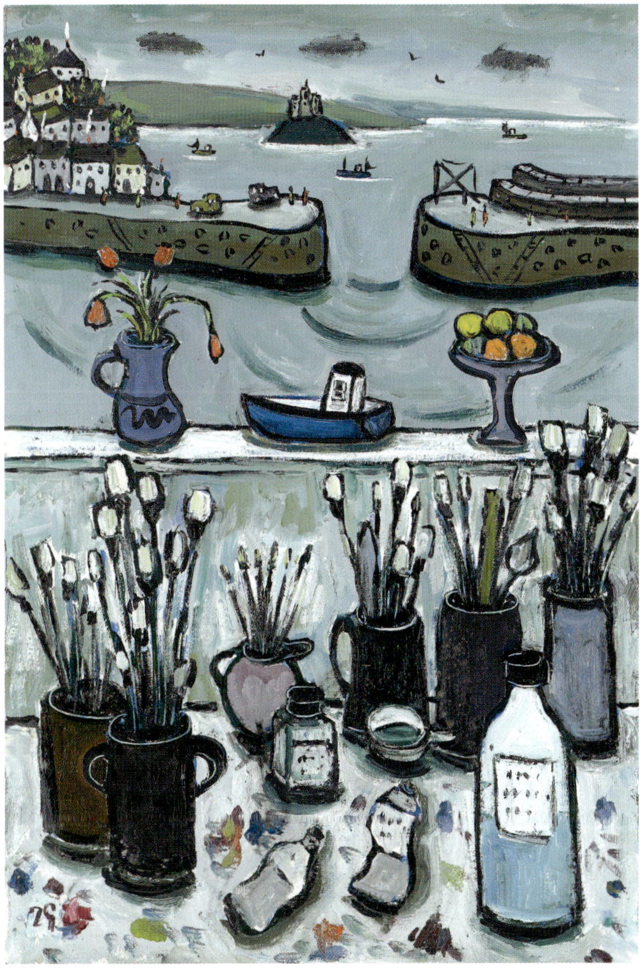
In My Studio at Mousehole